IMAGES
of America

RENO

On the Cover: The post–World War II years of the late 1940s, 1950s, and 1960s were boom times for downtown Reno, and few events illustrated that better than the annual Reno Rodeo Parade. Thousands of visitors and locals crowded downtown Reno for the annual Fourth of July celebration featuring horses, cowboys, Indians, and frequently, Hollywood celebrities. (Photograph courtesy of the Neal Cobb Collection.)

IMAGES
of America

RENO

Guy Clifton

ARCADIA
PUBLISHING

ISBN 978-0-7385-9326-5

Published by Arcadia Publishing
Charleston, South Carolina

Printed in the United States of America

Library of Congress Control Number: 2012938917

For all general information, please contact Arcadia Publishing:
Telephone 843-853-2070
Fax 843-853-0044
E-mail sales@arcadiapublishing.com
For customer service and orders:
Toll-Free 1-888-313-2665

Visit us on the Internet at www.arcadiapublishing.com

Dedicated to all those who call Reno home

Contents

ACKNOWLEDGMENTS

This book would not have been possible without the contributions of many people who not only embrace the history of Reno and Nevada but also work to preserve it. Editor Beryl Love of the *Reno Gazette-Journal* granted access to the newspaper's photographic archives, and Marilyn Newton, a *Gazette-Journal* photographer for nearly 50 years, helped find the negatives and prints from historic events—many of which she had taken herself. Great thanks to Reno historian Neal Cobb; former Reno newspaper publisher Warren Lerude; longtime Reno ad men Roy Powers, Mark Curtis, and Harry Spencer; and Jack Bacon, Colleen Rosencrantz, Lisa Foster, Eric Moody, Guy Rocha, Bill Griswold, Bill Pettite, Rill Riggio, Bob Carroll, Henry W. Thomas, and Buddy Garfinkle. A special thanks to Martina Beatty for her editing skills.

INTRODUCTION

G.A. Burns was not a resident of Reno in 1929, but he helped write the city's history just the same. In that year, Reno's city council sponsored a contest to come up with a city slogan to be displayed on the large metal arch spanning Virginia Street downtown. The arch had been erected to celebrate the Transcontinental Highways Exposition in 1927. With the event long over, the council decided it was time to revamp the arch and hosted the contest to create publicity for the bustling young city. Burns, a resident of Sacramento, earned $100 for the winning submission.

"The Biggest Little City in the World" was adopted as the city's slogan and has remained so ever since. The reason is simple: even before the slogan was adopted, Reno has always been a small city where big things happened.

In the summer of 1910, Reno became the focus of the sporting world. The fight between heavyweight champion Jack Johnson and former champion James J. Jeffries was originally planned for San Francisco, but just weeks before the fight was to take place, California's governor said it could not be held in the Golden State. Promoter Tex Rickard, facing financial ruin, acted quickly and moved the fight to Reno, then a bustling railroad town of 18,000. The city's population more than doubled by fight day on the Fourth of July, and newspapers from around the world covered the event with Reno as the dateline. A who's who of the boxing and journalism worlds converged on Reno for what was billed as "The Fight of the Century."

In early 1931, the Nevada Legislature passed, and Gov. Fred Balzar signed, two key bills that further changed Reno's history. The first legalized casino gambling, bringing gambling operations, which had previously been in the basements and back rooms of speakeasies, to Reno's downtown district, leading to the development of a casino core. It was not long before hotel-casinos with world-class entertainment became the norm. Starting in the 1950s, many of entertainment's top stars played in Reno's showrooms.

The second new law changed the residency requirement to obtain a divorce from three months to six weeks—the most liberal divorce laws in the country. Reno became known as the divorce capital of the world, with thousands of people from throughout the United States making their way to town to get "The Cure" or become "Reno-vated," as the Eastern papers called it. During the 1930s, more than 30,000 divorces were granted. Hotels, boardinghouses, and even specialty "divorce ranches" provided housing for the divorce seekers as they waited to establish their six weeks residency.

Reno, Nevada's largest city at the time, was the centerpiece of both the gambling and the divorce industries. Its wide-open, live-and-let-live attitude was criticized by much of the country, but it helped the state weather the Great Depression as other regions of the country struggled. The divorce trade remained an economic engine for Reno into the 1960s, and the casinos continue to drive the tourism industry today.

Sports have also been a mainstay in Reno for much of its history. From that gathering of the world's top fighters in 1910, virtually every heavyweight champion since has made his way through

Reno at one time or another. One of them, Jack Dempsey, a seminal figure of the "Roaring Twenties," made Reno his home for several years in the 1930s.

The Reno Rodeo, the city's longest-running special event, debuted in 1919 as a celebration to mark the end of World War I and remains one of the city's premier special events more than 90 years later. Known as "The Wildest, Richest Rodeo in the West," the annual event draws the top cowboys and cowgirls from across the country.

Along with entertainers, divorcees, cowboys, and cowgirls, Reno has also been a destination for politicians. From Teddy Roosevelt to Barack Obama, presidential candidates have sought to win votes in the swing state of Nevada. After all, since 1912, the state has voted with the winner of the presidential election every time with the exception of 1976, when it voted for Gerald Ford over Jimmy Carter—both of whom campaigned in Reno.

Even as the city has been in the national and international spotlight, even as it has grown from that bustling little railroad town into a metropolitan population of more than 400,000, Reno has kept its small-town feel. It's a place with distinctive neighborhoods and a city that celebrates the accomplishments of its favorite sons and daughters.

Reno is a unique place, well-deserving of its moniker, "The Biggest Little City in the World."

One

Favorite Sons and Daughters

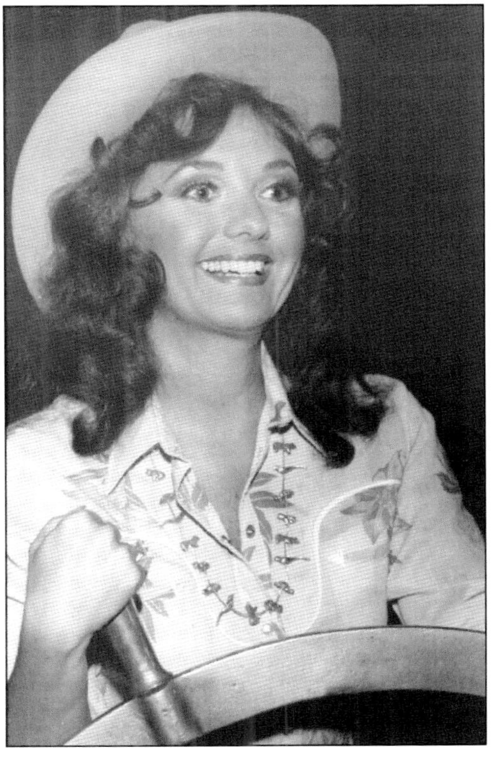

Dawn Wells, a Reno native and 1956 graduate of Reno High School, rose to national prominence for playing Mary Ann Summers on the television situation comedy *Gilligan's Island*, which ran from 1964 to 1967 and lives on today in syndication. She also made guest appearances in more than 20 other television series and several movies. After *Gilligan's Island*, she focused her career mainly on theater, spending the majority of the 1970s and 1980s touring in musical theater productions. She also remains close to her hometown in numerous charitable endeavors, including helping launch the Nevada Discovery Museum, which is targeted at youngsters. (Photograph courtesy of the *Reno Gazette-Journal*.)

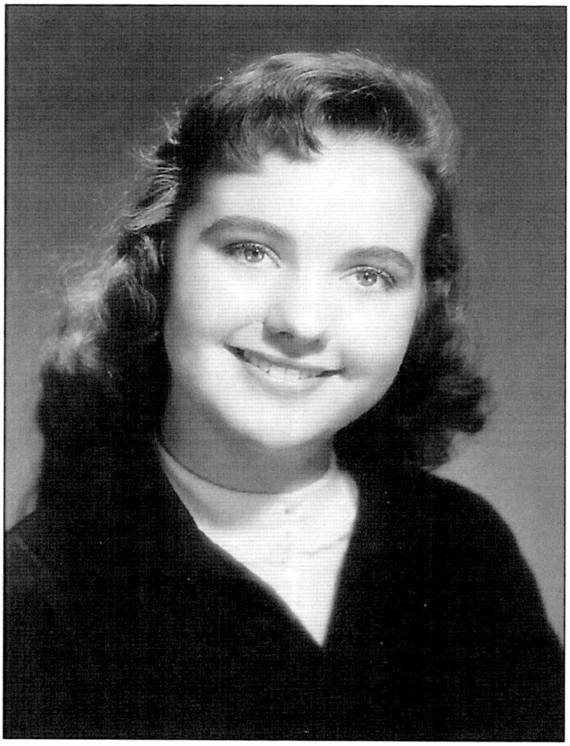

While majoring in theater at Stephens College in Columbia, Missouri, Dawn Wells ran for the crown of Miss Nevada. She won the pageant, held at the Reno High School auditorium on June 20, 1959. Her talent for the pageant was "a dramatic reading." She received a $1,000 scholarship from Pepsi-Cola and gifts from other Nevada businesses. Pictured with Wells, center, is runner-up Donna Jensen of Sparks (left) and Dianne Nelson of Boulder City, the second runner-up. (Photographs courtesy of *Reno Gazette-Journal*.)

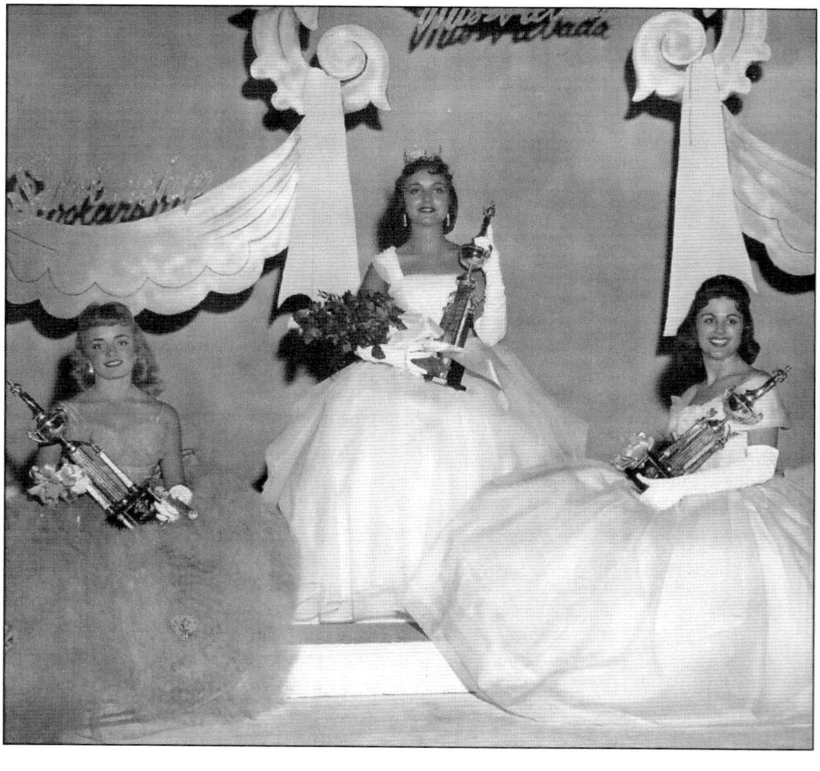

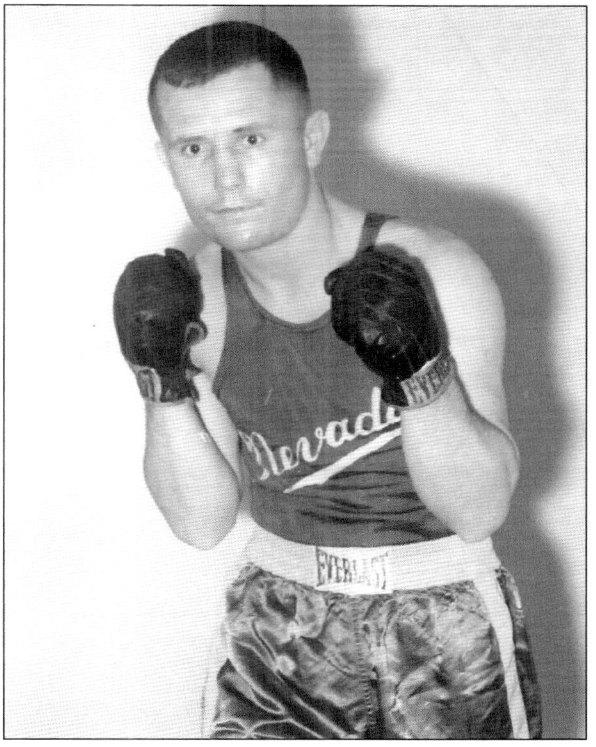

Before rising to fame as a boxing referee and the star of the *Judge Mills Lane* television show, Mills Bee Lane III was a former Marine who enrolled at the University of Nevada, Reno on a boxing scholarship. Lane won the 1960 NCAA welterweight title and qualified for the 1960 Olympic trials. He turned pro and amassed a 10-1 record before retiring and turning his attention to law. He served as a deputy district attorney in Washoe County then as Washoe County district attorney before being elected district court judge in Reno. All the while, he was a boxing referee, working more than 100 world championship fights. (Both photographs courtesy of the *Reno Gazette-Journal*; below, photograph by Marilyn Newton.)

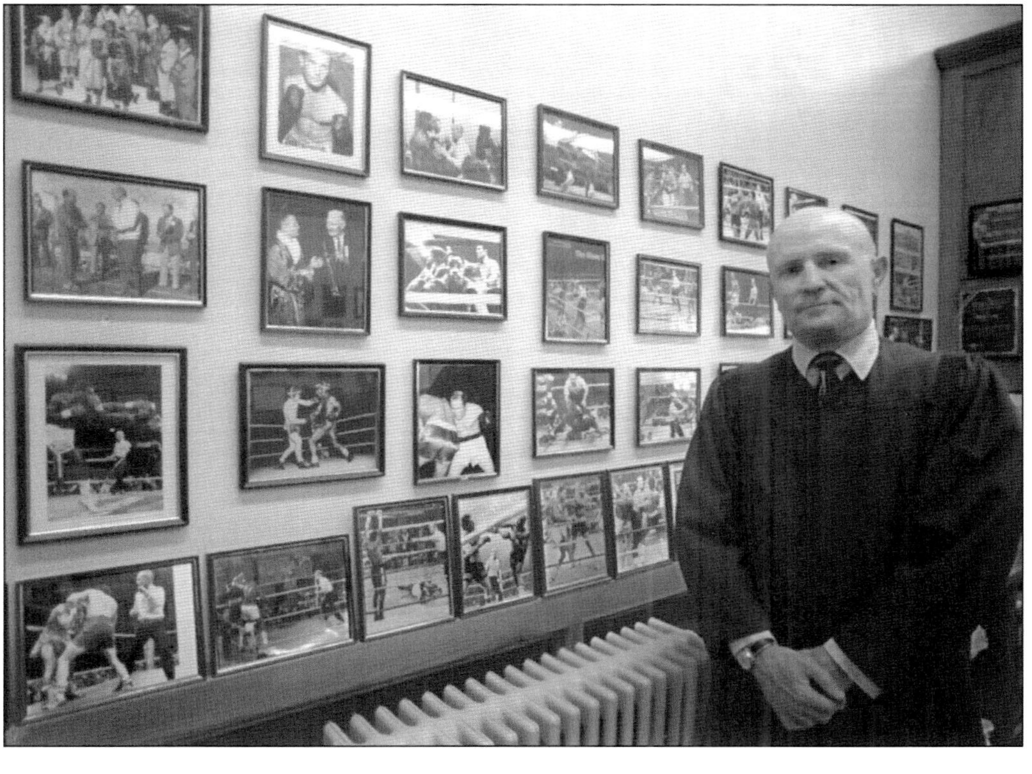

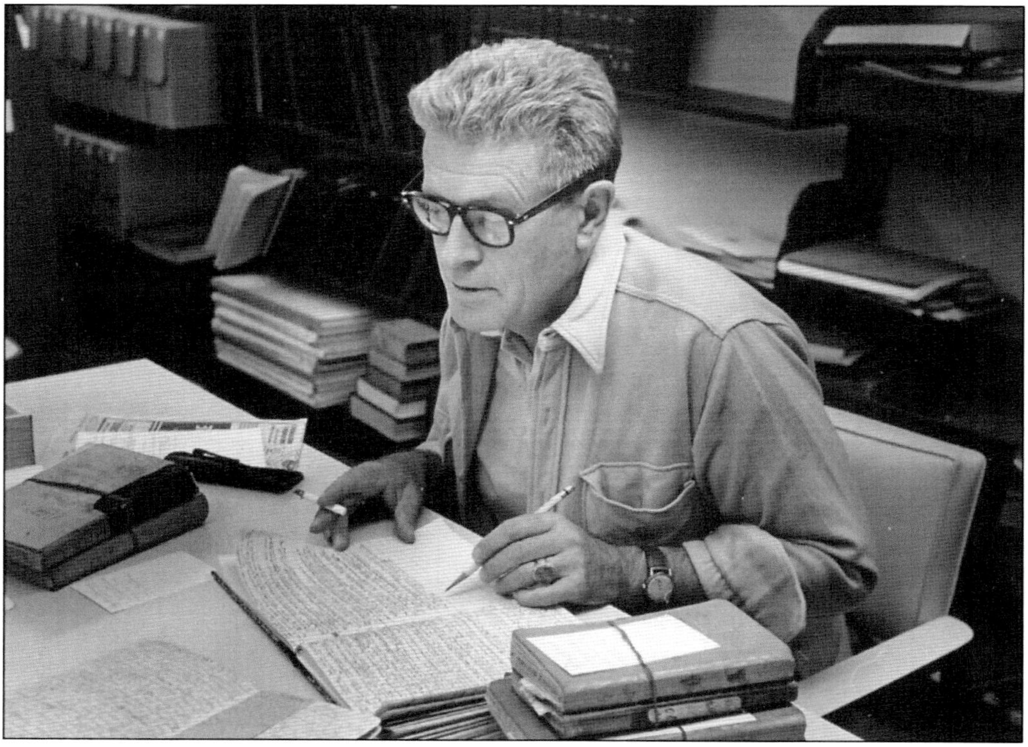

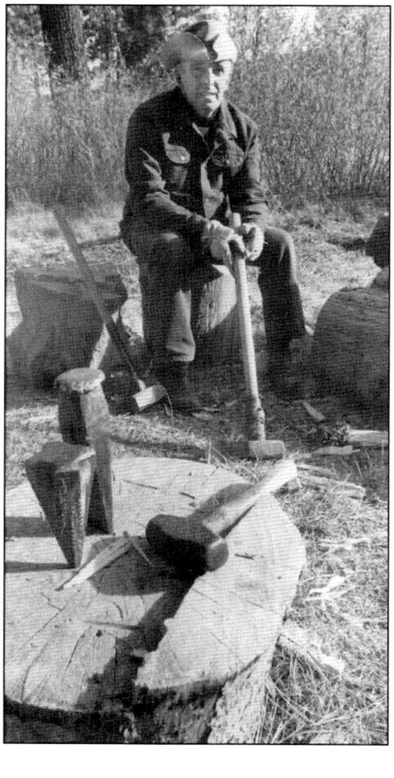

American novelist Walter Van Tilburg Clark grew up in Reno, where his father served as president of the University of Nevada. Clark attended Reno schools and the university before moving to New York to teach high school English and launch his fiction-writing career. His first published novel, *The Ox-Bow Incident*, came out in 1940 and was adapted into a movie starring Henry Fonda in 1943. Clark also published the novels *The City of Trembling Leaves*, about Reno, and *The Track of the Cat*. He returned to Reno in 1962 to teach at the university and remained until his death in 1971. (Photograph courtesy of *Reno Gazette-Journal*.)

Robert Laxalt, a journalist, professor, and author of 17 books, is perhaps best known for his novel *Sweet Promised Land*, which focused on the story of his father, a Basque sheepherder. Laxalt started his writing career as a newspaper reporter. Later, he was a featured writer for *National Geographic*. He founded the University of Nevada Press in 1964 and helped launch the Basque Studies program at the university. He taught writing at the University of Nevada and was the first occupant of the Distinguished Nevada Writer Chair. Also, he and Walter Van Tilburg Clark were the first inductees into the Nevada Writers Hall of Fame when it was established in 1988. (Photograph by Marilyn Newton, courtesy of the *Reno Gazette-Journal*.)

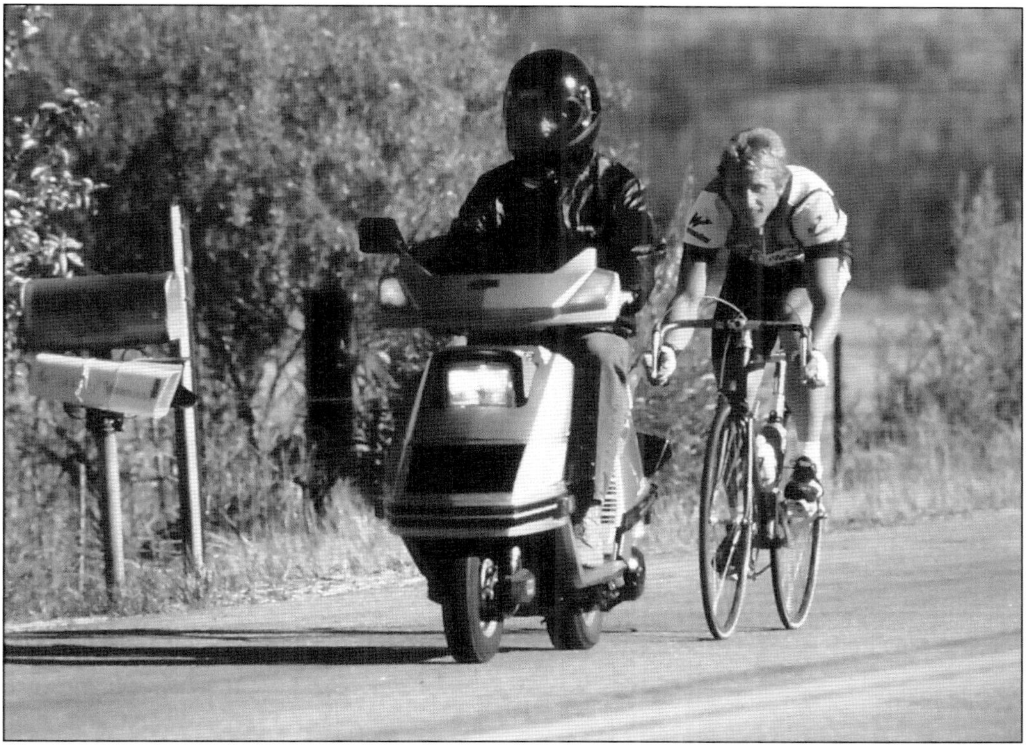

Greg LeMond is best known as the first American cyclist to win the Tour de France, a feat he first accomplished in 1986 and repeated in 1989 and 1990. Those victories came as no surprise in Reno, where residents regularly saw LeMond training on the windy, steep highways of Geiger Grade and Mount Rose Highway. Before turning professional, LeMond, who attended Wooster High School in Reno, was an accomplished junior racer, winning gold, silver, and bronze medals in the 1979 Junior World Championships in Argentina. He was selected for the 1980 US Olympic team but did not compete because of the boycott of the Moscow Games. He turned professional in 1981. (Photograph by Mark Crosse, courtesy of the *Reno Gazette-Journal.*)

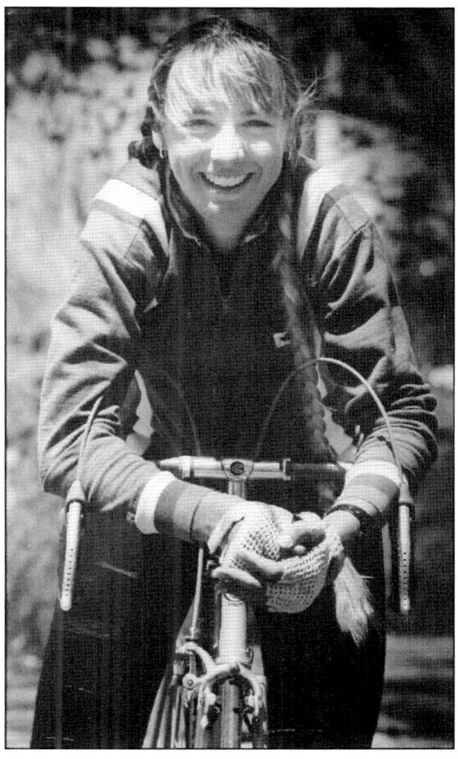

Just as Greg LeMond made a name for himself in men's cycling, Reno's Inga Thompson was doing the same in women's cycling. In a career stretching from 1984 to 1993, Thompson competed in two Olympic Games and won the United States National Road Race Championships four times: 1987, 1988, 1991, and 1993. She also helped the United States to the silver medal in the 1991 World Championships. (Photograph courtesy of the *Reno Gazette-Journal.*)

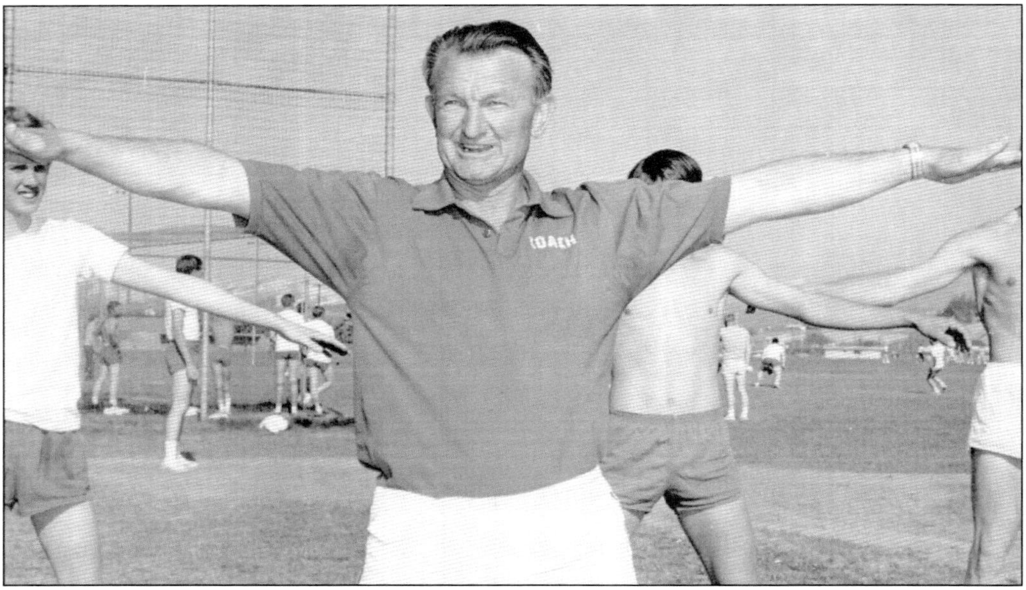

Bud Beasley was an athlete, coach, and teacher who influenced thousands of Reno youngsters in his 70-year career as an educator. He played football at the University of Nevada, which he graduated from in 1934, and also played professional baseball in the Pacific Coast League in the summers. However, his true calling was teaching and coaching, a vocation he continued throughout his life in Reno. An elementary school in Sparks and the athletic complex at Reno High School are named in his honor. (Photograph courtesy of the *Reno Gazette-Journal.*)

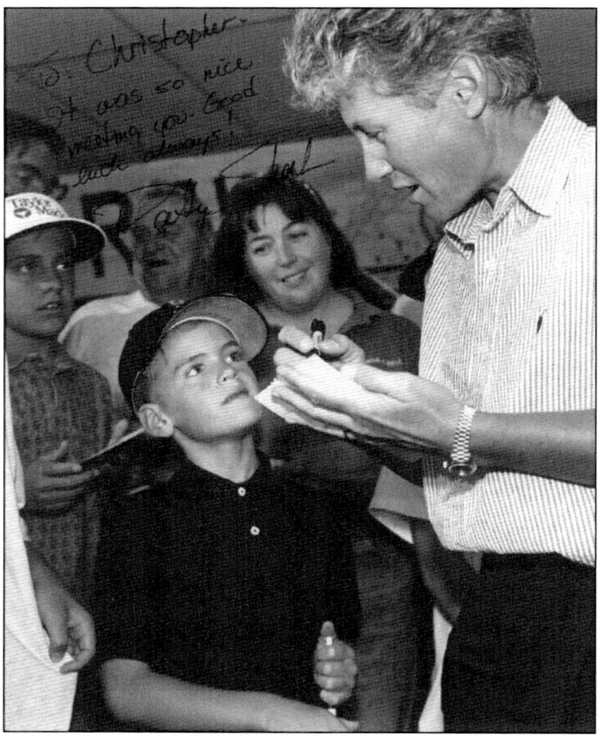

Before turning professional in 1980, Patty Sheehan won three straight Nevada High School golf championships, three straight Nevada State Amateurs, and the national collegiate championship. She joined the Ladies Professional Golf Association in 1981, and she earned Rookie of the Year honors on her way to a hall-of-fame career. Sheehan, who attended Reno's Wooster High School and still lives in Reno, won 35 LPGA tournaments, including six major championships. Here she signs an autograph for Reno youngster Christopher Cobb after winning her first US Open. (Photograph courtesy of William Cobb Collection.)

Marion Motley is the only player in the history of the University of Nevada, Reno to be inducted into the Pro Football Hall of Fame. A native of Canton, Ohio, Motley came to Nevada in 1941 and played two seasons. In 1946, he was one of four African American players to break professional football's color barrier. Motley starred for the Cleveland Browns in the All America Football Conference and the NFL. He was inducted to the Pro Football Hall of Fame in 1969 and was an inaugural member of the University of Nevada's Athletic Hall of Fame. (Photograph courtesy of University of Nevada, Reno Athletics.)

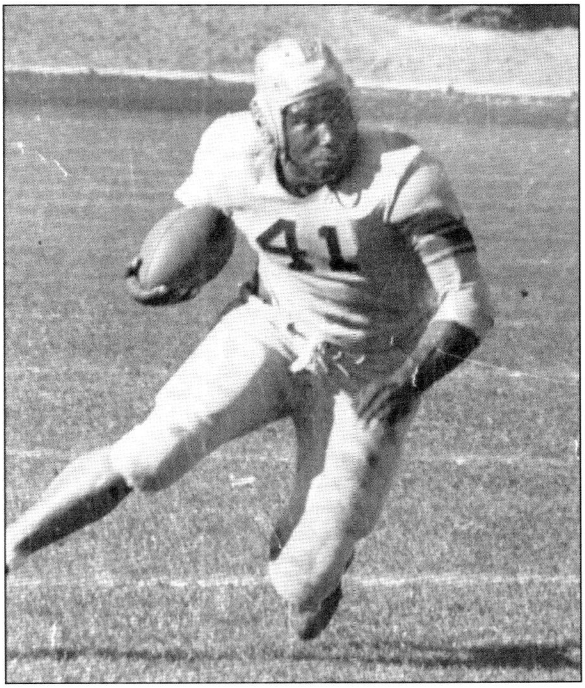

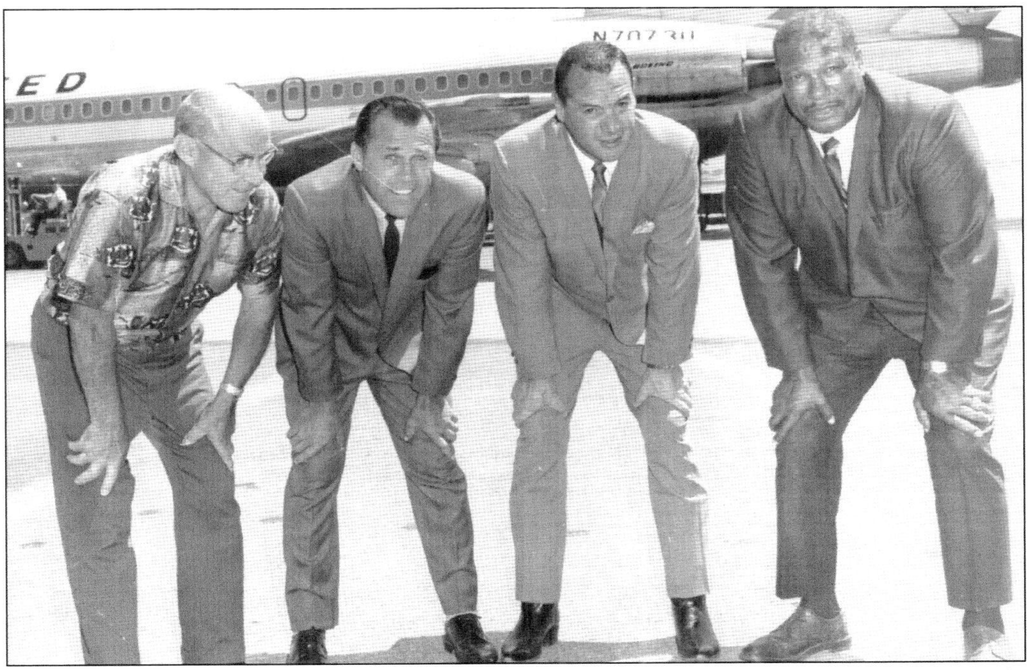

Dubbed "Nevada's all-time backfield," James "Rabbit" Bradshaw, Tommy Kalmanir, Stan Heath, and Marion Motley were among the inaugural inductees into the University of Nevada Athletic Hall of Fame. Bradshaw was Nevada's first-ever All-American, while Kalmanir, Heath, and Motley went on from Nevada to careers in professional football. (Photograph courtesy of University of Nevada Special Collections, Ty Cobb Collection.)

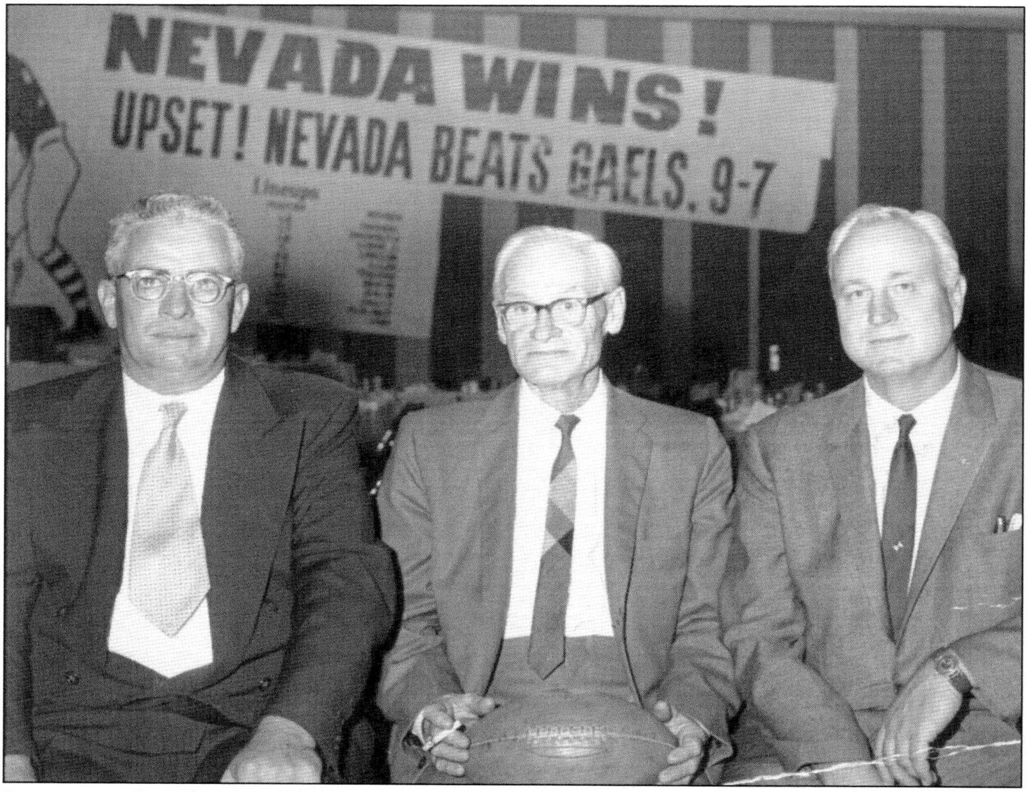

Long remembered as one of the greatest victories in University of Nevada football history was the 9-7 win over the nationally ranked St. Mary's Gaels in 1934. The heroes of the game included center Tom Cashill (left), who had the game-winning drop kick; coach Brick Mitchell (middle); and fullback George Tharp, who scored the team's only touchdown. The team was honored at the 25-year reunion of the game at the Riverside Hotel in 1959. (Photograph courtesy of University of Nevada Special Collections, Ty Cobb Collection.)

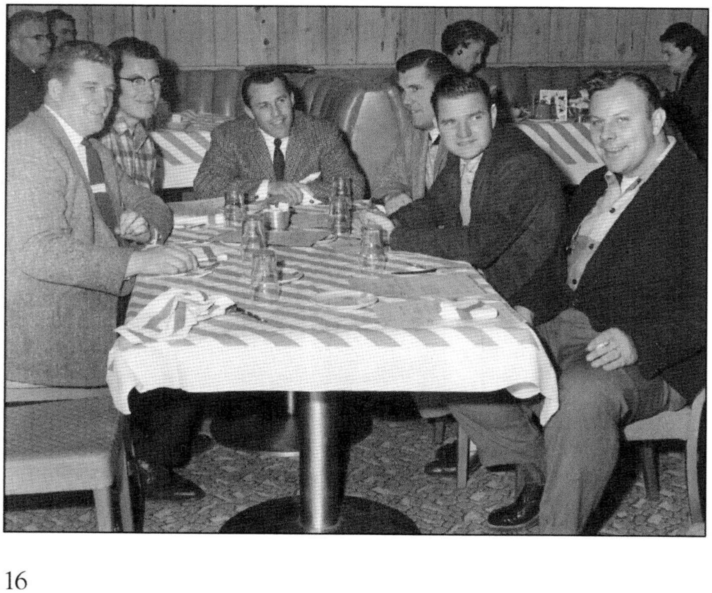

Longtime Reno newspaperman Rollan Melton (far right) visited with former University of Nevada football standouts, from left to right, Max Dodge, Bob Corley, Tommy Kalmanir, James "Buster" McClure, and Dick Trachok in 1958 to reminisce on the 10-year anniversary of Nevada's 1948 bowl team. (Photograph courtesy of Marilyn Melton Collection.)

Jimmie Olivas came to the University of Nevada as a football player but made his claim to fame in the boxing ring. Olivas was the national collegiate welterweight champion in 1931 and qualified for the US Olympic trials, but a serious knee injury derailed his attempt to make the team. He went on to spend 35 years as the coach of the University of Nevada boxing team, coaching several national championship teams and dozens of individual national champions. (Photograph courtesy of the *Reno Gazette-Journal.*)

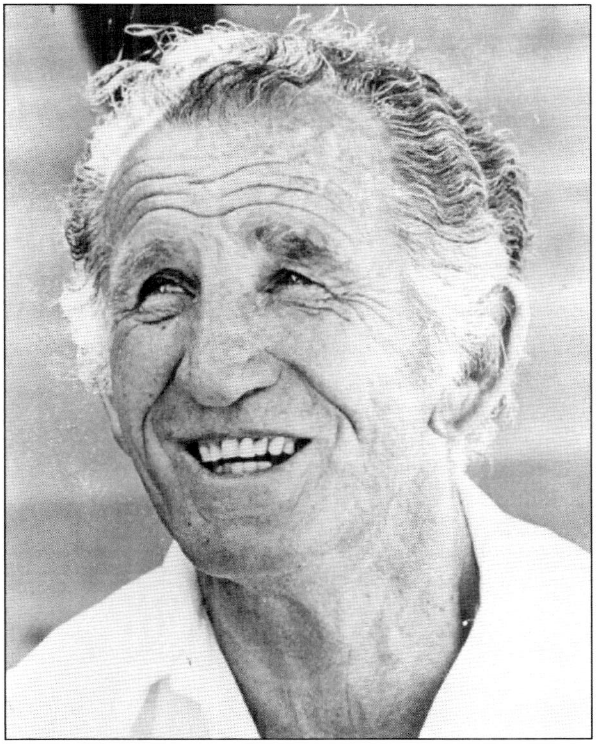

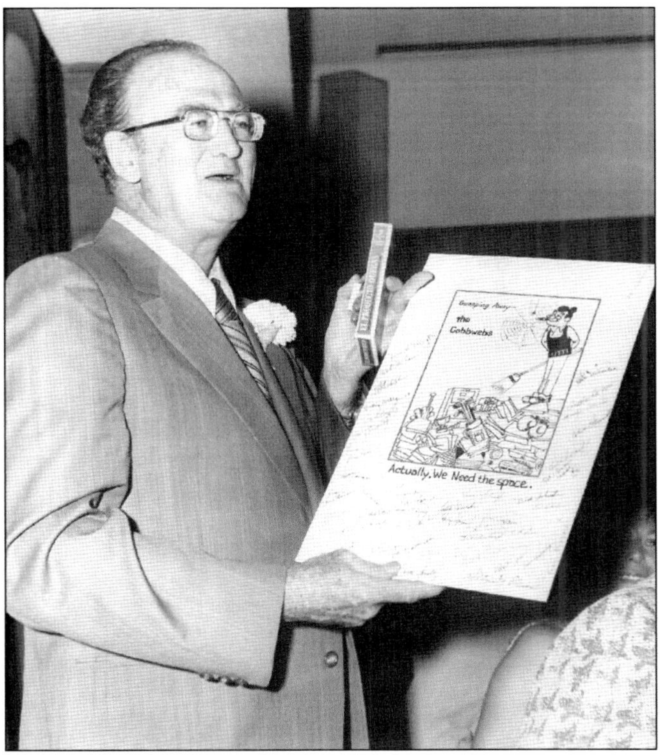

Ty Cobb grew up in Virginia City and attended college at the University of Nevada, Reno before embarking on a lifelong career as a newspaperman. Cobb began working at the *Nevada State Journal* as a sportswriter in 1938 and spent stints as the newspaper's sports editor, managing editor, and associate editor before his retirement in 1975. After retirement and despite failing eyesight, Cobb continued to write a regular column for the *Reno Gazette-Journal* until his death in 1997. (Photograph courtesy of the *Reno Gazette-Journal.*)

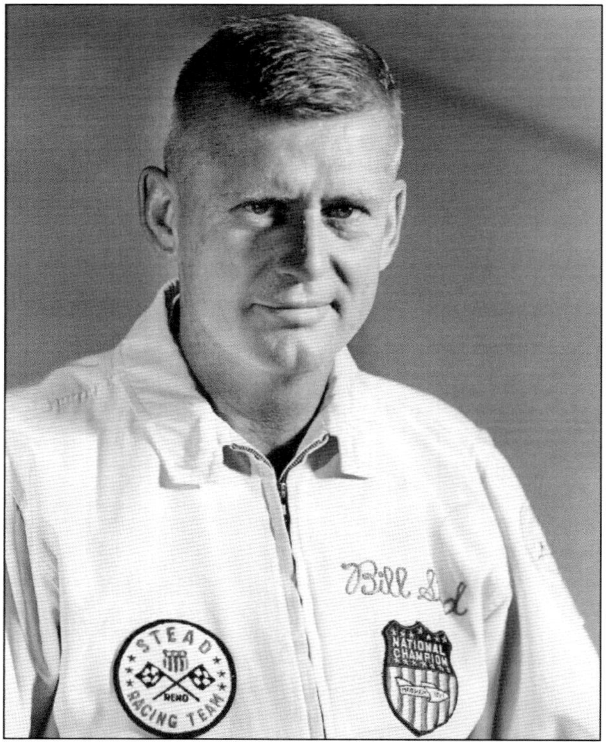

Bill Stead grew up a cowboy on his family's ranch but gained national attention as one of the top hydroplane racers in the country in the 1950s and 1960s. A decorated pilot in World War II, Stead was also the driving force in resurrecting the National Championship Air Races, which had previously been held in Cleveland. The first Reno National Championship Air Races were held near his ranch in Spanish Springs in 1964 and were later moved to Reno-Stead Airfield. Bill Stead died when his racing airplane crashed in Florida in 1966. (Photograph courtesy of the *Reno Gazette-Journal*.)

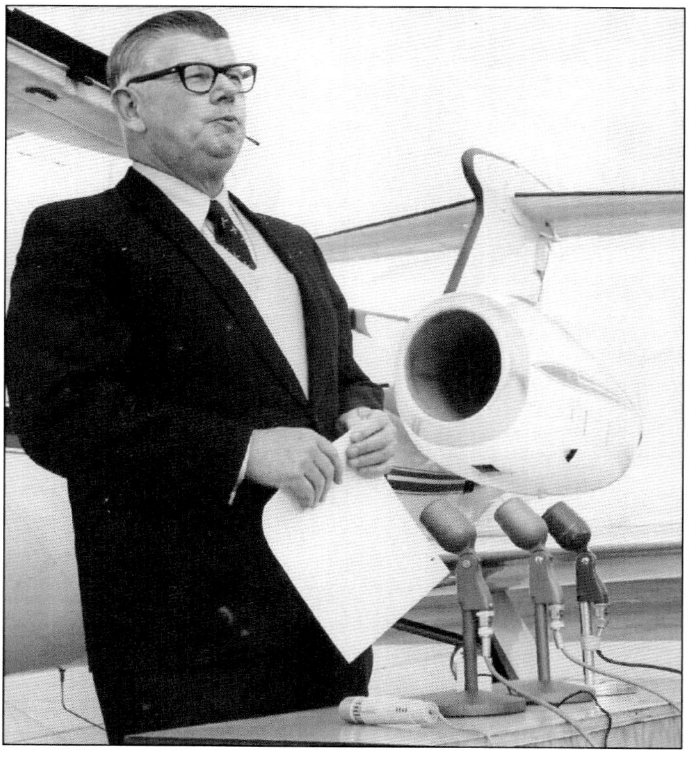

Bill Lear made contributions to the aviation industry so epic that most are taken for granted today. He developed airplane radio systems and navigation and autopilot systems, including those used on aircraft in World War II and Korea. In 1960, he launched the idea for a jet-powered business plane and the Lear Jet was born. Lear's innovative mind also introduced the car radio and the eight-track tape player. He died in Reno in 1978 at age 75. His widow, Moya, gave millions of dollars to the Reno community through her philanthropic efforts. (Photograph courtesy of the *Reno Gazette-Journal*.)

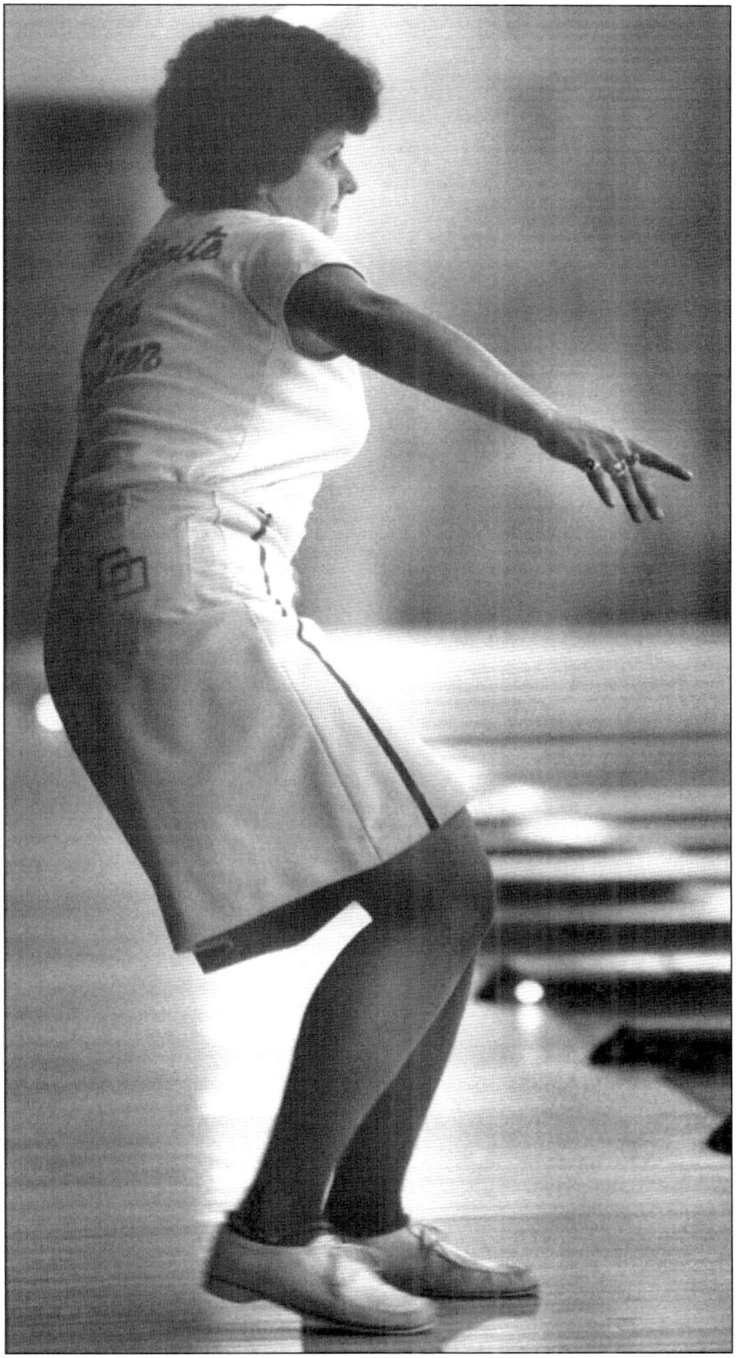

Pam Buckner was a high school teacher when she launched a professional bowling career and became the most accomplished Reno bowler. Buckner won 22 professional titles and 14 local women's bowling association titles. She also won the prestigious US Bowling Congress Queens title in 1976. Buckner is enshrined in four bowling halls of fame, and a professional tournament is named in her honor. (Photograph courtesy of the *Reno Gazette-Journal.*)

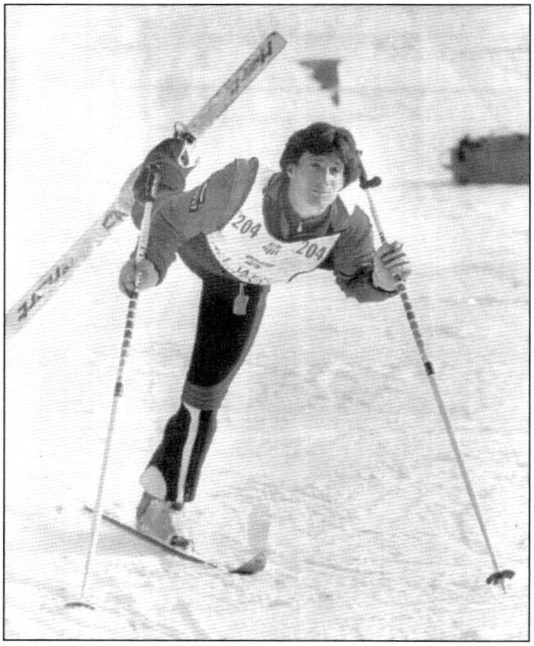

Reno's Lane Spina helped bring competitive freestyle skiing to the international forefront in the late 1980s and early 1990s. He won medals in the 1988 Calgary Olympics and the 1992 Albertville Olympics. In 1991, he captured the Freestyle World Championships in Lake Placid, New York. (Photograph courtesy of the *Reno Gazette-Journal.*)

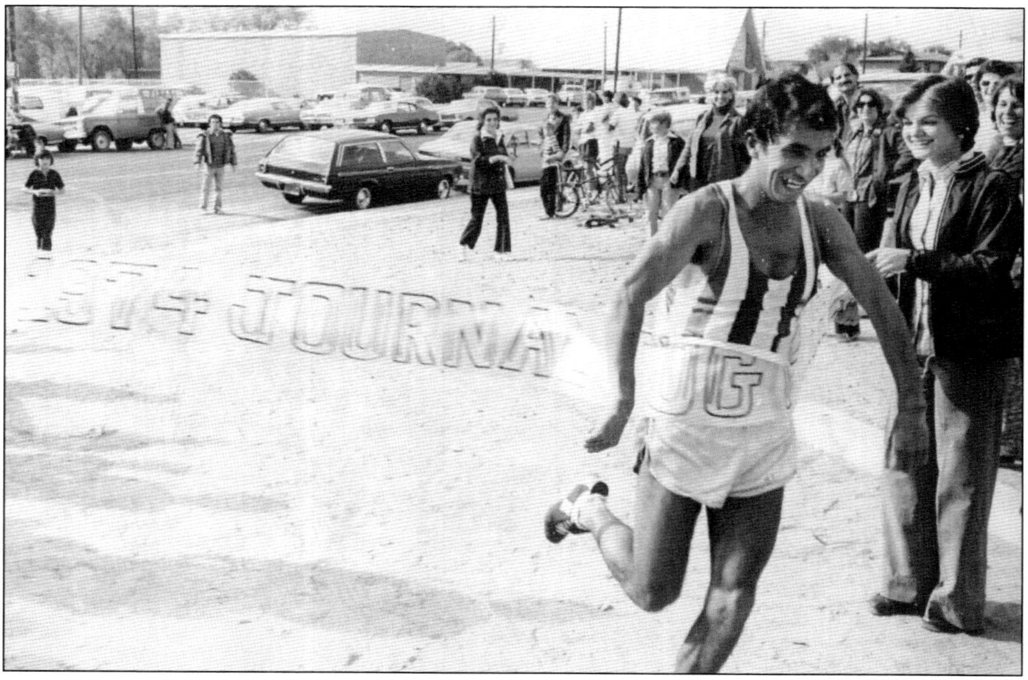

Coming to Reno from his native Colombia to run track for the University of Nevada, Domingo Tibaduiza became one of the dominant distance runners in the world in the 1970s and 1980s. He represented Colombia in four consecutive Summer Olympics—1972, 1976, 1980, and 1984—and also qualified in the 5,000 meters in 1976. In 1982, he won the prestigious Berlin Marathon. Here he is shown winning his adopted hometown's Journal Jog, one of many such victories for him and his distance-running family. (Photograph courtesy of the *Reno Gazette-Journal.*)

Two

Businesses and Businesspeople

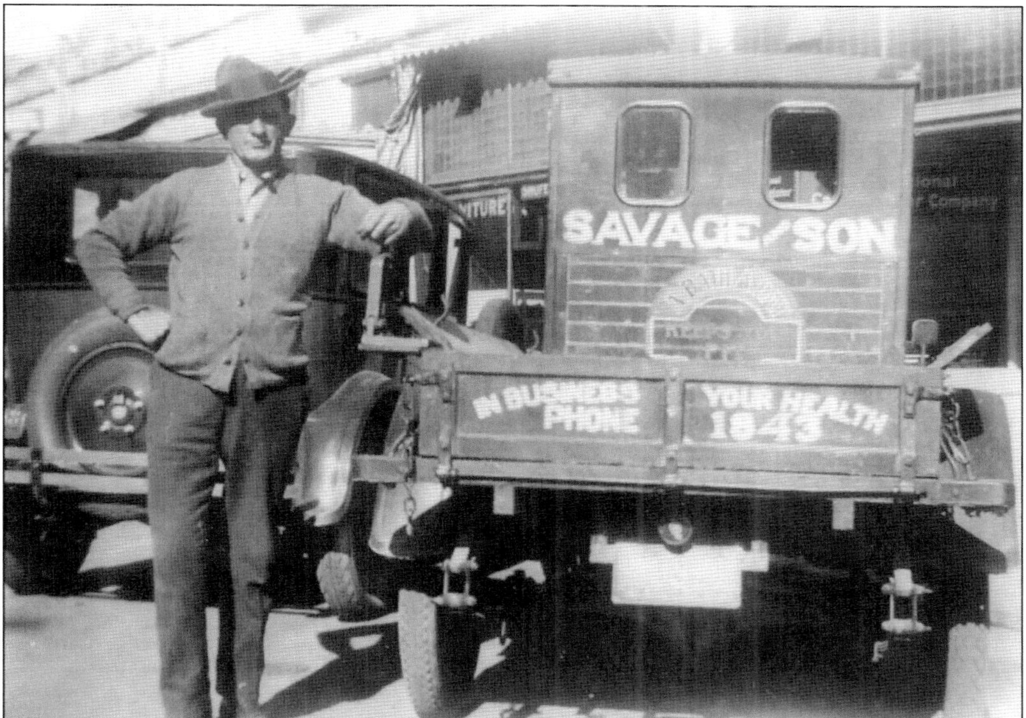

Savage & Son was founded in Reno as a one-man plumbing business in 1893 by Frank Charles Savage. The business holds business license No. 10 and is the city's longest continuously operating family business. Frank Savage passed it to his son, Leonard Charles Savage, who passed it to his son, L.J., who passed it to sons Len and Pete, who operate the business today. (Photograph courtesy of Savage & Son, Inc.)

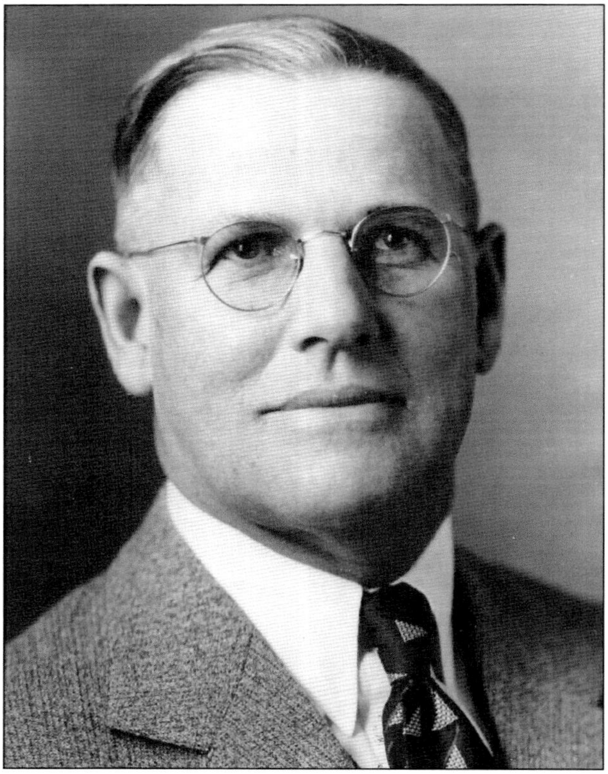

In 1905, Reno native Ed Chism (left) converted an old milk house on the family's ranch into an ice cream factory, making about 25 gallons a day, which he distributed around Reno in a horse-drawn wagon. In 1916, Chism bought his first ice cream truck, a Ford Model T with a canvas top that became well-recognized throughout the Truckee Meadows. In 1933, the ever-expanding company added soft drinks to its lineup. After Ed Chism's death in 1956, family members continued to operate the business, which eventually became the 7-Up Bottling Company. (Photographs courtesy of the *Reno Gazette-Journal*.)

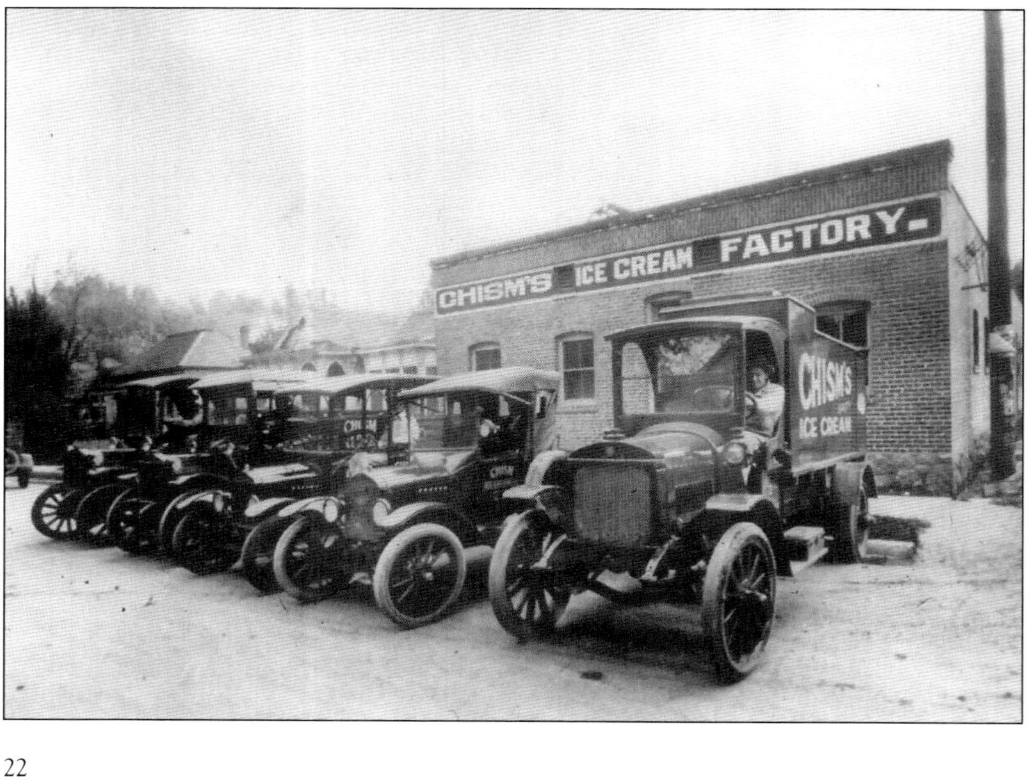

In June 1938, brothers Chet and Link Piazzo, the sons of Italian immigrants, opened the Sportsman at 358 North Virginia Street, building the business into one of the most popular and venerable sporting goods stores in northern Nevada. For decades, hunters, fishermen, athletes, and schools filled their needs at the Sportsman, which operated for more than 70 years. Chet and Link also had a popular television show, *Sportsman's Trails*, in which they shared films of their hunting and fishing adventures. (Photographs courtesy of the *Reno Gazette-Journal*.)

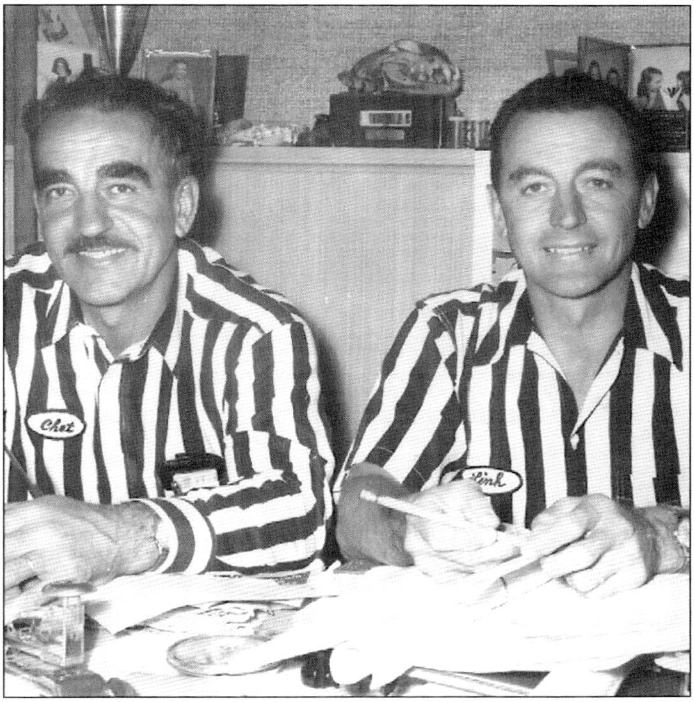

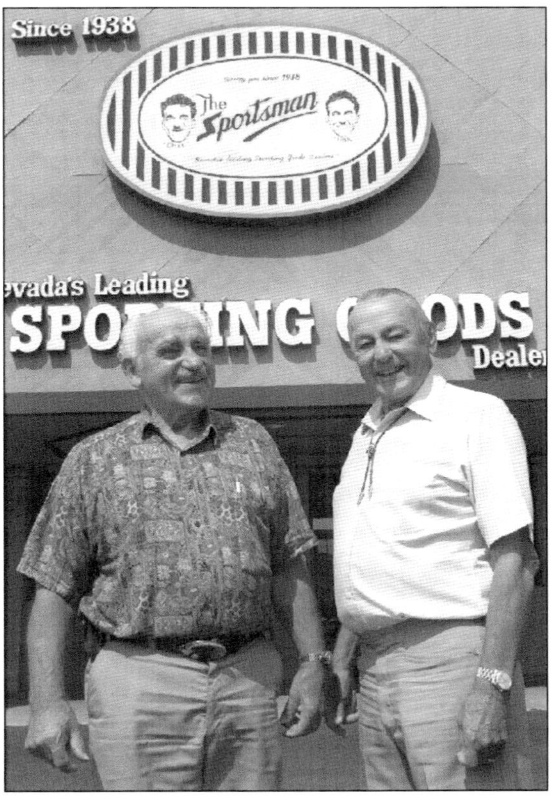

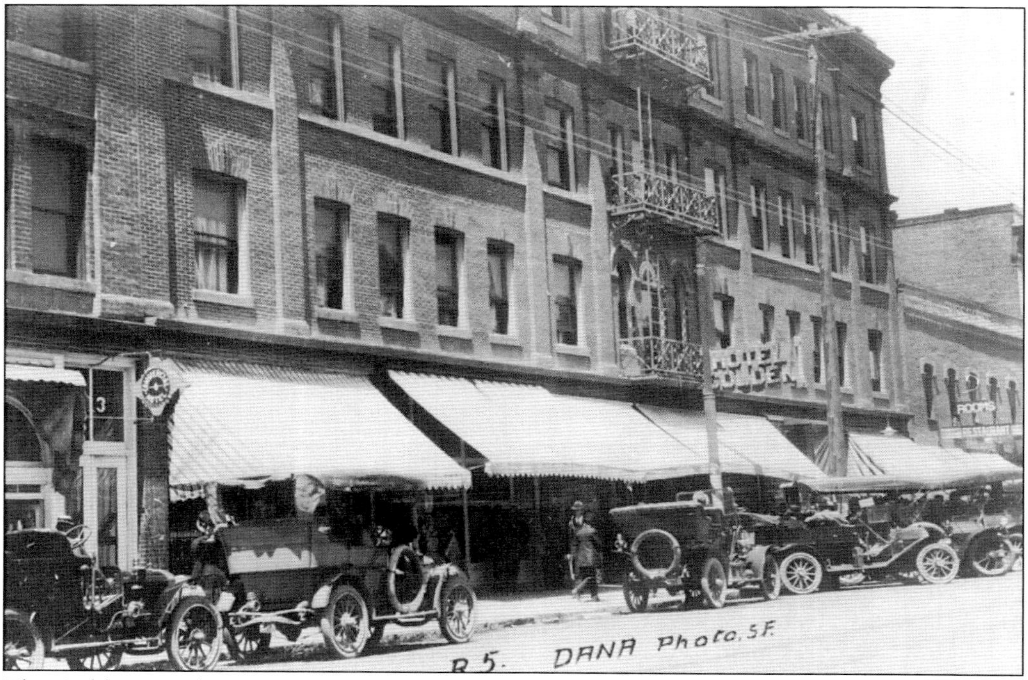

The Golden Hotel, named for its owner, Frank Golden Sr., was built in 1906 on Reno's North Center Street. Conveniently located near the city's railroad depot, the hotel was a favorite spot of visitors to the city. In 1910, it was Tex Rickard's headquarters as he promoted "The Fight of the Century" between heavyweight boxing champions Jack Johnson and Jim Jeffries. By 1952, the hotel, which had added a casino, had 400 employees and the largest payroll in downtown Reno. On April 3, 1962, a fire completely destroyed the building and killed six people. At the time, it was the deadliest fire in the city's history. (Above, photograph courtesy of Jack Bacon Collection; below, photograph courtesy of the *Reno Gazette-Journal*.)

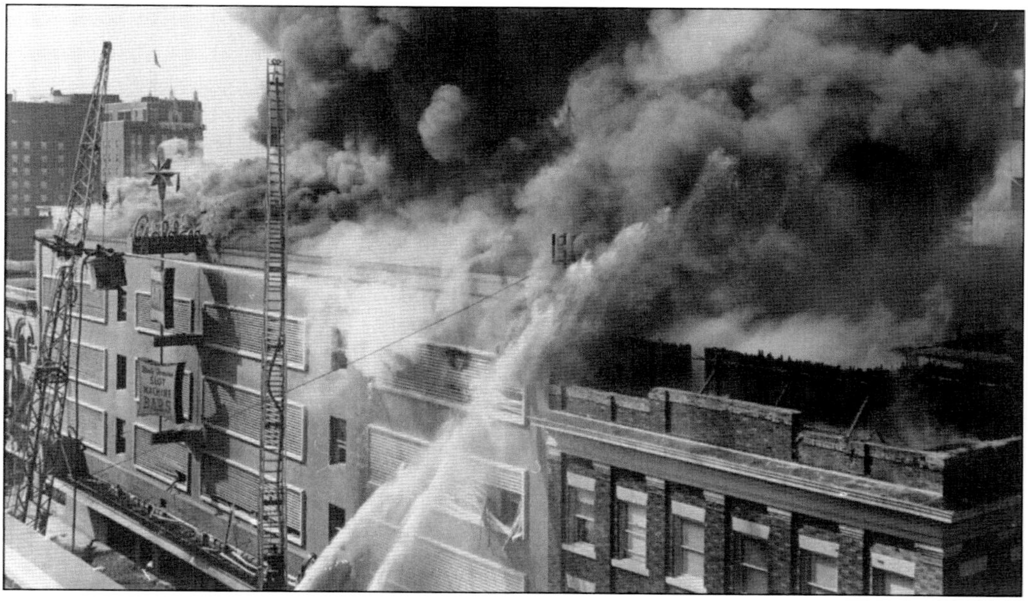

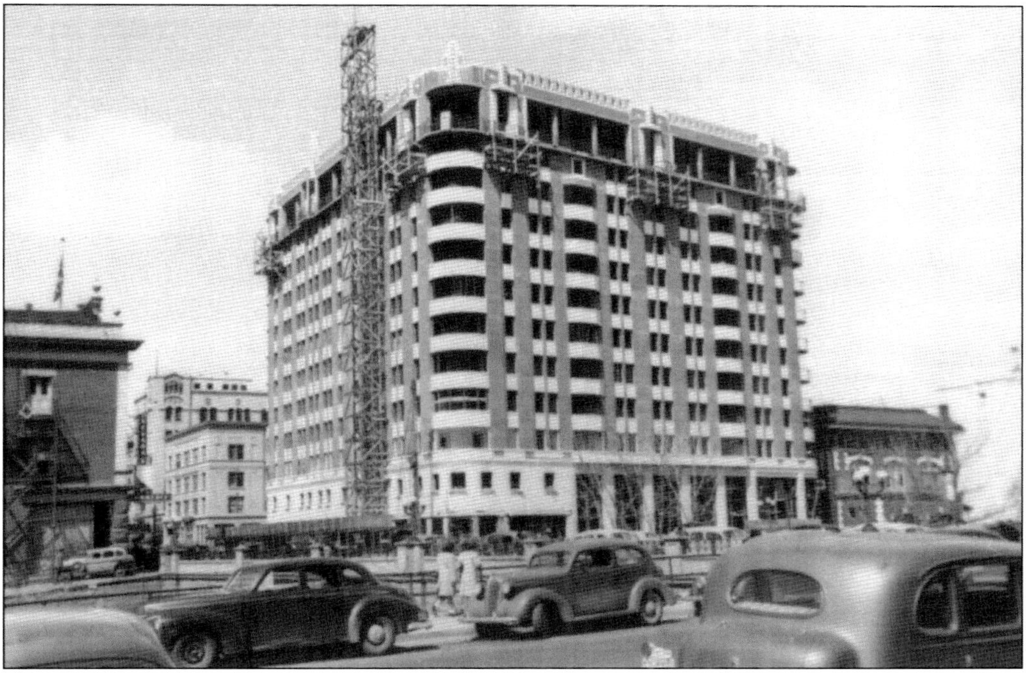

In 1945, Gladys Mapes and her son, Charles W. Mapes Jr., announced plans to construct a hotel in downtown Reno. The Mapes Hotel opened on December 17, 1947, with 300 hotel rooms and 12 stories, making it the tallest building in the state at the time. Over the next three decades, the Mapes attracted the biggest stars from the world of entertainment and became the headquarters for the making of the film *The Misfits*, starring Marilyn Monroe, Clark Gable, and Montgomery Clift. In 1982, after 35 years, the cash-strapped hotel closed its doors for the final time. Preserving the hotel became a political battle over the next two decades, but the hotel was imploded on January 30, 2000. (Both photographs courtesy of the *Reno Gazette-Journal*; below, photograph by Marilyn Newton.)

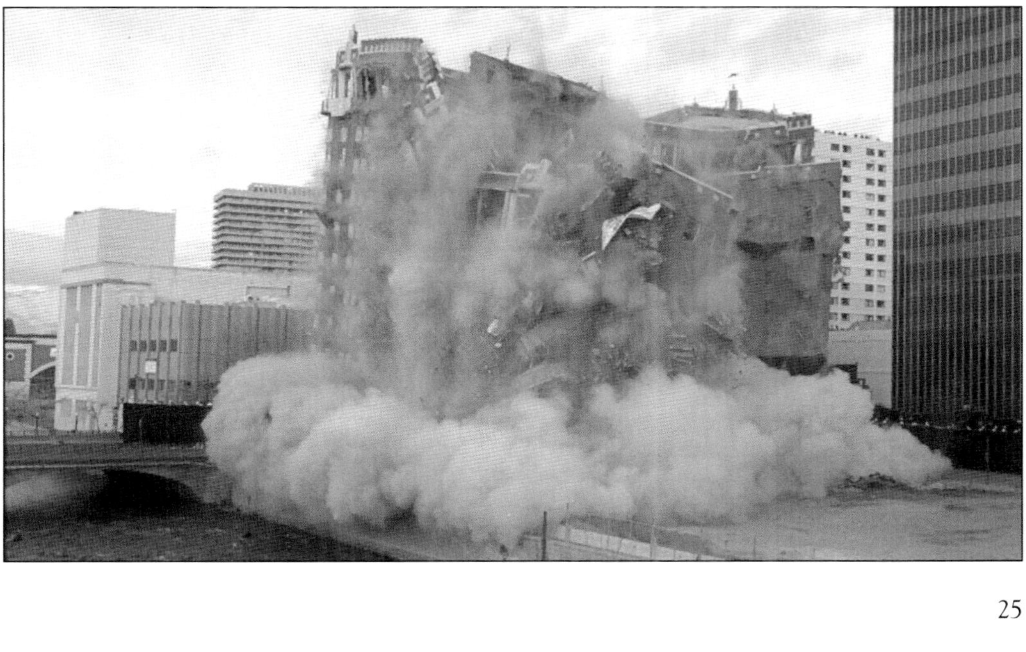

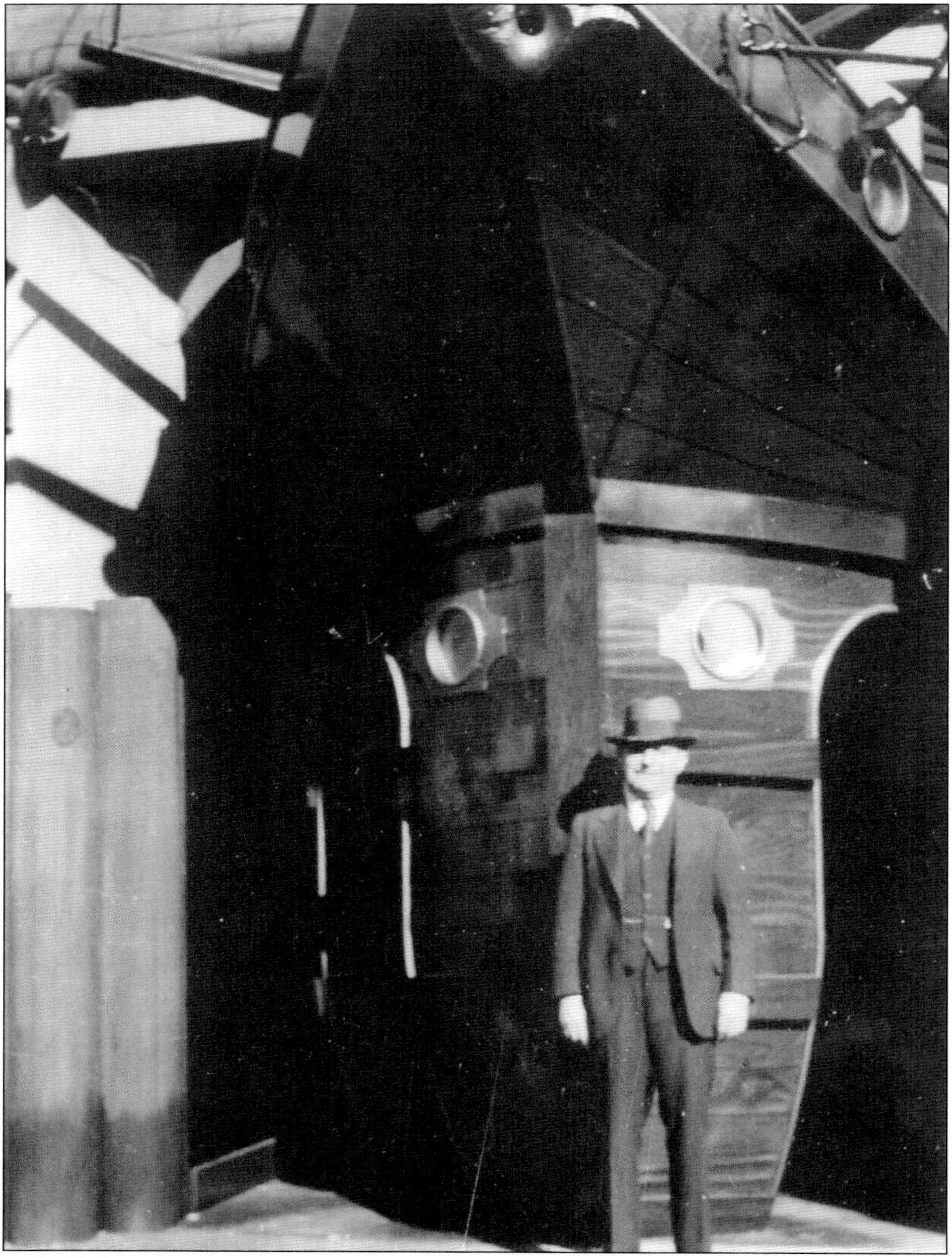

Nick Abelman was a major figure in Nevada mining and gaming throughout the first half of the 20th century. After owning clubs and mining interests in Tonopah, he moved to Reno and became involved in many ventures when gambling was legalized in 1931. He owned the ornate Ship & Bottle Club, the Stateline Country Club, and the Waldorf Club. He also operated the Riverside Hotel for 15 years. Abelman died in 1951. (Photograph courtesy of Bill Pettite Collection.)

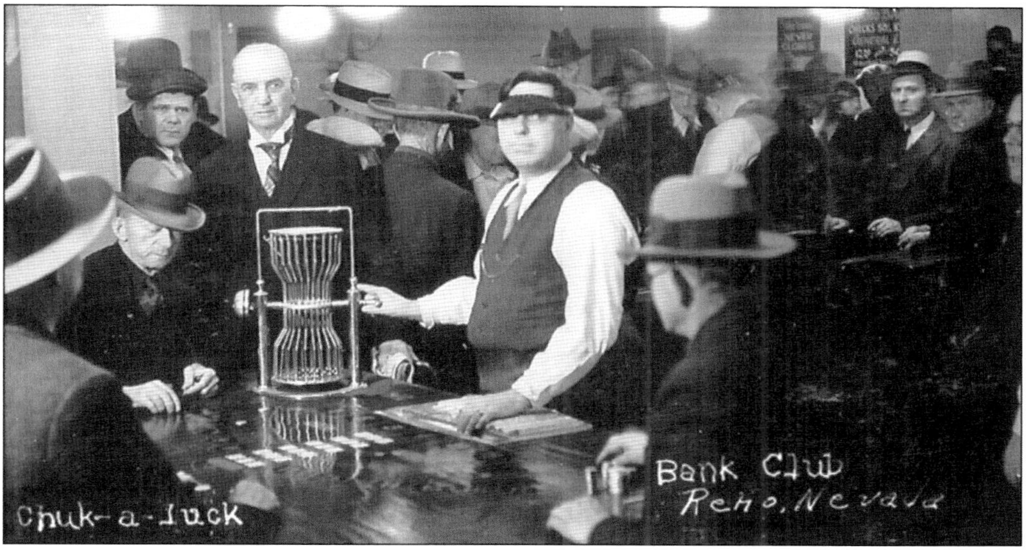

The Bank Club, located at 239 North Center Street, was the second officially licensed casino when Nevada legalized gambling in 1931—the first was the Owl Club on Commercial Row. The Bank Club had operated illegally in the basement of the same building for years but moved its operations upstairs when gambling was legalized. Among its supporters was Mayor E.E. Roberts (center), who promoted Reno's live-and-let-live attitude and pushed for the end of Prohibition. (Photograph courtesy of Colleen Rosencrantz Collection.)

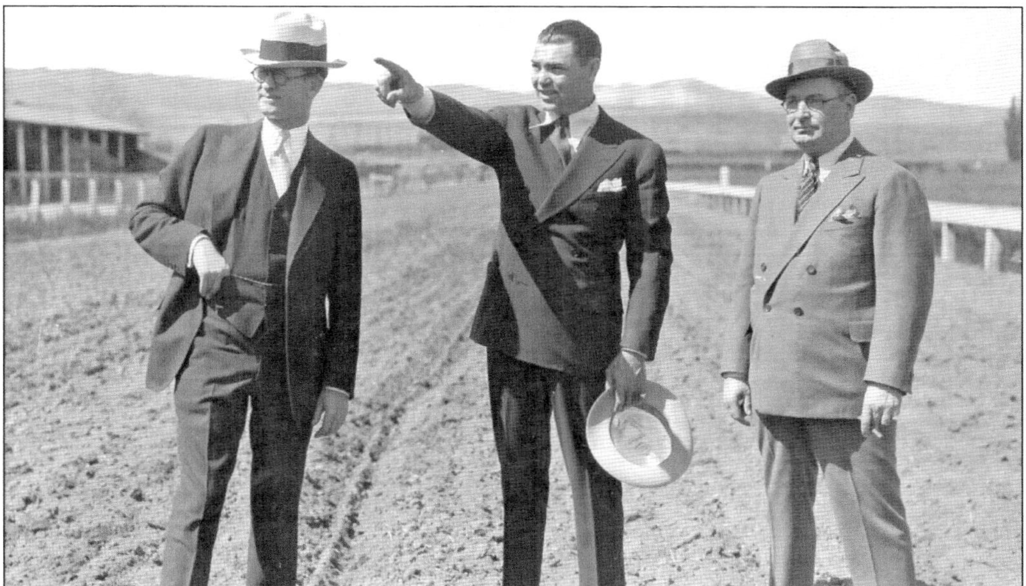

Bill Graham (left) and James McKay (right) stand here with former heavyweight boxing champion Jack Dempsey at the Reno Race Track. The racetrack was owned by the Bank Club, along with several other speakeasies and the city's red-light district, known as "the Stockade." The partners were a powerful force in the early years of Reno gambling but were sent to federal prison for mail fraud in 1938. They returned to Reno after being pardoned by Pres. Harry Truman. (Photograph courtesy of Colleen Rosencrantz Collection.)

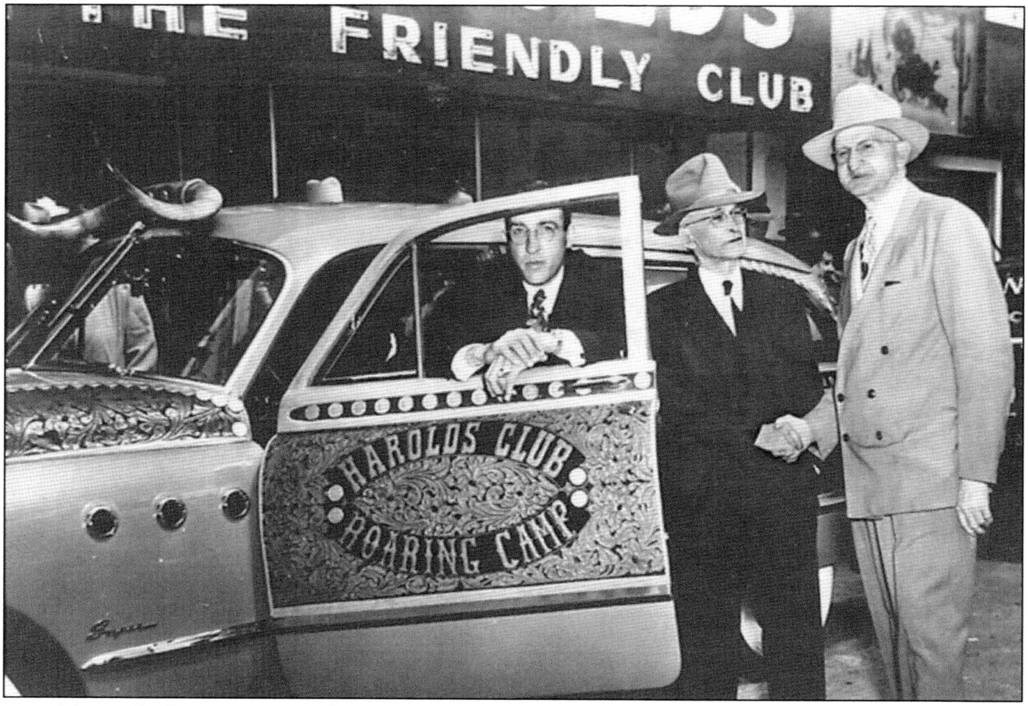

Harold Smith (left) borrowed $500 from his father, Raymond I. "Pappy" Smith (right), to open Harolds Club at 236 North Virginia Street in 1935. The casino operated at that location for the next 60 years. They are pictured here with fellow downtown businessman George Southworth. Harolds Club, under the ownership of the Smith family, was known for its large, loyal, and friendly staff. The casino achieved worldwide acclaim through some creative advertising ventures. In the 1940s, signs reading "Harolds Club or Bust" were put up at locations throughout the United States and near military bases around the world. (Photographs courtesy of Neal Cobb Collection.)

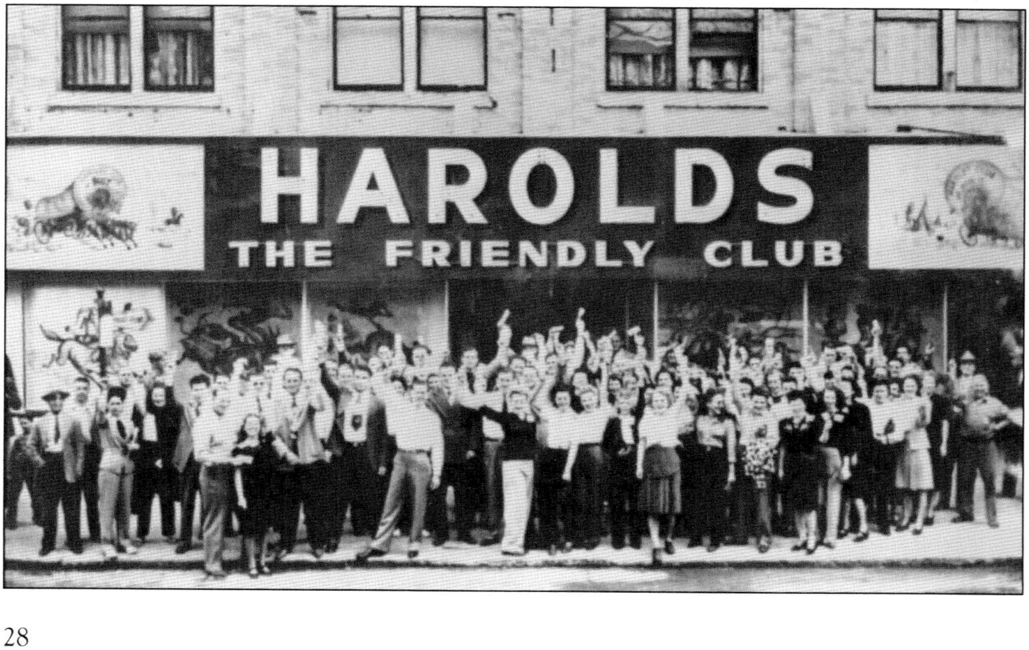

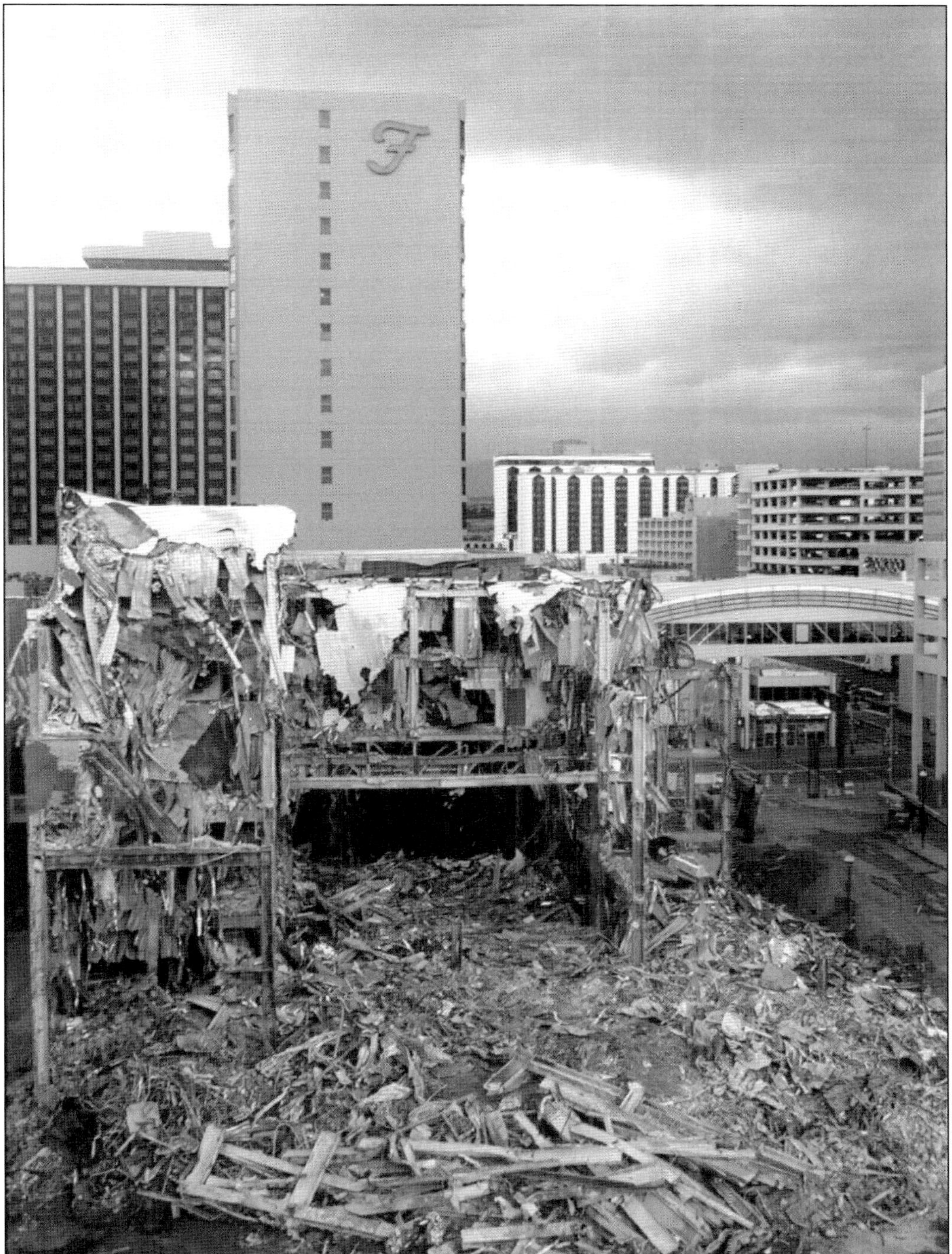

The Smith family sold Harolds Club to billionaire Howard Hughes in 1970. Ownership changed hands several times after that, and the club closed for good in 1997. The property was ultimately bought by Harrah's, who imploded the building. The area is now a plaza. (Photograph by Jean Dixon, courtesy of the *Reno Gazette-Journal*.)

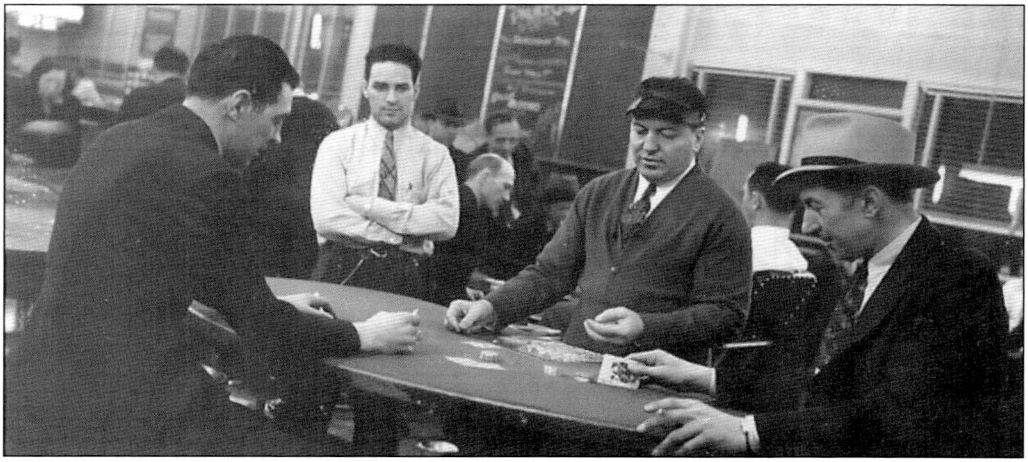

Silvio Petricciani, second from left, followed his father, John "Slot Machine Johnny" Petricciani into the gaming business at the Palace Club in the 1930s and became known as one of the top dice and faro dealers in the business. World War II service briefly interrupted his career, but he returned to Nevada after the war and held management positions at casinos in Las Vegas and Reno over the next 40 years. A civic leader, he was also a founder of the National Championship Air Races. (Photograph courtesy of Petricciani family.)

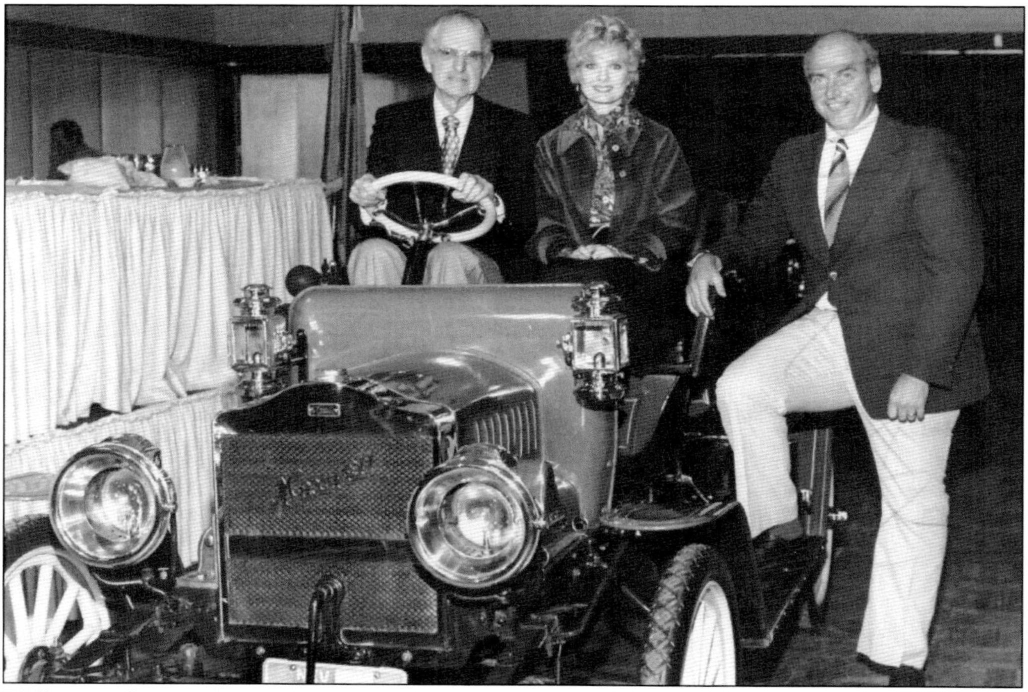

William Fisk Harrah, pictured with his wife, Scherry, and Gov. Mike O'Callaghan, arrived in Reno in 1937 and opened a bingo parlor at 124 North Center Street. Over the next 40-plus years, he built a gambling empire, focusing on top-notch entertainment and exemplary customer service. Harrah also collected vintage automobiles, and his name lives on in both his casinos and the Harrah Collection at the National Automobile Museum in Reno. (Photograph courtesy of the *Reno Gazette-Journal*.)

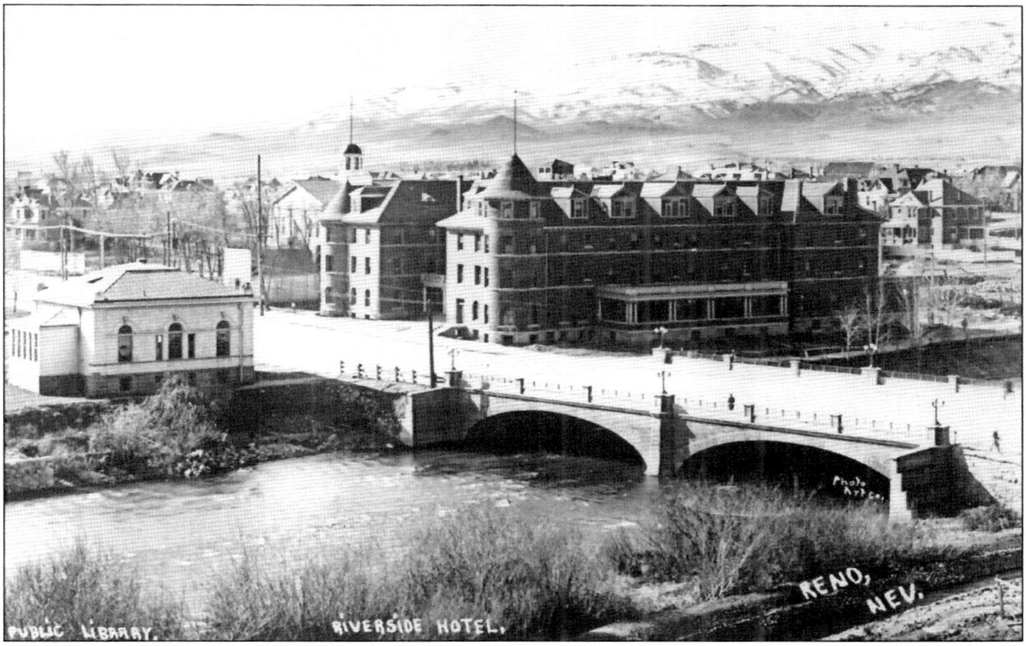

The Riverside Hotel existed in one form or another virtually from Reno's inception. A 1920s version of the hotel was destroyed by fire, but it was rebuilt using the design of noted Reno architect Frederic DeLongchamps in 1927. Located on the banks of the Truckee River, the hotel became the focal point of the divorce trade in Reno, as it was situated next door to the Washoe County Courthouse. (Photographs courtesy of the *Reno Gazette-Journal*.)

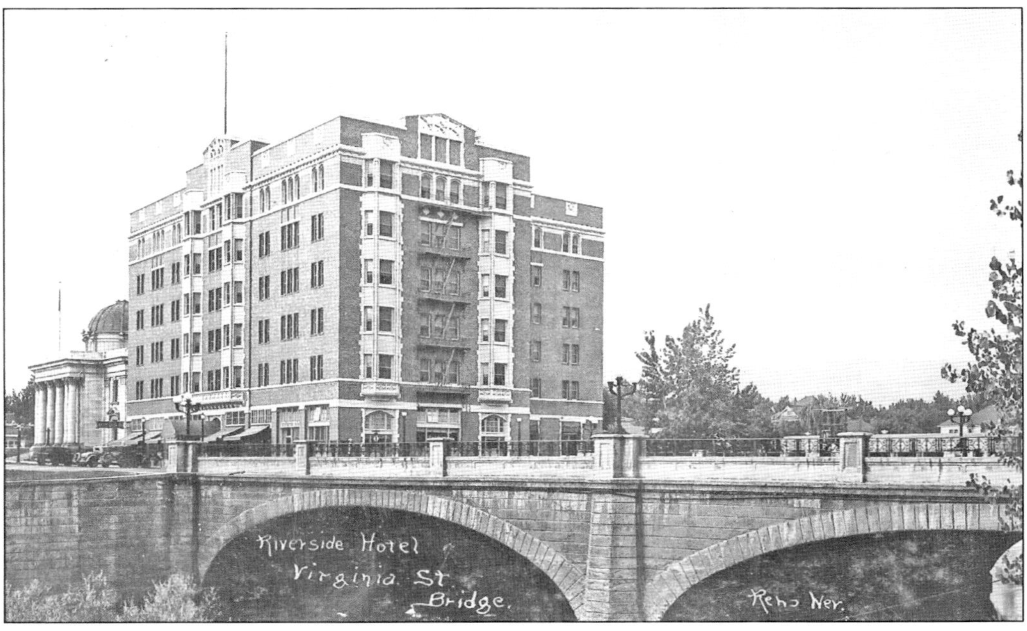

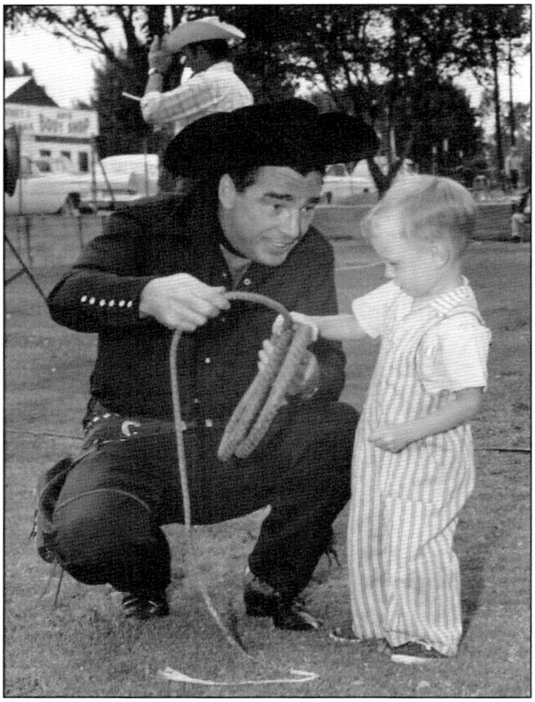

Lash LaRue rose to cinematic fame as a cowboy who could flick the six-gun out of a villain's hand with a lash of his bullwhip. He appeared in more than 100 movies and television shows, including the television series *Lash of the West* in 1952 and 1953. In October 1962, LaRue left Hollywood and moved to Reno. He bought the El Ruth Motor Court and changed the name to LaRue Lodge, which was widely photographed because of its sign that read "Truckers, Salesmen, Divorcees Welcome." LaRue was married nine times, including to Reno native Josephine Clark (below), who acted in Western films and television shows under the name Reno Browne. (Photographs courtesy of the *Reno Gazette-Journal*.)

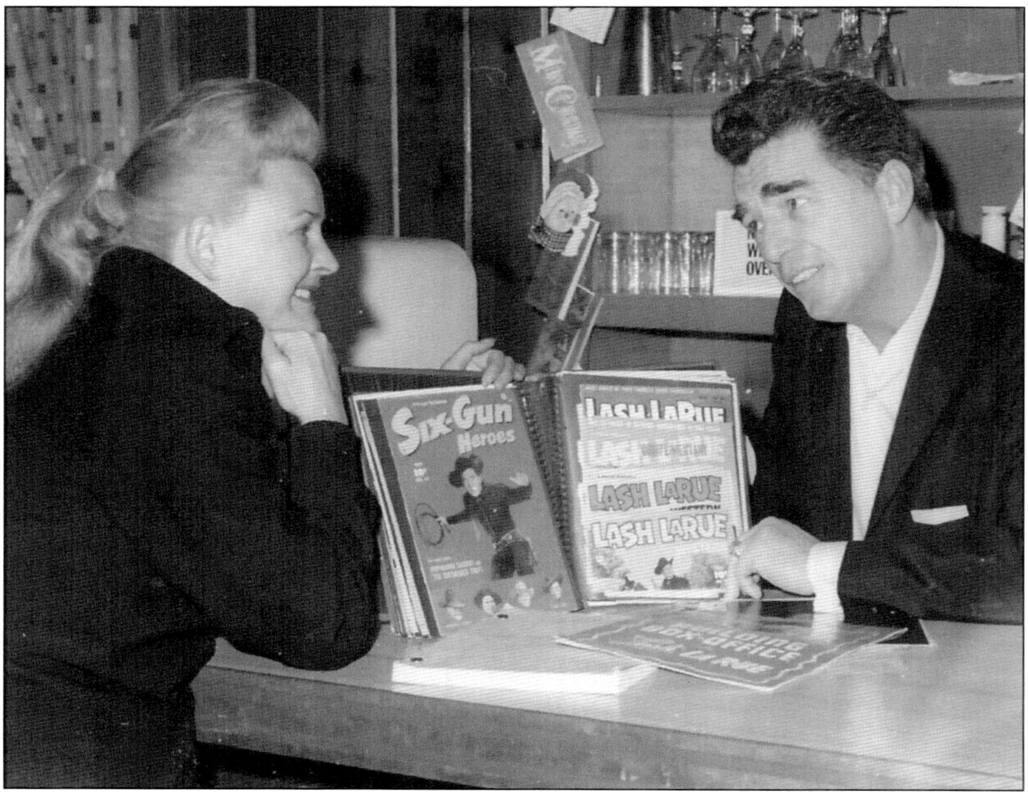

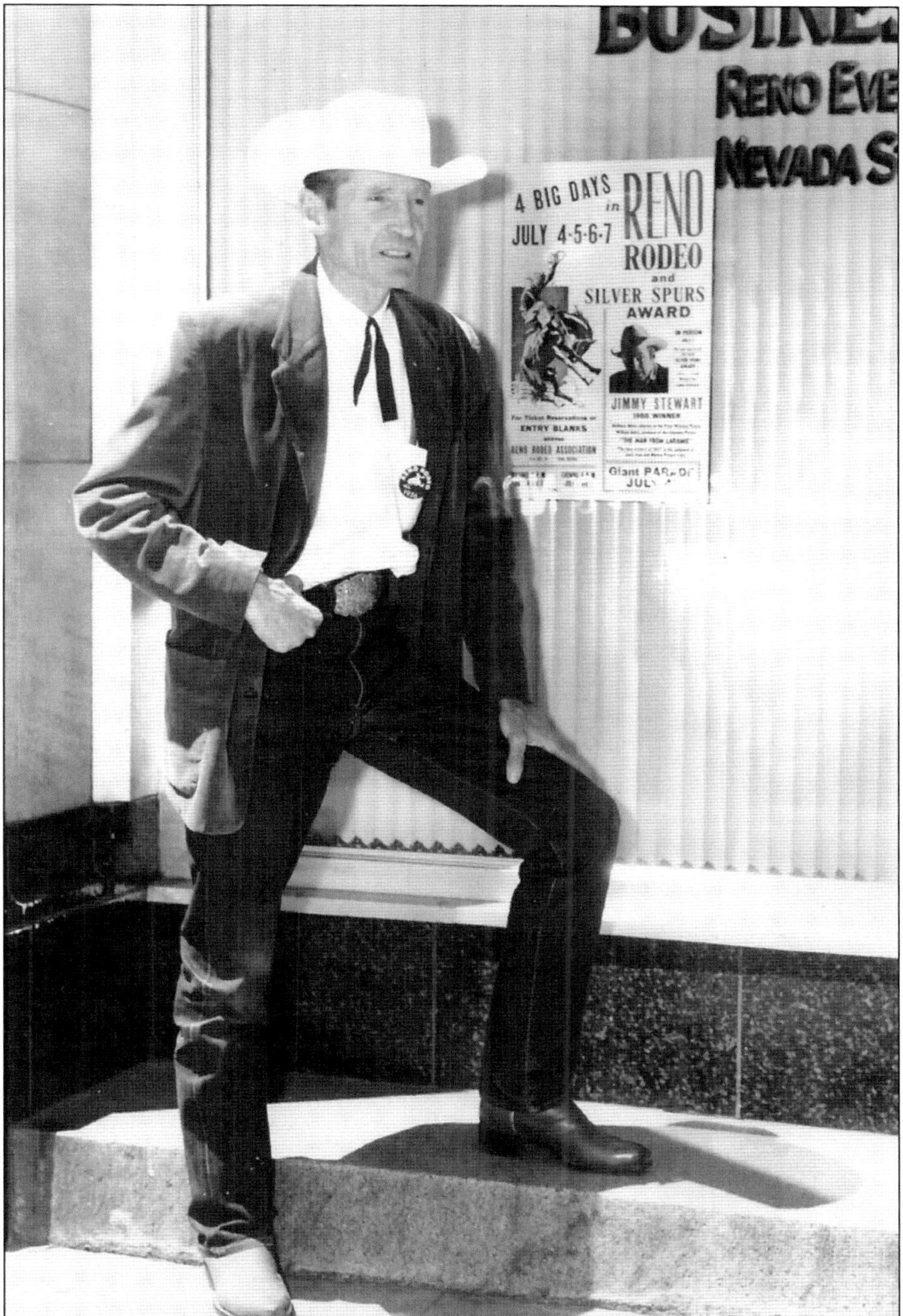

The Reno Printing Company was founded in 1907. Harry Frost, a former star running back for the University of Nevada, had a part-time job there in the late 1920s. Several years later, he married the owner's daughter, and they took over operating the company in 1931, running it for many years before retiring. Frost was also a civic leader and longtime supporter of the university and the Reno Rodeo. (Photograph courtesy of the *Reno Gazette-Journal*.)

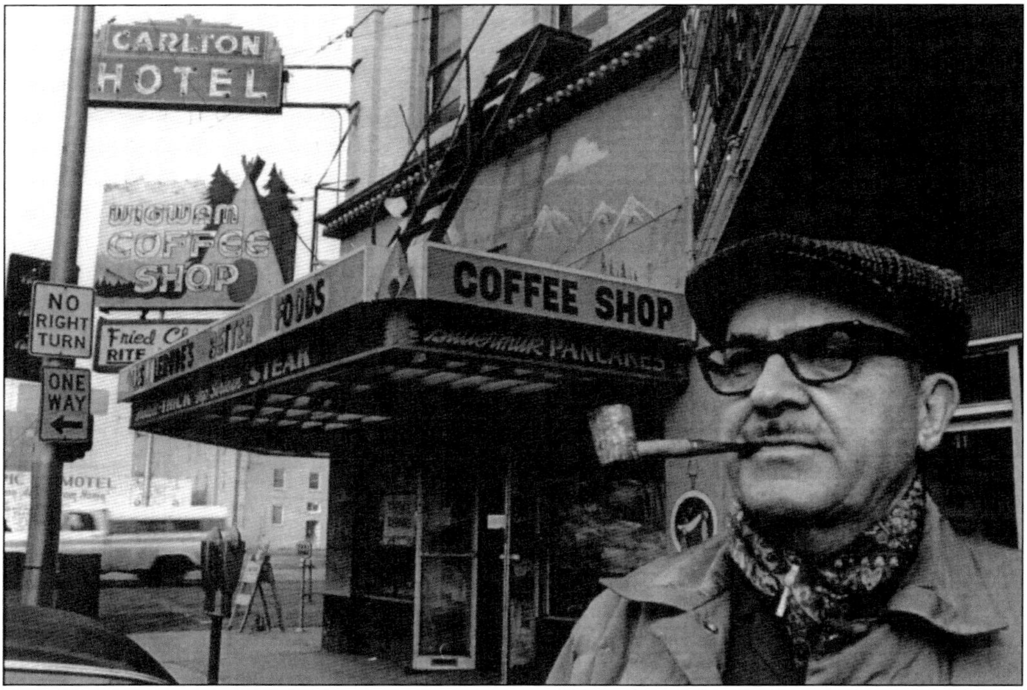

Restaurateur Les Lerude opened the landmark Wigwam restaurant at Second and Sierra Streets in 1934. Filled with signs and catchy slogans, the restaurant was a local favorite for more than 30 years. The house specialty was hot apple pie with butter sauce, a recipe Lerude kept secret for years before finally making it available to the public. He operated the restaurant until 1972. (Photograph courtesy of Warren Lerude.)

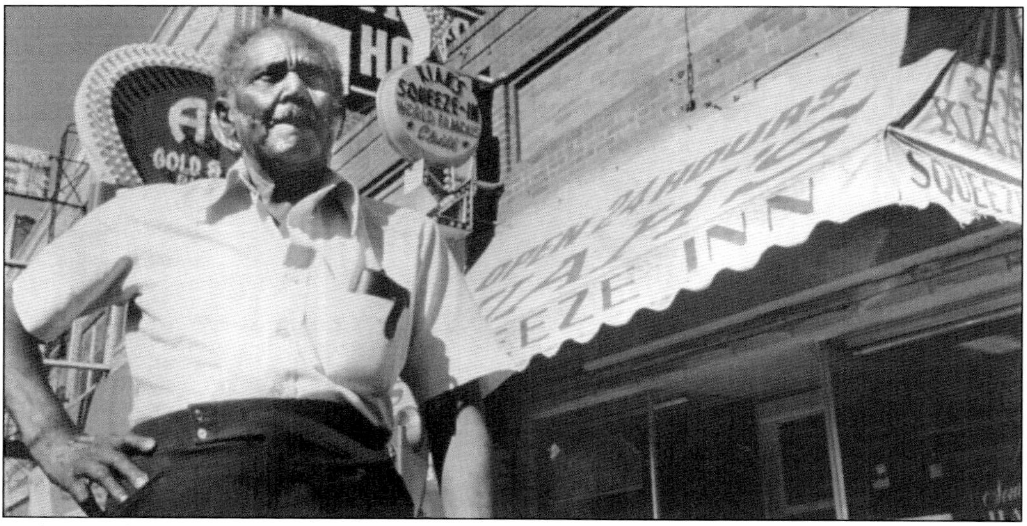

Kiah Lumpkin, owner of the Kiah's Squeeze Inn on North Virginia Street, was the first African American business owner in the downtown core. The restaurant became a favorite haunt for celebrities performing at the Reno clubs and for those enjoying a late night on the town. Lumpkin had a sign behind the counter that read "Kiah, World's Greatest Cook." (Photograph courtesy of the *Reno Gazette-Journal*.)

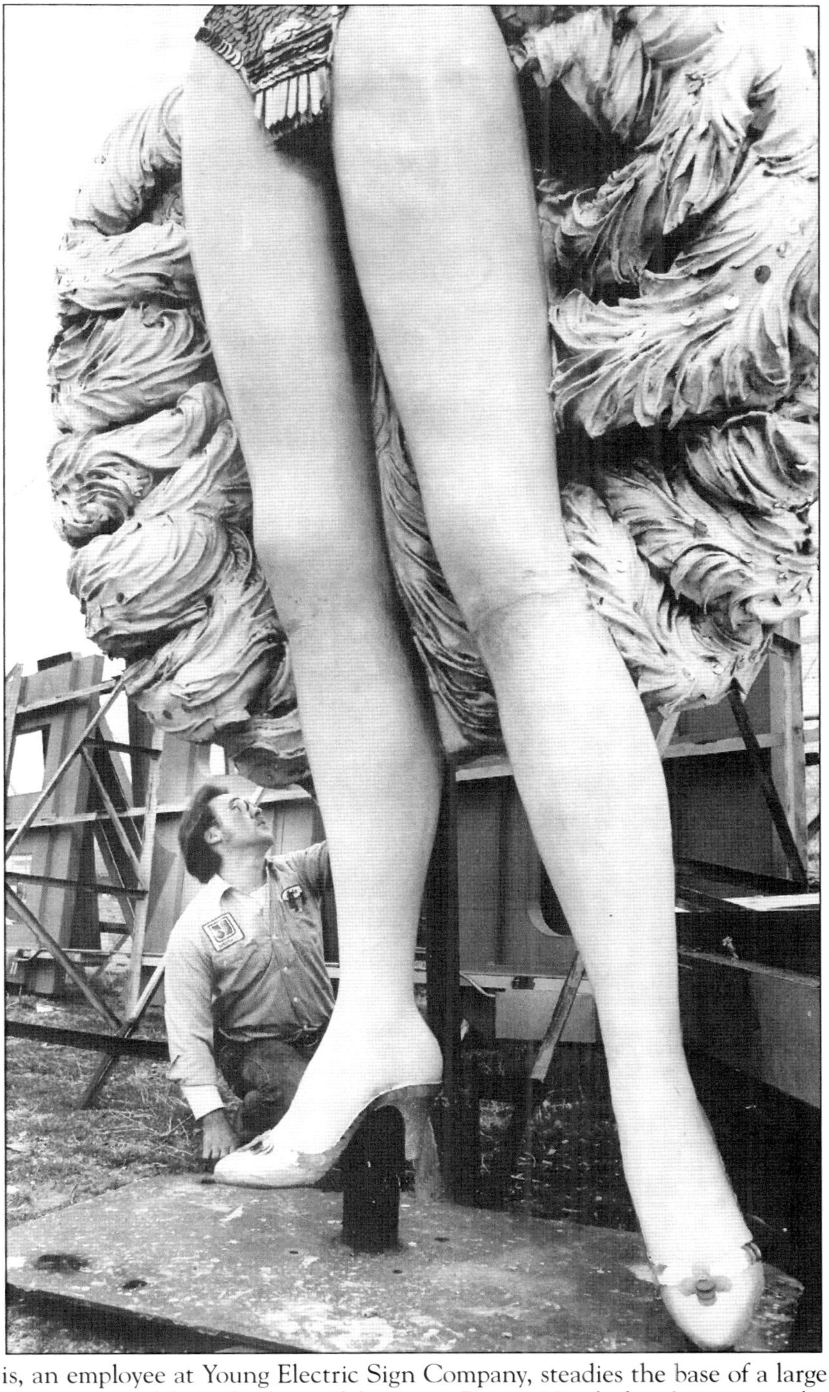

Jake Davis, an employee at Young Electric Sign Company, steadies the base of a large showgirl statue that was removed from the front of the Prima Donna Hotel after the property became the Flamingo Hilton on Virginia Street in 1982. The large statue was transported north on Kietzke Lane via truck and on to the sign company storage yard. (Photograph by Jean Dixon, courtesy of the *Reno Gazette-Journal*.)

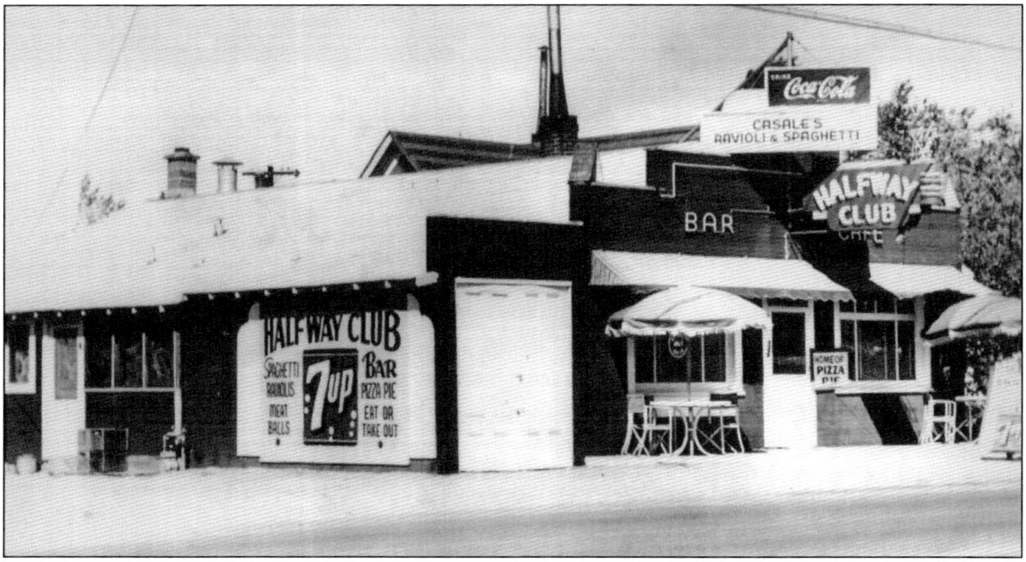

The Halfway Club on East Fourth Street, so named because it was located roughly halfway between Reno and Sparks, started life as a roadside fruit stand owned by John and Elvira Casale in 1937. In 1940, they started selling ravioli, and in 1942, the restaurant that still stands today began operating. John and Elvira's daughter, Inez Stempeck, has been making homemade ravioli and meatballs at the restaurant for more than 60 years. (Above, photograph courtesy of Inez Stempeck; below, photograph by Marilyn Newton, courtesy of the *Reno Gazette-Journal*.)

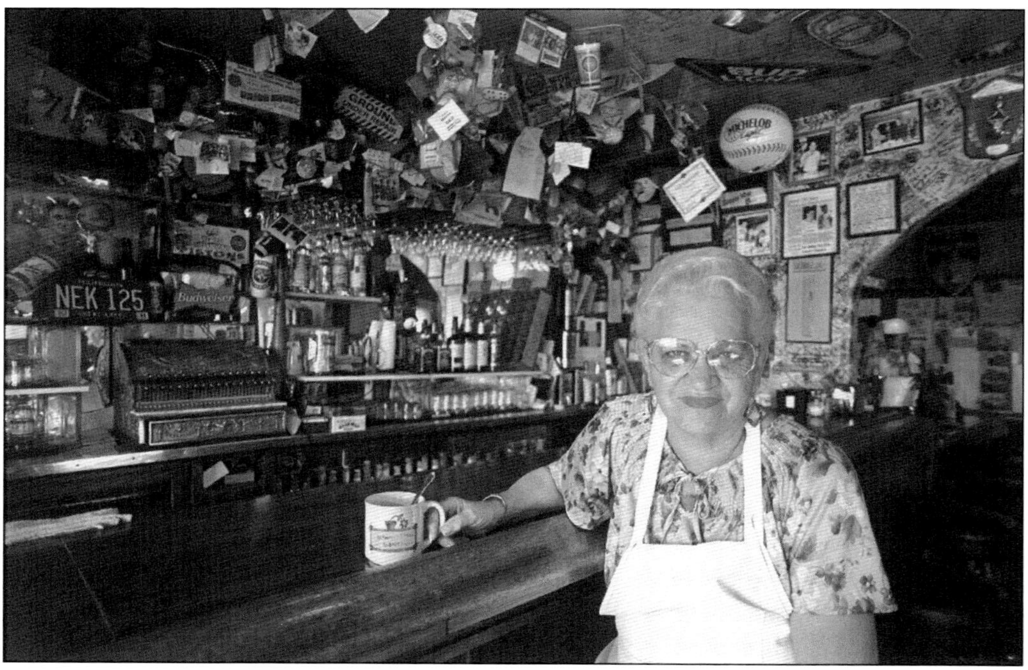

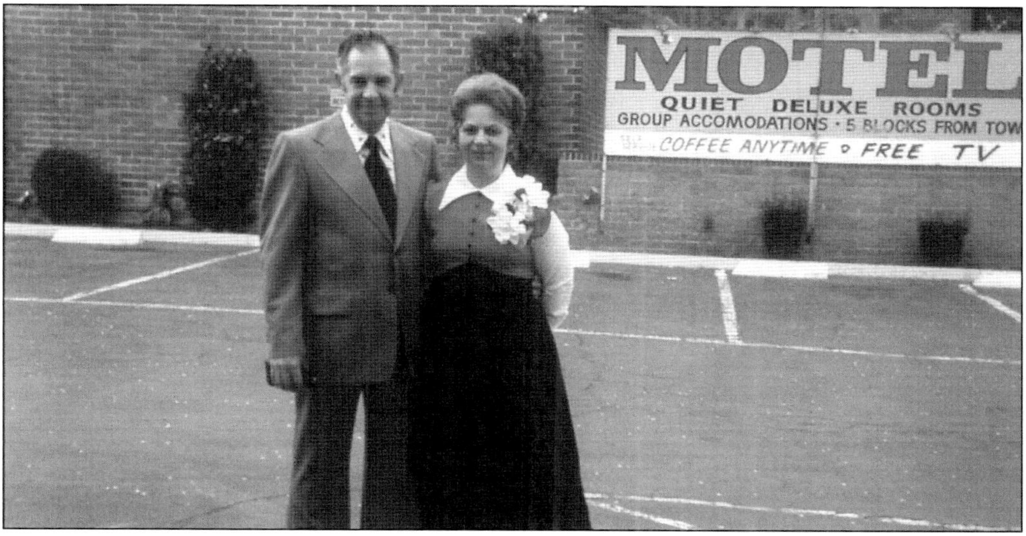

Lewis and Georgia Foster stand in front of their Silver Dollar Motor Lodge on the corner of Eighth and North Virginia Streets. The Fosters owned and operated the business from 1968 until their retirement more than 20 years later. It served as a convenient spot for visitors who wanted to access downtown Reno without staying in one of the casino-hotels. (Photograph courtesy of the Foster family.)

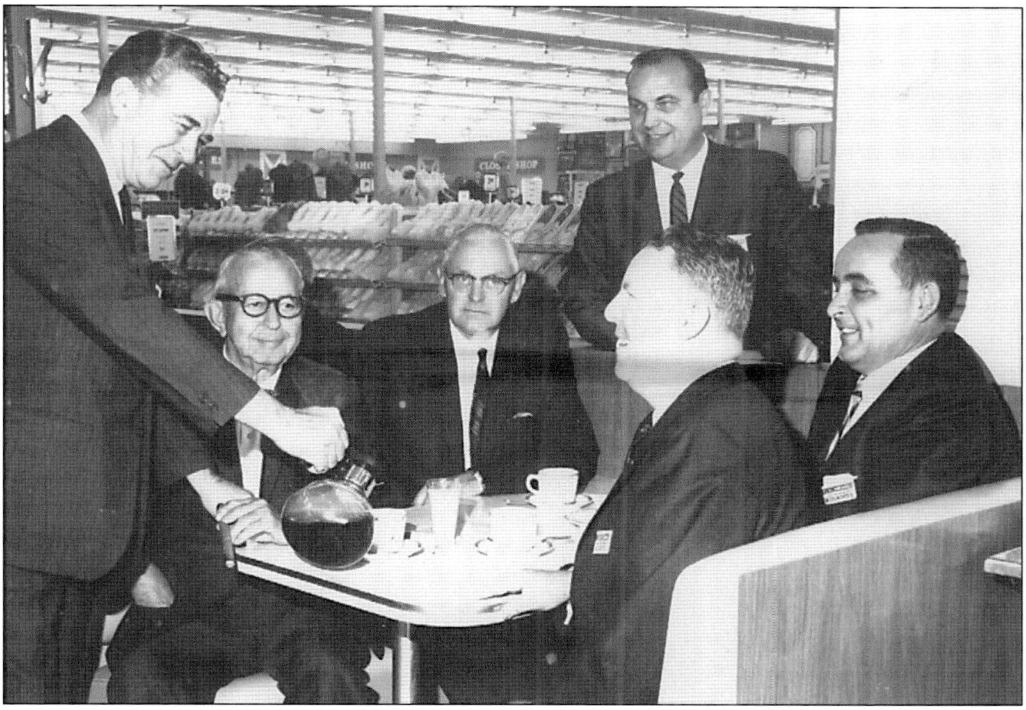

The coffee shop inside the Woolworth store in Park Lane Mall became a regular meeting place for groups of Reno businessmen in the 1960s and 1970s. This group includes, from left to right, H.M. Swift, Dr. Bart Hood, Mayor Roy Bankofier, Chuck Charlton, H.P. Smith, and Paul O'Driscoll. (Photograph courtesy of the *Reno Gazette-Journal*.)

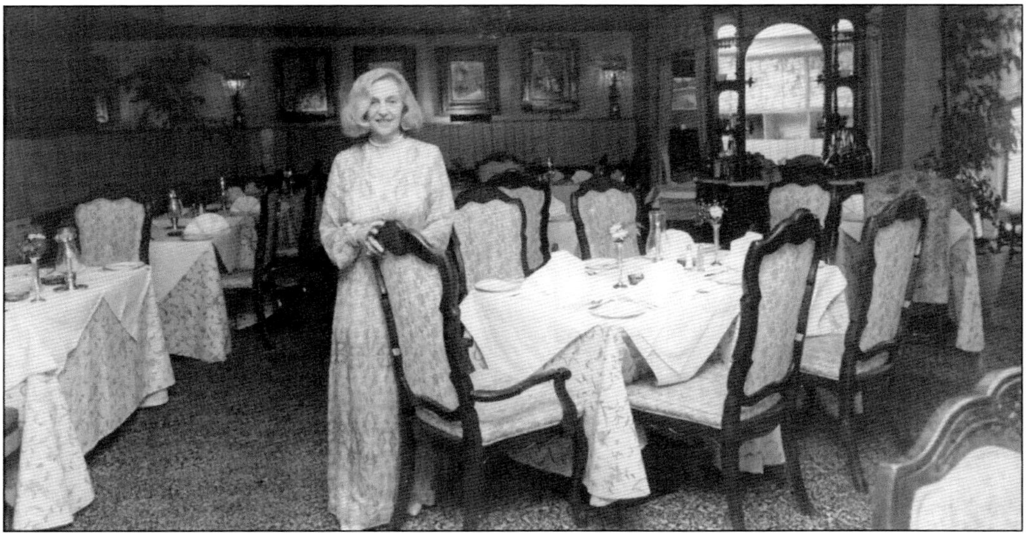

Cebe Loomis and her husband, Frandsen "Bud" Loomis, built the Bundox Restaurant and adjoining River House Motor Hotel in 1956 on property Bud purchased along the banks of the Truckee River in downtown Reno in 1938. The Bundox, at 2 Lake Street, was decorated with jade and other Far East artifacts the Loomises had collected on their travels. It was a favorite fine dining spot for locals and visiting celebrities for more than 30 years. (Photograph by Marilyn Newton, courtesy of the *Reno Gazette-Journal*.)

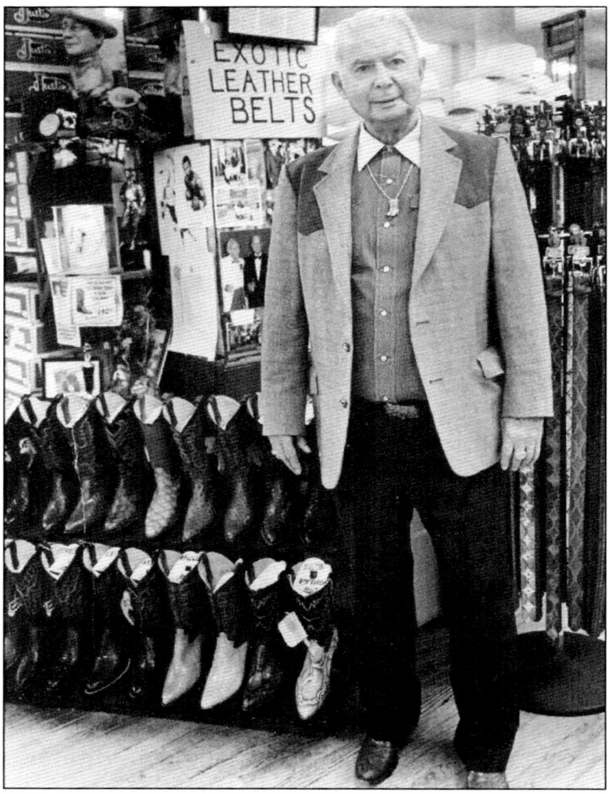

Founded in 1919 by George Parker on Center Street, Parker's Western Wear was a Reno institution up until the family-owned business closed for good in 2000. Harry Parker, seen here, bought the business from George Parker's widow in 1958 and moved it to 151 North Sierra Street. Harry and his brother, Mush, were well known downtown civic leaders. The store served ranchers, cowboys, visitors, and celebrities ranging from Clark Gable to Whoopi Goldberg. (Photograph by Jean Dixon, courtesy of the *Reno Gazette-Journal*.)

Three

UNDER THE ARCH

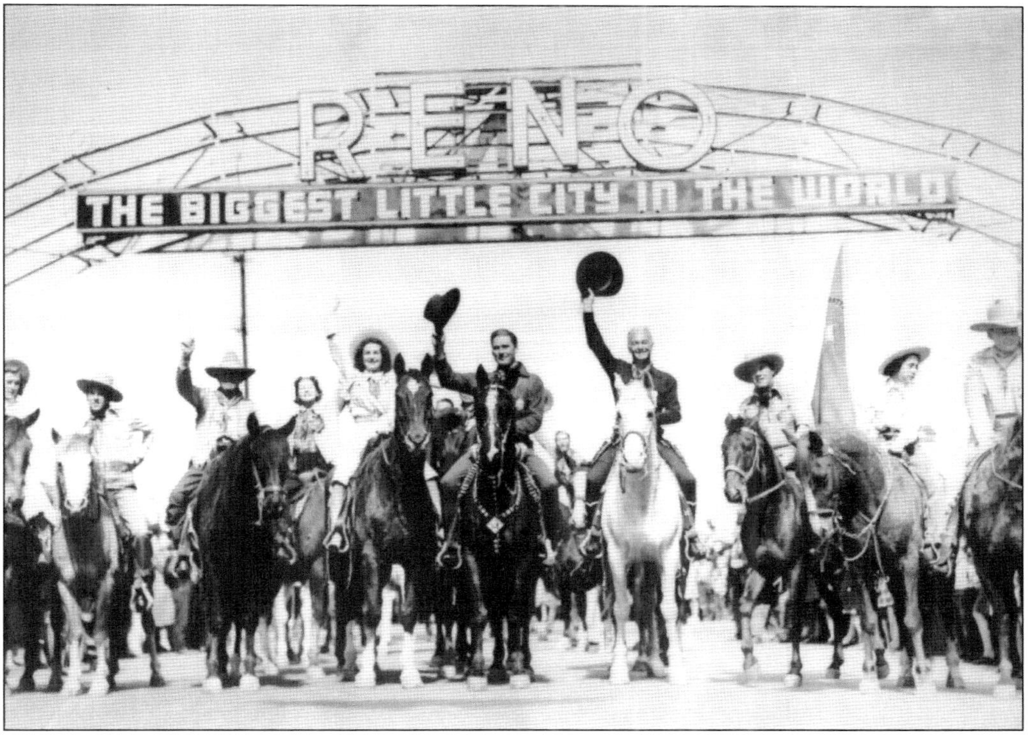

The arch across Virginia Street in downtown Reno has been the city's signature landmark since 1926 and a feature in thousands of photographs taken of Reno through the years. In 1940, Hollywood stars celebrating the premiere of the movie *Virginia City* struck a pose in front of the arch. All the stars of the film and other actors under contract to Warner Brothers were required to attend the premiere. Those pictured include Ronald Reagan (second from left), Errol Flynn (center, on the dark horse), and William Boyd (center, on the white horse). (Photograph by Jerry Cobb, courtesy of the Neal Cobb Collection.)

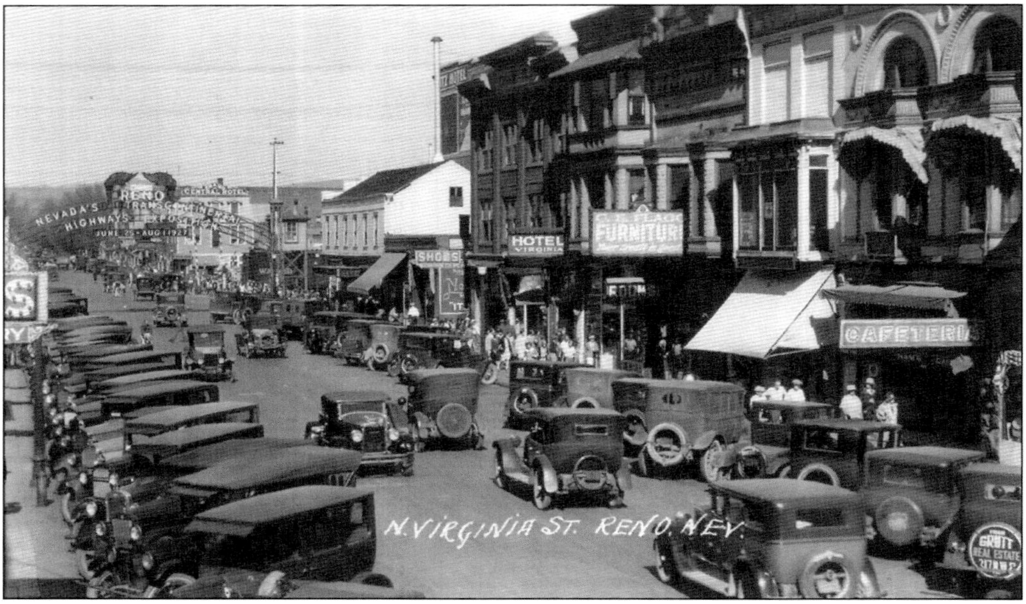

The first Reno Arch was erected in 1926 at the intersection of Virginia Street and Commercial Row to publicize the Transcontinental Highways Exposition, which celebrated the completion of the Lincoln and Victory Highways. The exposition was held from June 25 to August 1, 1927, at Idlewild Park in Reno. After the exposition, Reno's city fathers voted to keep the arch as a permanent fixture in the city. The torches from the original arch were maintained, and the slogan "The Biggest Little City in the World" was added after the slogan contest in 1929. (Photographs courtesy of the Neal Cobb Collection.)

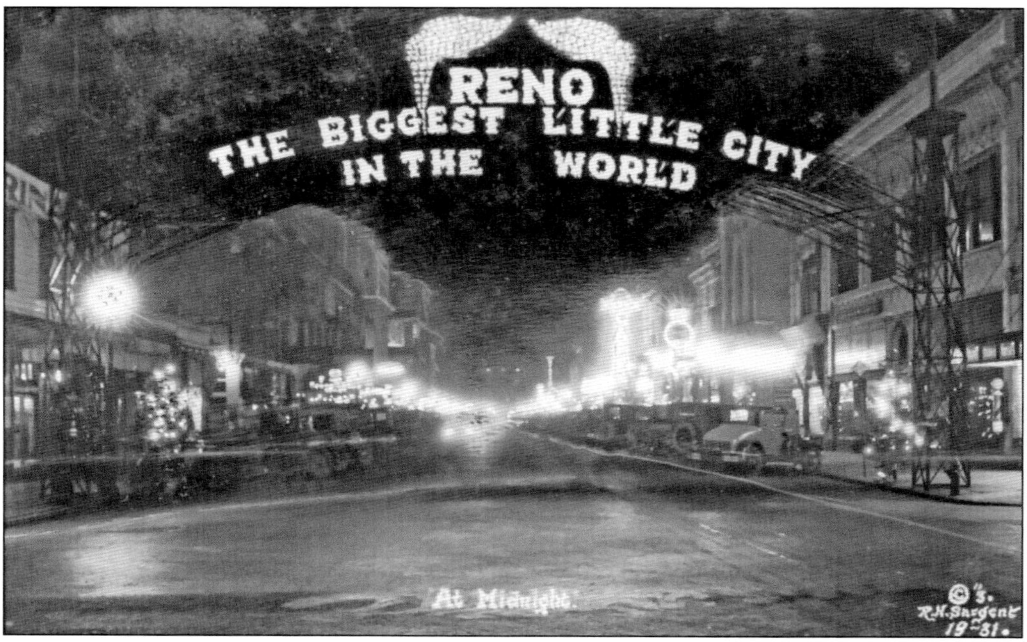

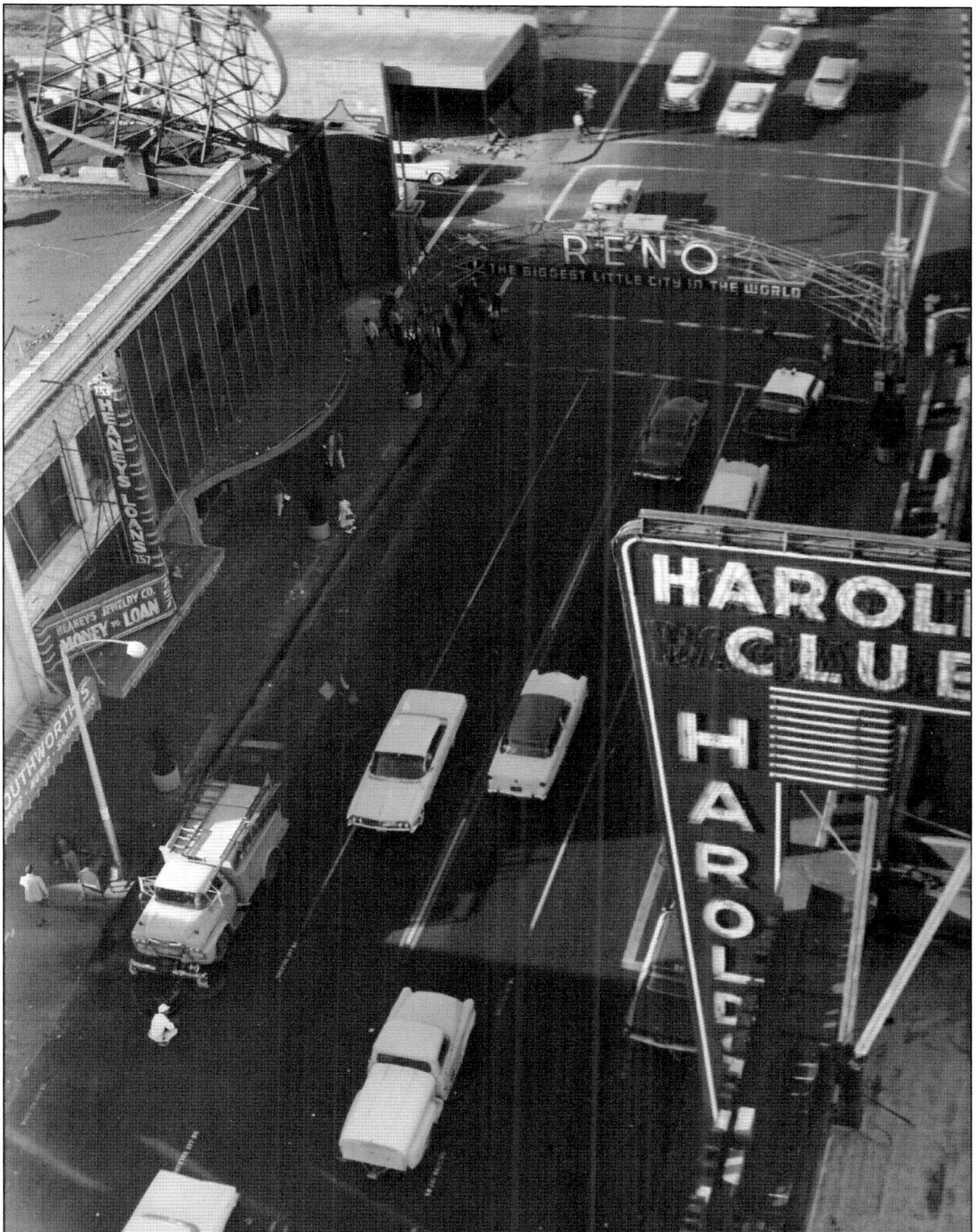

The third version of the Reno Arch, as seen here from the roof of Harolds Club, spanned Virginia Street in 1935. At first, it did not include the slogan "The Biggest Little City in the World," but after a public outcry, the slogan was added once again. This version of the arch stood for more than 30 years and moved to several locations after a more modern arch was introduced in 1963. Today, it spans Center Street near the National Automobile Museum. (Photograph courtesy of the Neal Cobb Collection.)

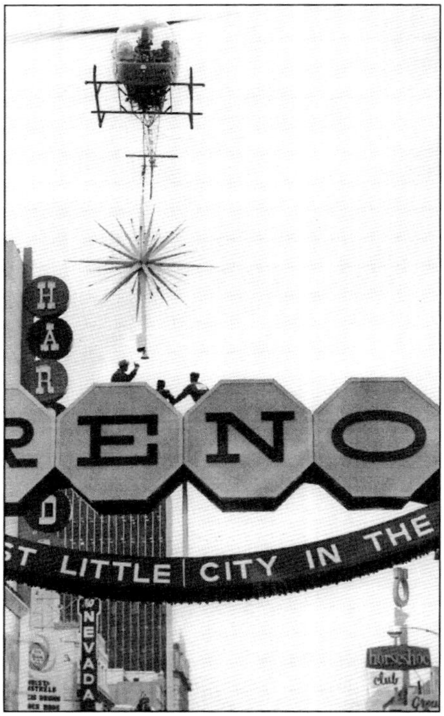

In 1963, a group of downtown casino owners decided the long-standing Reno Arch was outdated "and a bit of an eyesore when contrasted to the modern building fronts on Virginia Street." The casino group, which included Harolds Club, the Prima Donna, the Nevada Club, Poor Pete's, and the Horseshoe, said they would not only pay for a modern arch but also pay to operate it for the first five years. The new version was put into place on New Year's Eve 1963. A helicopter mounted the snowflake atop the new arch, which continued to be a focal point for the city's special events, including the National Championship Air Races. (Photographs courtesy of the *Reno Gazette-Journal*.)

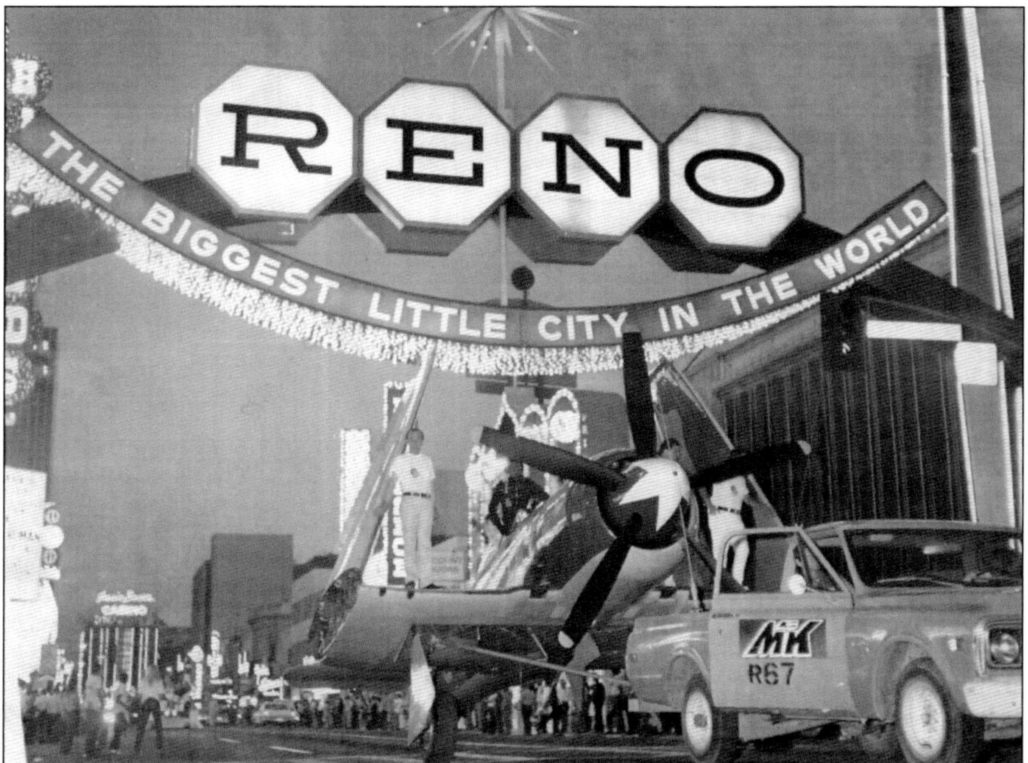

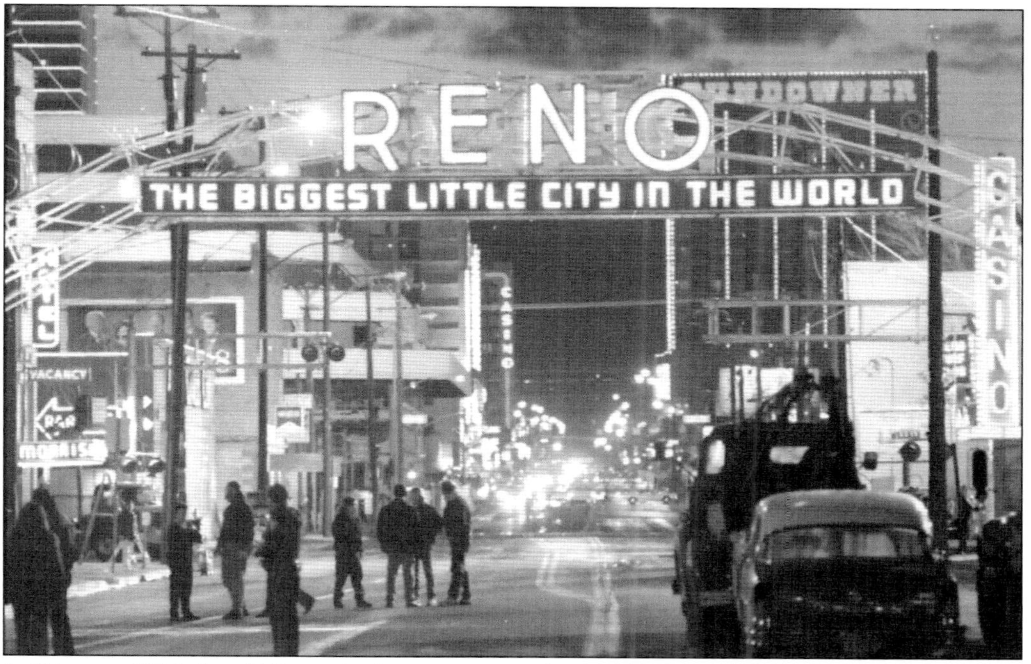

In February 1994, the old Reno Arch was temporarily moved to Fourth Street in downtown Reno to be used as a prop in the movie *Ty Cobb*, starring Tommy Lee Jones as the Hall of Fame baseball player. The movie also starred Robert Wuhl and Lolita Davidovich. (Photograph by David B. Parker, courtesy of the *Reno Gazette-Journal*.)

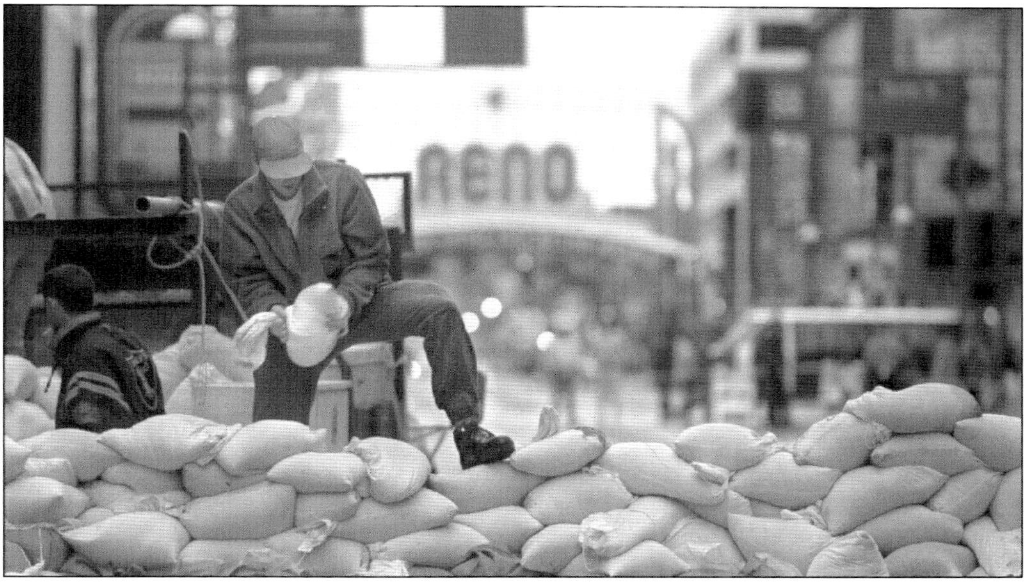

The Reno Arch was the backdrop for Reno's great New Year's flood of 1997, when a warm rain melted a large snowpack and sent water from the Truckee River over its banks and into many low-lying neighborhoods, including downtown Reno. Here, Will Sapperfield of Reno helps volunteers create a sandbag barrier across Virginia Street just north of First Street. (Photograph by David B. Parker, courtesy of the *Reno Gazette-Journal*.)

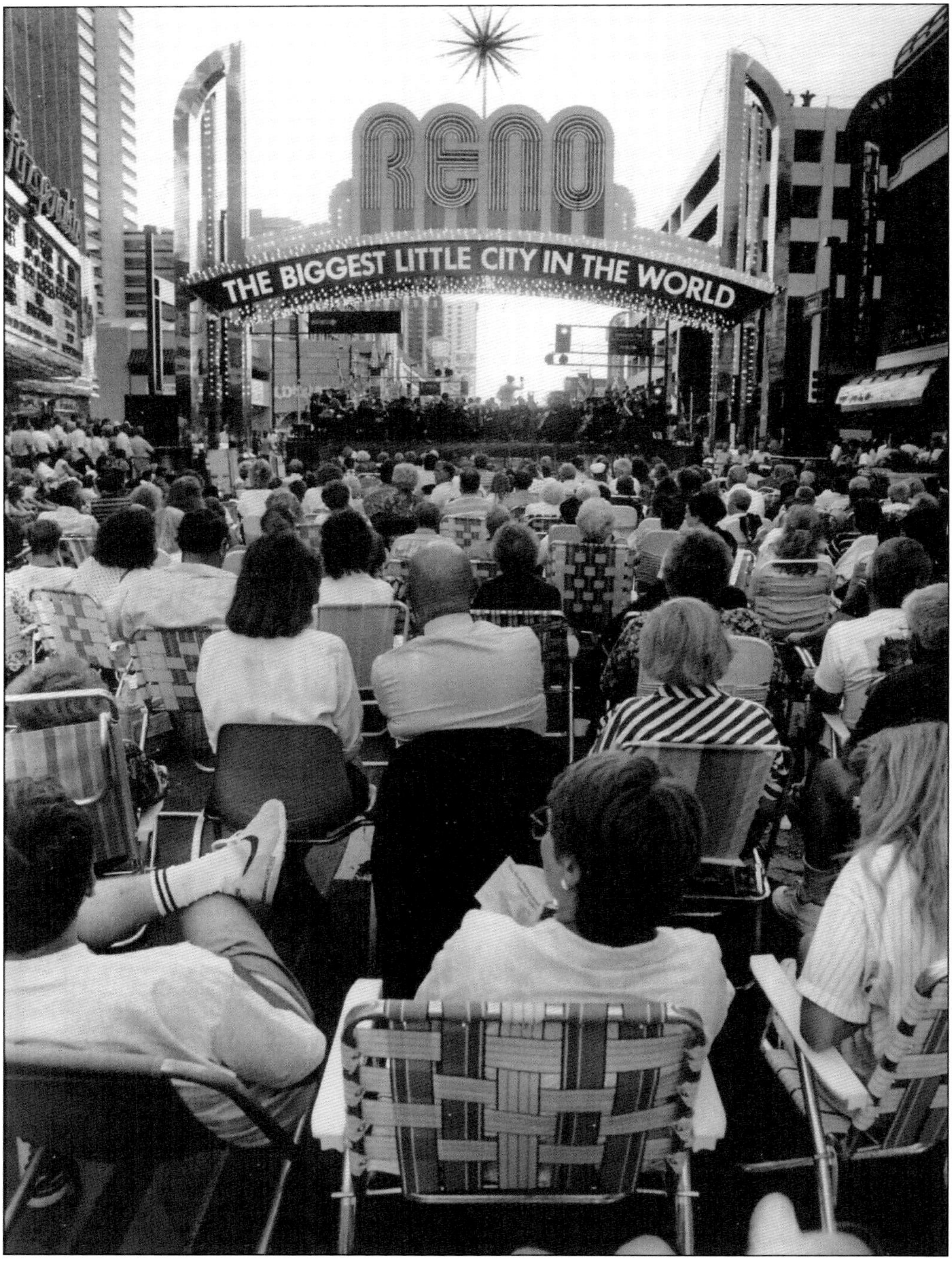

The present-day Reno Arch was dedicated on Virginia Street on August 8, 1987, with a modern look but the same traditional theme, including the "The Biggest Little City in the World" slogan. The arch contains 2,076 light bulbs. It continues to be an attraction for numerous special events, including this performance of the Reno Philharmonic Orchestra on July 13, 1991. (Photograph by David B. Parker, courtesy of the *Reno Gazette-Journal*.)

Four

WELCOME, MR. PRESIDENT

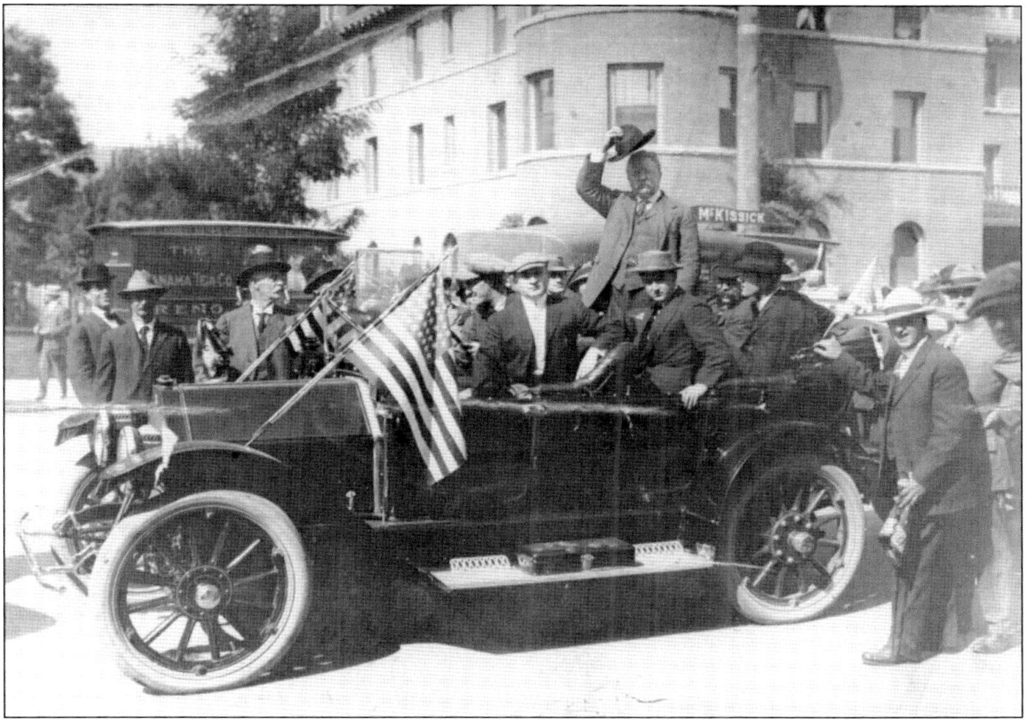

Theodore Roosevelt was the second president to visit Reno—Rutherford B. Hayes was the first, in 1880. Roosevelt arrived in Reno via train from California on May 19, 1903, at 7:30 a.m., passing through on his way to Carson City to deliver an address on the steps of the state capitol. After the speech, he returned to Reno, talked to supporters at the Washoe County Courthouse, and then traveled by car to the University of Nevada campus for a brief speech to students. (Photograph courtesy of the Nevada Historical Society.)

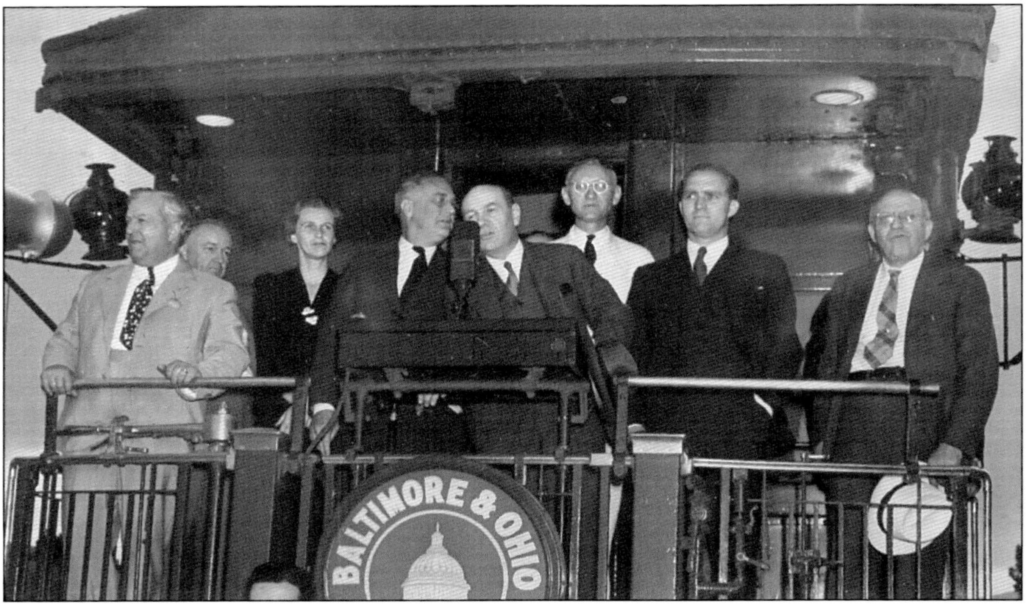

Pres. Franklin D. Roosevelt, sharing the microphone with Gov. Richard Kirman, stopped in Reno during a whistle-stop campaign trip through Nevada. Traveling westbound, Roosevelt made stops in Carlin, Imlay, and Sparks before delivering his speech in Reno. Also traveling with Roosevelt and Kirman was Sen. Patrick McCarran (far left). (Photograph courtesy of the Nevada Historical Society.)

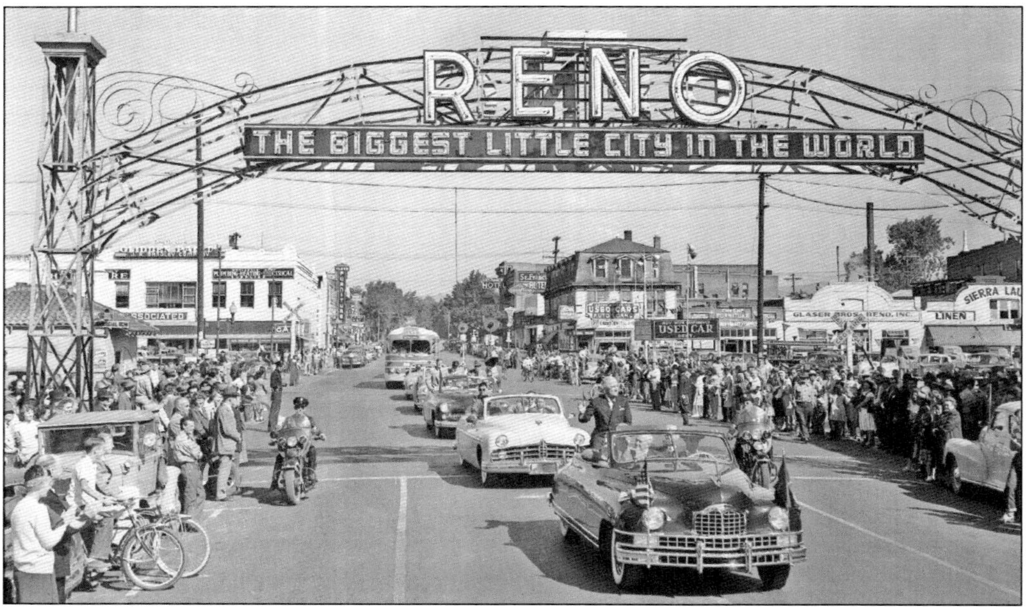

Pre. Harry S. Truman made a pass through Reno, and under the famous Reno Arch, while seeking election in 1948. He also returned to Reno as a former president in October 1960 for a speech in support of Democratic presidential candidate John F. Kennedy at the University of Nevada. Newspapers noted that "Give 'em Hell" Harry gave a fiery speech in support of Kennedy. (Photograph courtesy of the *Reno Gazette-Journal*.)

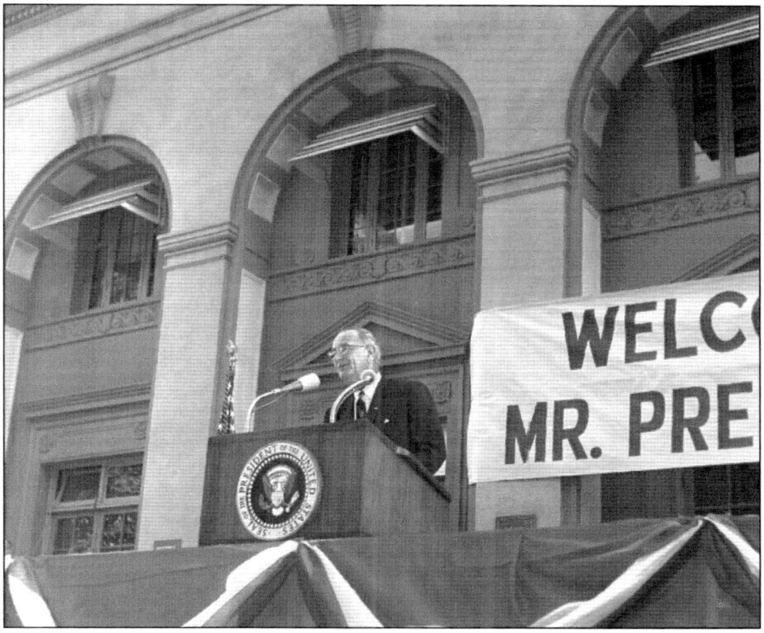

Pres. Lyndon B. Johnson became the first president to travel to Reno aboard Air Force One when he touched down for a campaign stop on October 12, 1964. Nevada's top Democrats, including US senators Alan Bible and Howard Cannon and Gov. Grant Sawyer, joined Johnson for his campaign appearance at the State Building in downtown Reno. (Photograph by Marilyn Newton, courtesy of the *Reno Gazette-Journal*.)

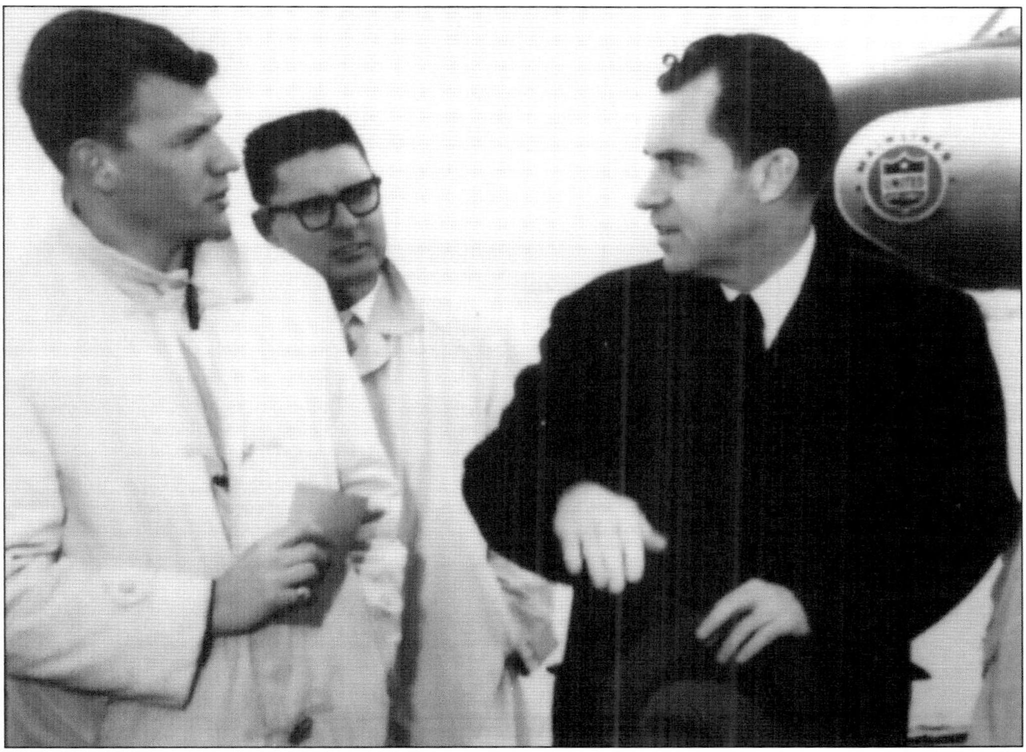

Vice Pres. Richard M. Nixon touched down at the Reno airport on February 18, 1960, on his way to nearby Squaw Valley Ski Area to officially open the Winter Olympic Games. The opening ceremony had to be delayed because a massive Sierra snowstorm caused a traffic nightmare between Reno and the ski resort. (Photograph courtesy of Bob Carroll Collection.)

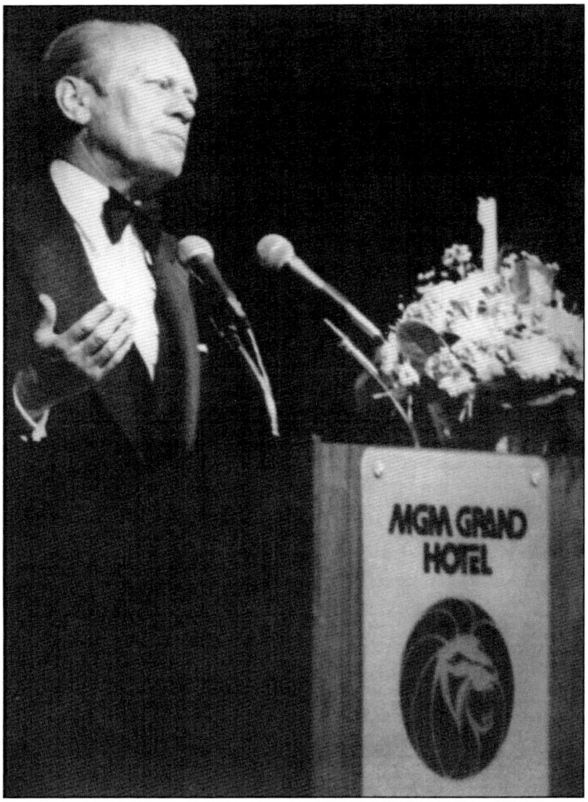

Pres. Gerald Ford visited Reno on several occasions, including as a candidate in 1976. Ford won Nevada but lost the election to Jimmy Carter—the only time in the 20th century that Nevada voters did not vote for the eventual winner. Ford also traveled to Reno to headline a cancer fundraiser in 1982 at the MGM Grand Hotel and again for the Safari Club convention in 1984. (Photograph courtesy of the *Reno Gazette-Journal*.)

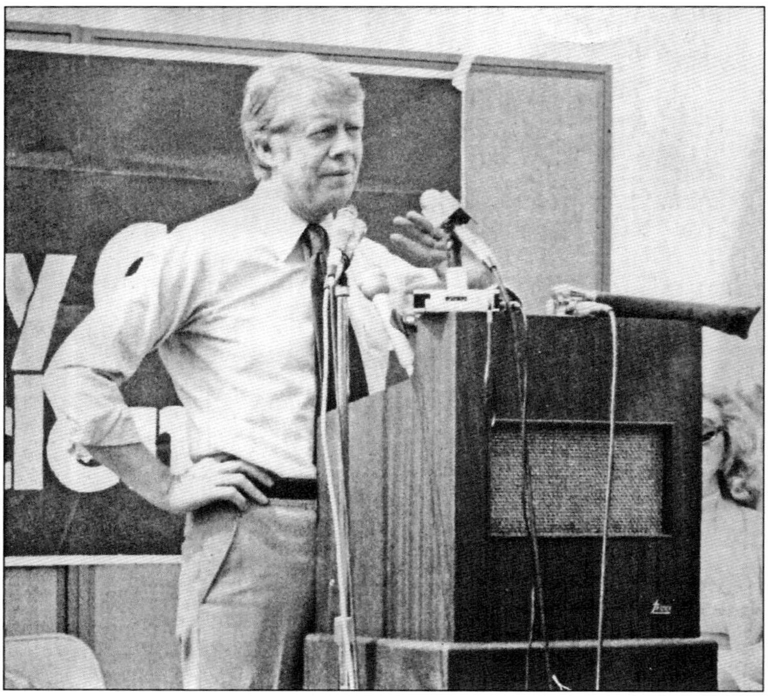

Jimmy Carter visited Reno's Park Lane Mall on May 21, 1976, as he was seeking the Democratic nomination for president. While Carter would go on to win the nomination, he was not received warmly in Nevada; four days after Carter's visit, Nevada sent its support to California governor Jerry Brown by a 2:1 margin. (Photograph courtesy of Jack Bacon Collection.)

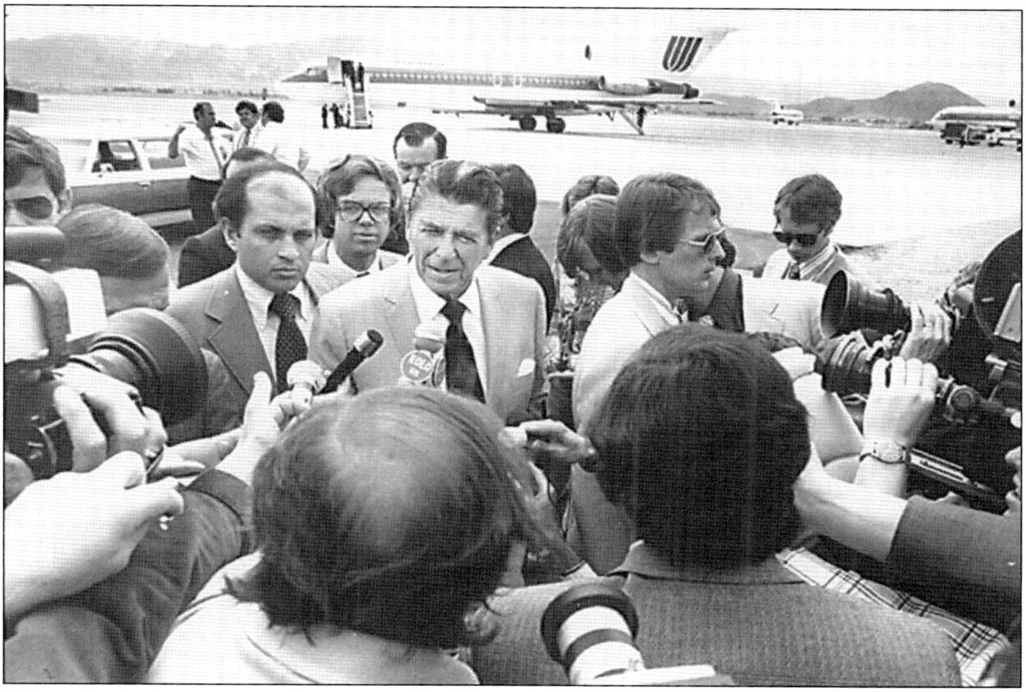

If Reno had a favorite president, it was likely Ronald Reagan, the former California governor and best friend of former Nevada governor and US senator Paul Laxalt. Reagan made a number of trips to Reno, Lake Tahoe, and Carson City, including a campaign stop during the 1976 presidential election when he took on Gerald Ford and was met by a throng of media at the Reno airport. In 1984, Reagan became the first president since Theodore Roosevelt to appear on the University of Nevada campus (below). Behind Reagan is Laxalt, with Gov. Robert List at far right. (Photographs courtesy of the *Reno Gazette-Journal*.)

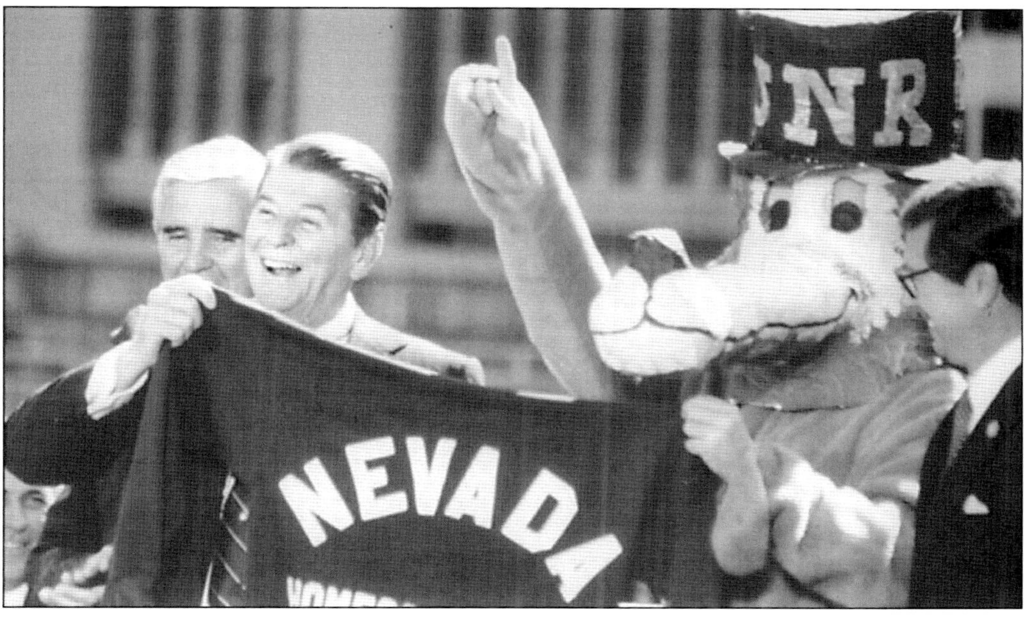

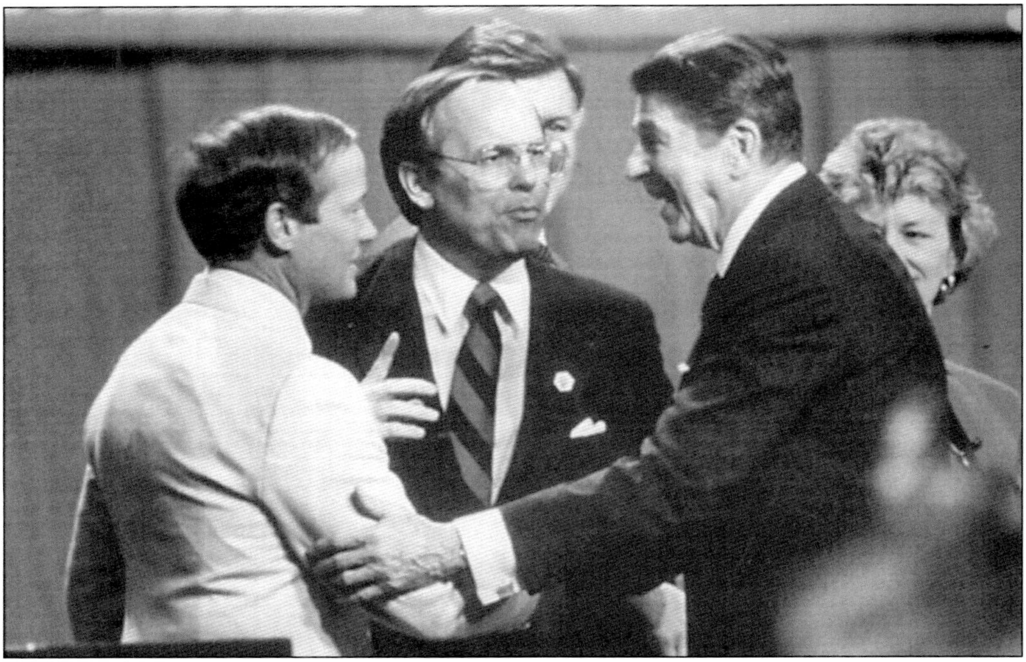

In 1986, Ronald Reagan returned to the University of Nevada campus (above) for another address and shook hands with University of Nevada football coach Chris Ault. Between Reagan and Ault is Republican National Committee chairman Fran Fahrenkopf, who also worked as a political science professor at the University of Nevada. Below, Reagan, always a lover of horses, accepts a Reno Rodeo belt buckle from Reno businessman Jack Bacon. The buckle remains on display at the Ronald Reagan Presidential Foundation and Library in Simi Valley, California. (Above, photograph courtesy of the *Reno Gazette-Journal*; below, photograph courtesy of Jack Bacon Collection.)

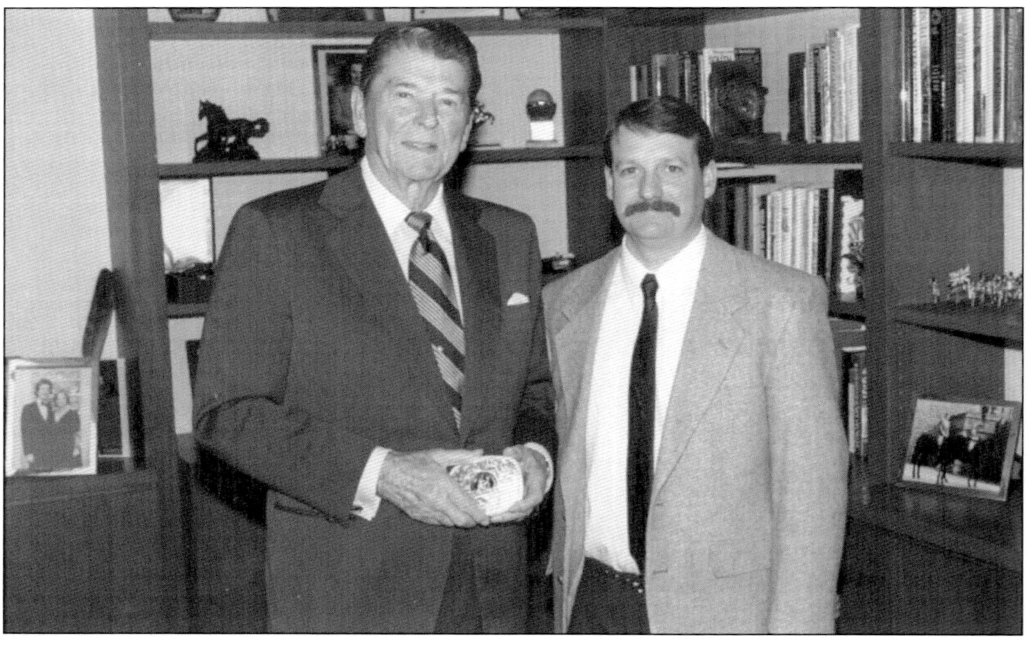

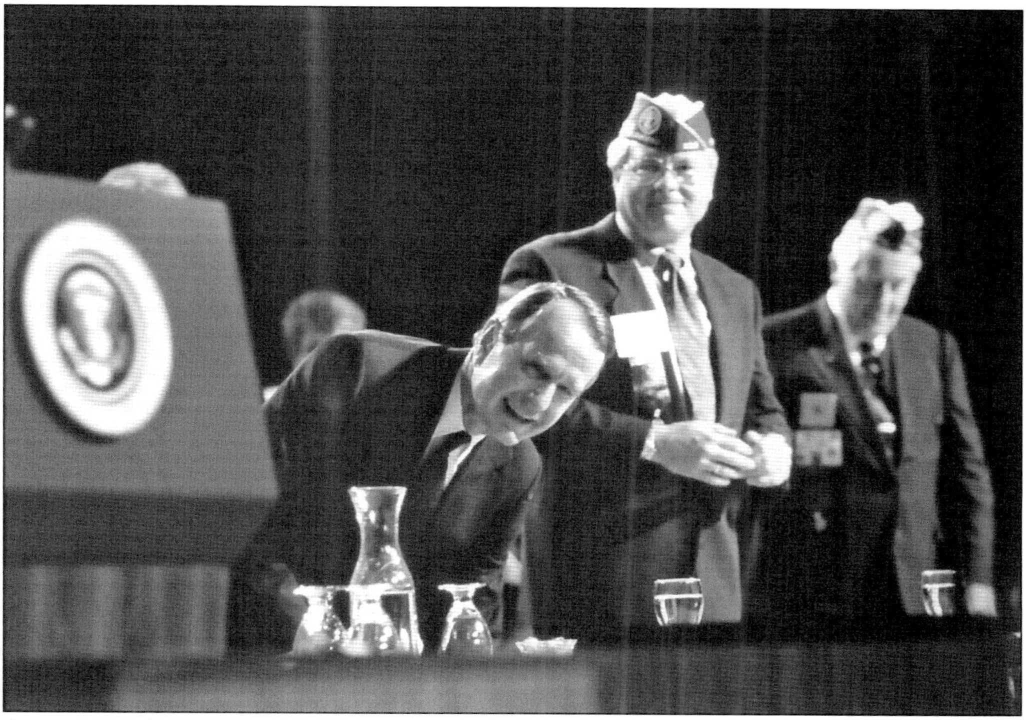

As vice president, George H.W. Bush made trips to Reno to campaign and raise funds for his presidential campaign. As president, he came to Reno to address this conference of the Disabled American Veterans in 1992. He also returned several times during his post-presidency to address the Safari Club International convention at the Reno-Sparks Convention Center. (Photograph by Craig Sailor, courtesy of the *Reno Gazette-Journal*.)

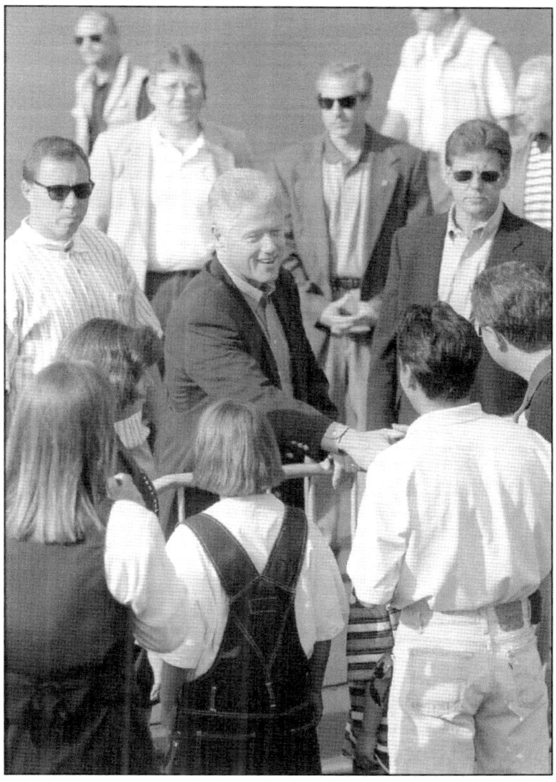

Pres. Bill Clinton is greeted by well-wishers at Reno-Tahoe International Airport after Air Force One landed there on the morning of July 26, 1997. Clinton was whisked by motorcade to Lake Tahoe, where he joined Vice Pres. Al Gore and leaders from both Nevada and California for the inaugural Lake Tahoe Summit, a conference on environmental issues affecting the Lake Tahoe Basin. Clinton also returned to Reno to campaign for his wife, Hillary, during her presidential run in 2008. (Photograph by Joe Gosen, courtesy of the *Reno Gazette-Journal*.)

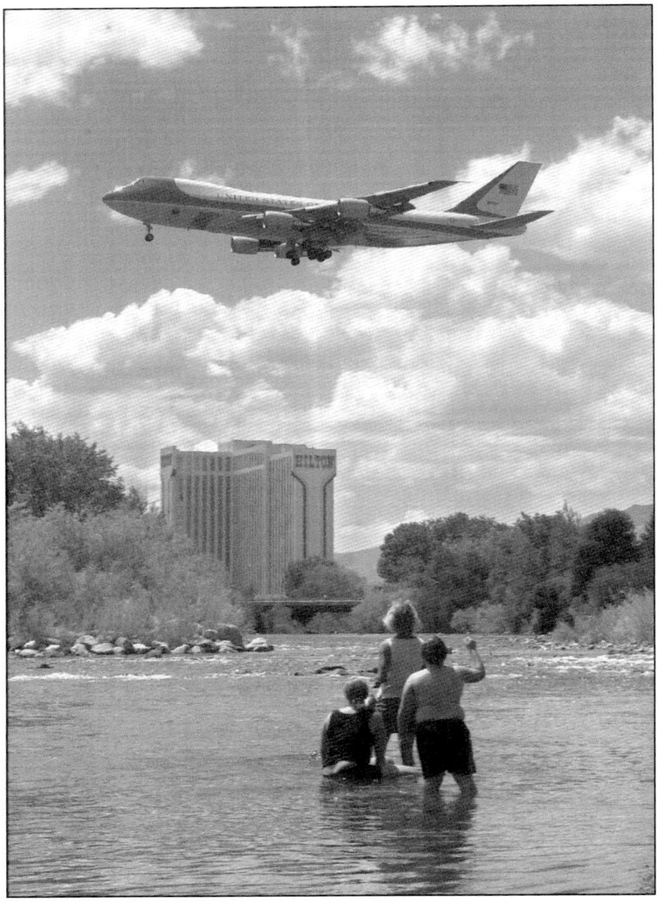

On October 14, 2004, just a few weeks before the election, Pres. George W. Bush traveled to Reno on Air Force One to make a campaign pitch to Reno voters during a rally at Rancho San Rafael Regional Park. As usual, Nevada was a swing state in the presidential election, and Bush faced a challenge from Sen. John Kerry, but he carried the state and the election. (Left, photograph by Tim Dunn, courtesy of the *Reno Gazette-Journal*; below, photograph by Andy Barron, courtesy of the *Reno Gazette-Journal*.)

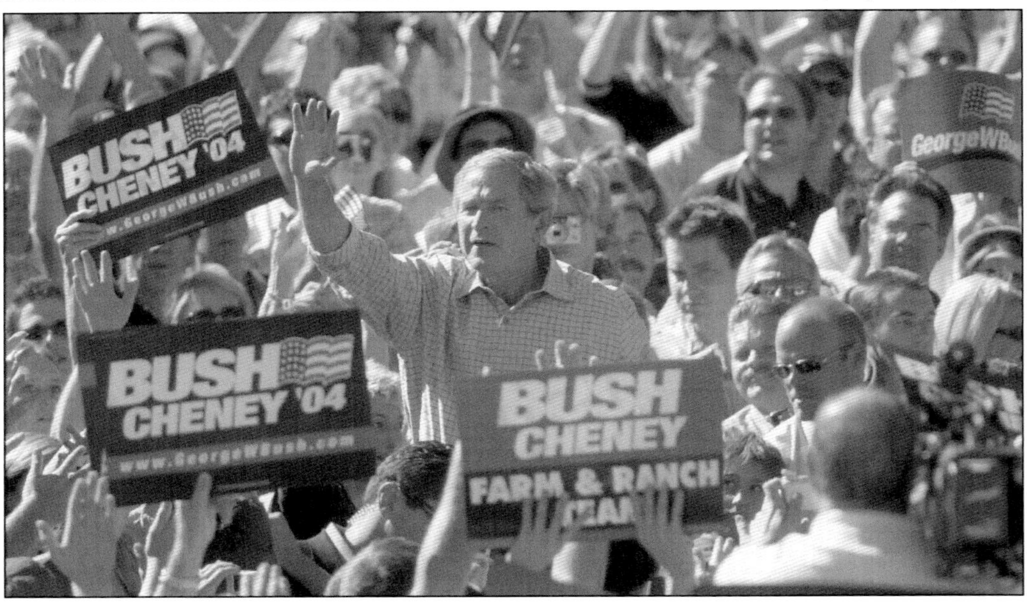

Five

Famous Faces

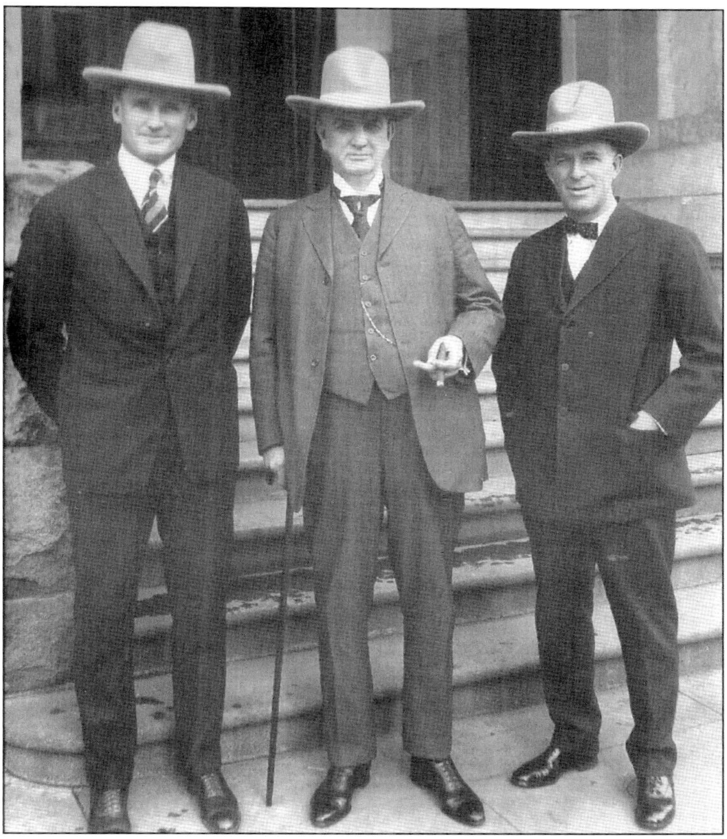

When he was not pitching for the Washington Senators in the 1920s, Hall of Famer Walter Johnson (left) spent his off-seasons in Reno at the South Virginia Street home of his father-in-law, Reno mayor E.E. Roberts (center). Johnson loved the wide-open spaces of Reno and hunting at Roberts's lodge in nearby Spanish Springs. Johnson's hunting partners were Roberts and the Reverend Brewster Adams (right). (Photograph courtesy of Henry W. Thomas.)

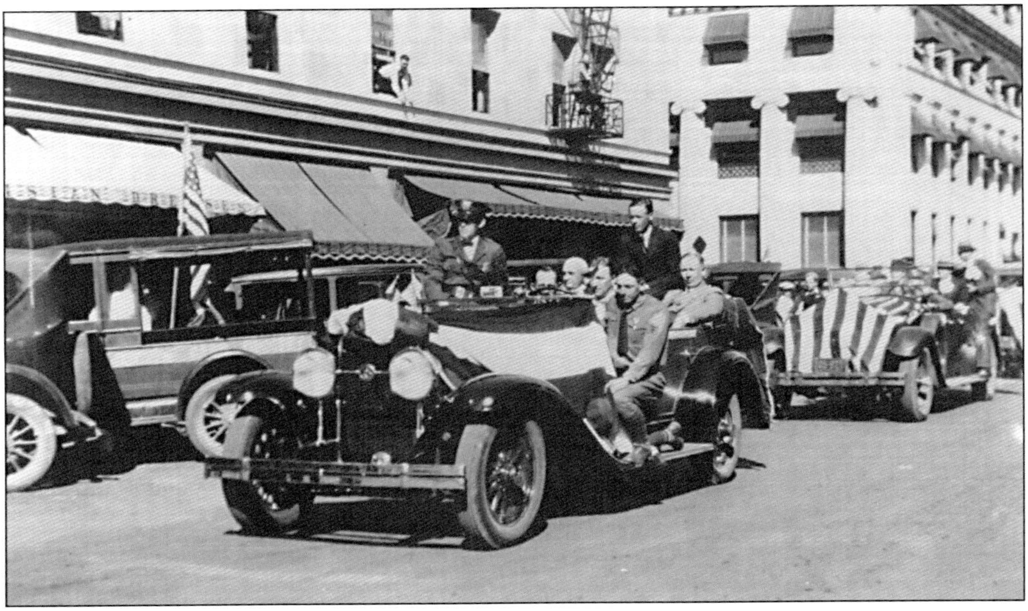

In 1927, four months after his historic solo flight from New York to France, Charles Lindbergh and his plane, the *Spirit of St. Louis*, touched down at Reno's airport as part of an 82-city whirlwind tour. Lindbergh was welcomed by Mayor E.E. Roberts and guarded by the University of Nevada cadet corps with the help of the University of Nevada football team. Lindbergh was put into a car for a parade from the airport to Idlewild Park, where 3,000 schoolchildren waited. Lindbergh attended another rally in his honor that night at Powning Park and spent the night at the Riverside Hotel. (Photographs courtesy of the Nevada Historical Society.)

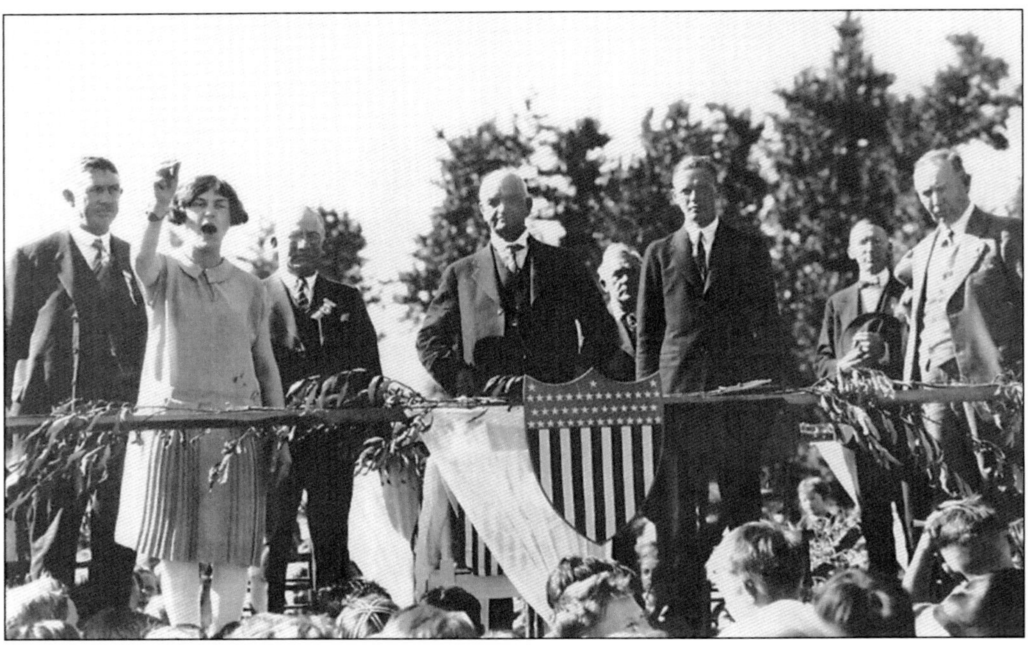

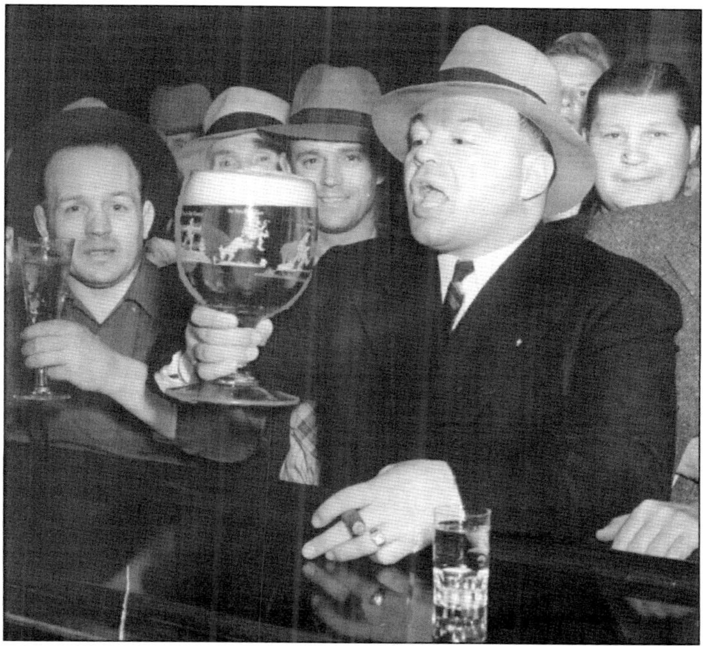

In 1939, heavyweight boxer Tony Galento came to Reno for an exhibition bout put on by promoter Harry Myerfield at a small arena on East Plaza Street. However, Galento seemed more interested in drinking from this large goblet at the bar at the Bank Club, which had a placard reading "Reserved for Two-Ton Tony." Galento finished the beer-filled goblet several times, along with a few cigars, before enjoying a plate of Chinese food at the Dog House on Center Street. (Photograph courtesy of University of Nevada Special Collections.)

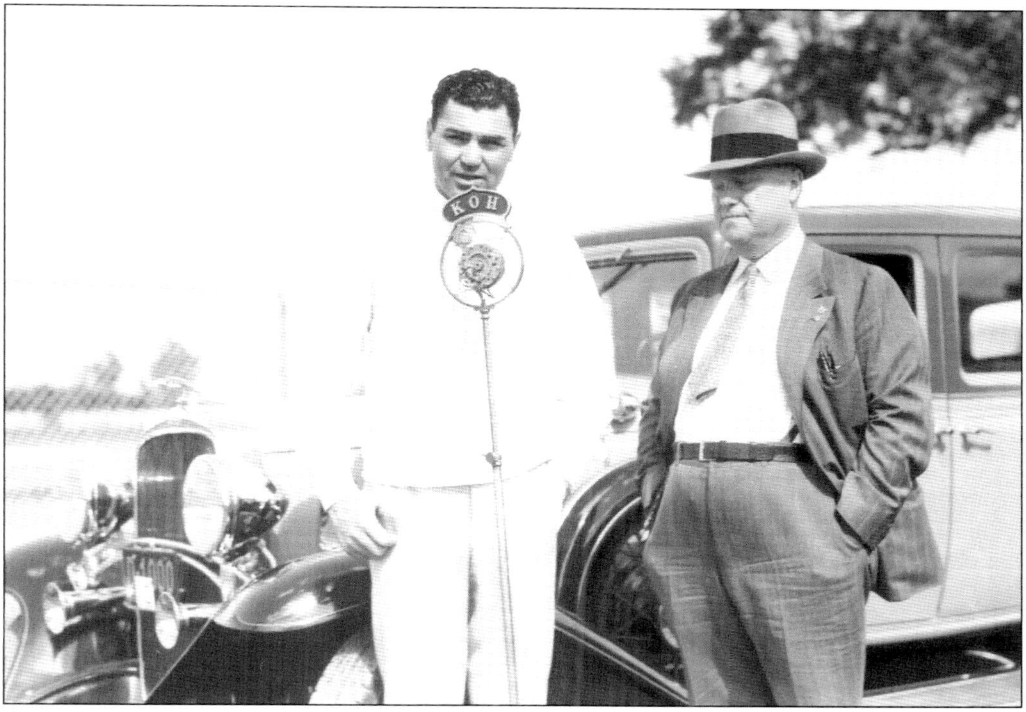

On April 10, 1931, Jack Dempsey arrived in Reno for what he called "six weeks rest." That night, in an interview on Reno's KOH Radio with Earl Leif, the Nevada manager of United Press, Dempsey assured Leif that he was not in town to obtain a divorce from his wife, Estelle Taylor. A day later, Dempsey filed for divorce at the Washoe County Courthouse. (Photograph courtesy of University of Nevada Special Collections, Ty Cobb Collection.)

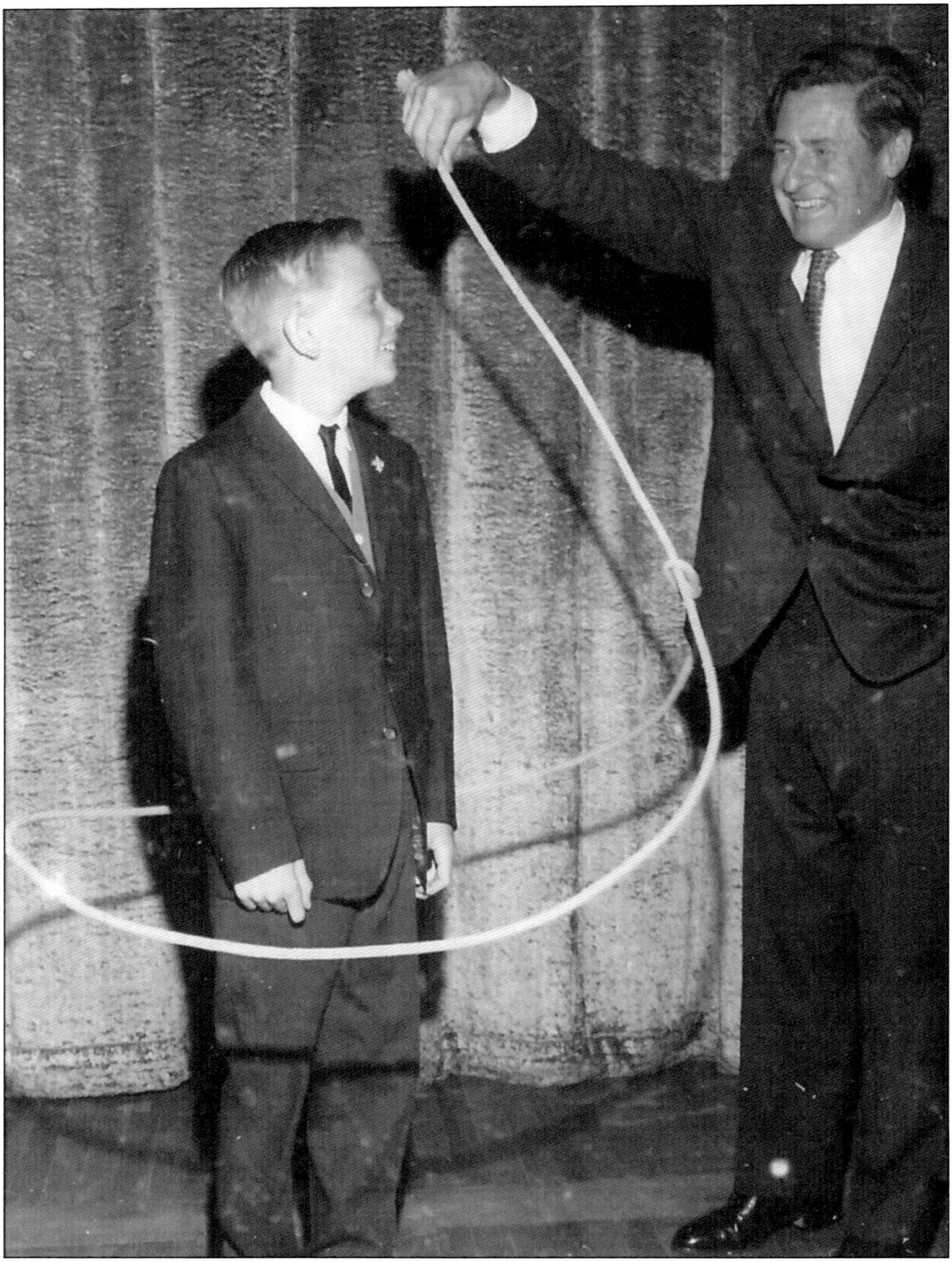

Scott Jamieson, a fifth-grader at Veterans Elementary School in Reno, approached trick roper Will Rogers Jr., the son of the famous American humorist, for an autograph on April 6, 1964, and ended up being part of the "Destiny" variety show held inside the State Building at Powning Park. The show had a Vaudeville theme with slapstick, tap dancers, comedians, singers, and Rogers showing off his rope tricks. (Photograph by Marilyn Newton, courtesy of the *Reno Gazette-Journal*.)

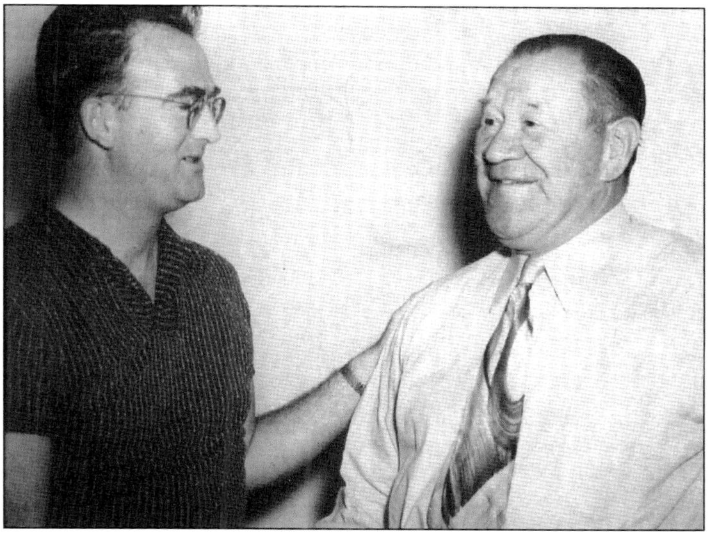

Jim Thorpe, voted the world's greatest athlete in the first half of the 20th century, was a Las Vegas club owner when he visited *Nevada State Journal's* longtime sports editor Ty Cobb in Reno in 1952. Thorpe had also been in town during World War II and visited students at Reno High School, but this was Thorpe's final trip; he died in 1953. (Photograph courtesy of William Cobb Collection.)

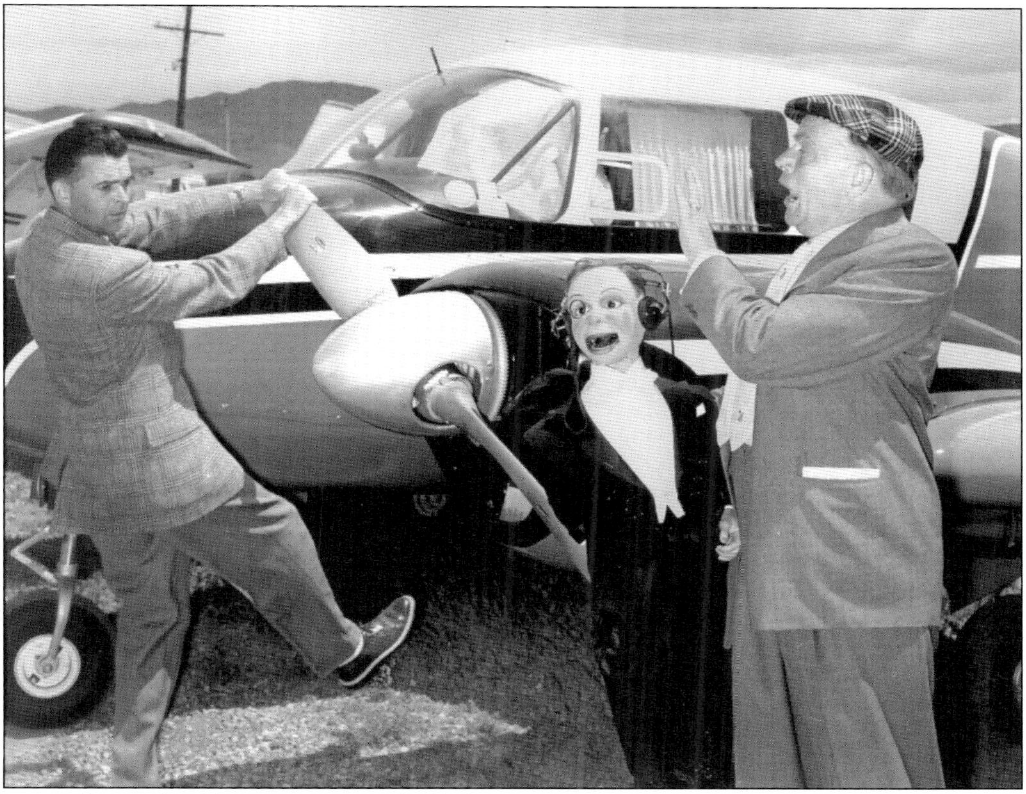

Riverside Hotel publicist Roy Powers (left) clowns around with famed ventriloquist Edgar Bergen and his dummy Charlie McCarthy in June 1957. In addition to appearing nightly at the Riverside, Bergen also performed for children's groups around town, including to a crowd of more than 2,000 youngsters at Wingfield Park. Advertisements for the Riverside show featured a large drawing of Charlie McCarthy and the words "Incidentally, Edgar Bergen is here, too." (Photograph courtesy of the Roy Powers Collection.)

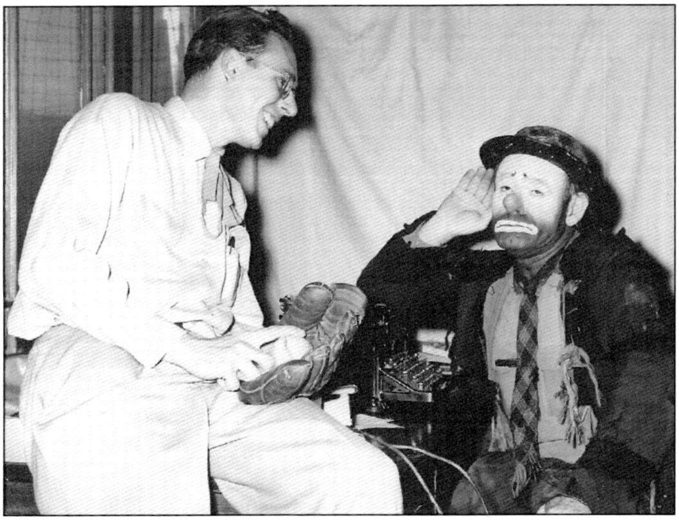

The famed circus clown Emmett Kelly, who developed his character "Weary Willie" during a long career with Ringling Brothers and Barnum & Baily Circus, left the circus in 1956 to perform as the mascot for the Brooklyn Dodgers. It was in that role in 1956 that he appeared in Reno. The Reno Silver Sox were a minor-league affiliate of the Dodgers, and Kelly chatted with Silver Sox business manager Bob Nitsche (left). (Photograph courtesy of Steve Sneddon Collection.)

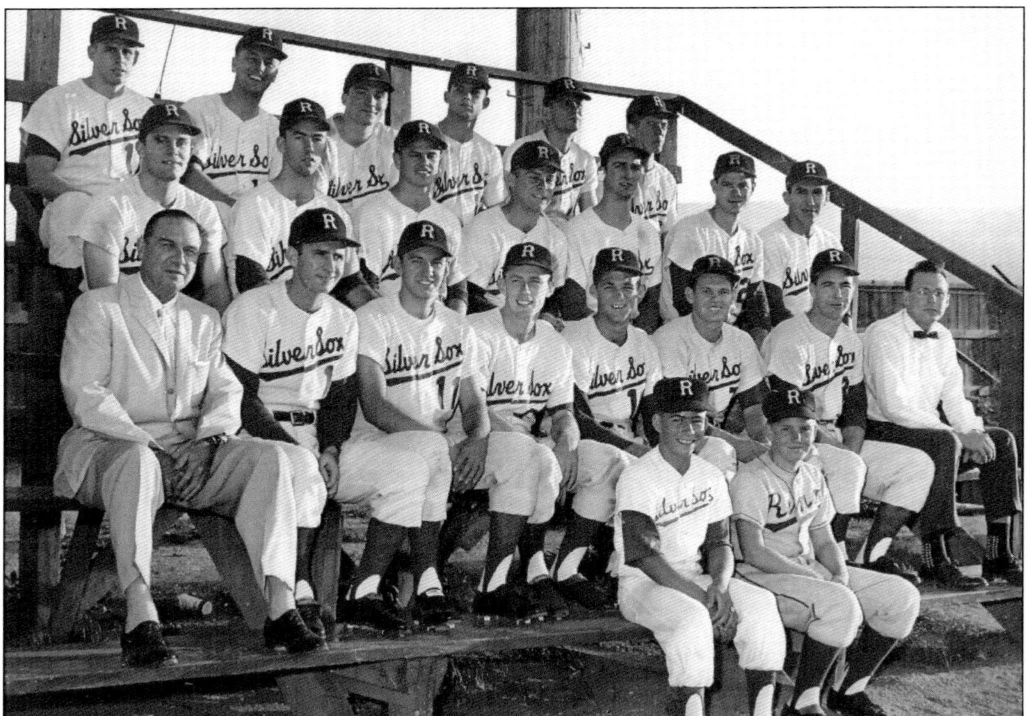

The 1960 Reno Silver Sox were the California League champions, finishing with a record of 89-51. Second baseman Bobby Cox (fourth row, second from right) went on to manage the Atlanta Braves to a World Series title. The rest of the team included, from left to right, (first row) batboys Jimmy Bender and Tommy Myers; (second row) Ben Edwards (president), Tom Saffell (manager), Richard Crowe, Ron Cronan, Bud Curtin, Bob Arrighi, Joe Penland, and Bob Nitsche (business manager); (third row) Tom Richards, Thad Tillotson, Tommy Wells, Tom Murray, Phil Graf, Lowell Barnhart, and Camilo Estevis; (fourth row) Jim Ward, Ron Boone, Al Ferrara, John Van Ornum, Bobby Cox, and Jimmy Shinn. (Photograph courtesy of Steve Sneddon Collection.)

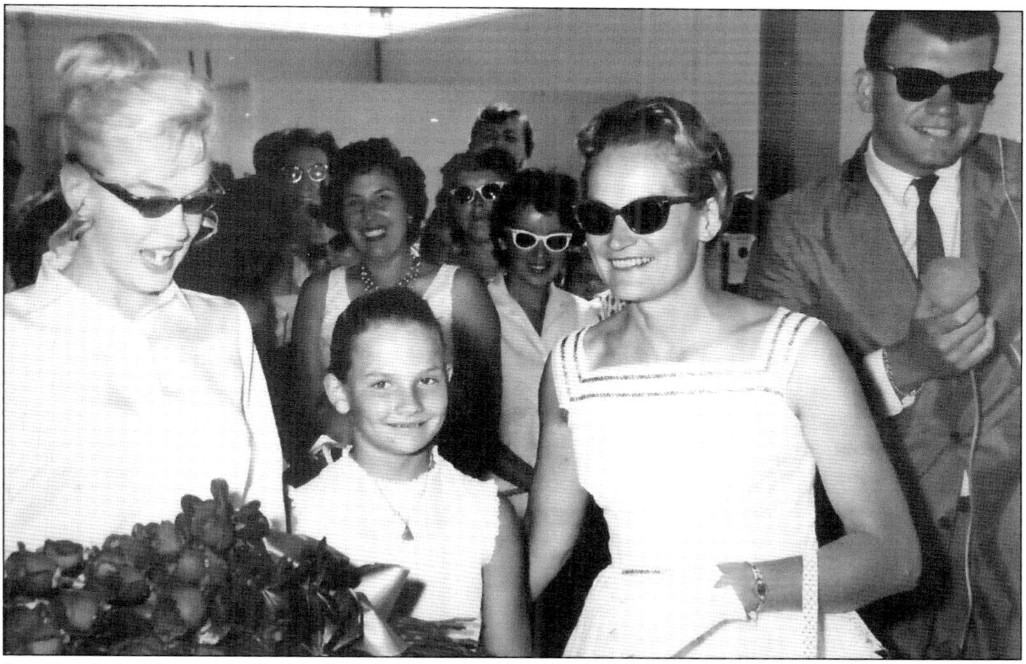

Marilyn Monroe arrived in Reno in 1960 to star in her husband Arthur Miller's movie *The Misfits* along with Clark Gable and Montgomery Clift. Monroe was met at the Reno airport by Nevada's first lady, Bette Sawyer, and radio and television newsman Bob Carroll, in sunglasses. During filming, Monroe flashed a smile for a local newspaper photographer (right). (Above, photograph courtesy of Bob Carroll Collection; right, photograph by Marilyn Newton, courtesy of the *Reno Gazette-Journal*.)

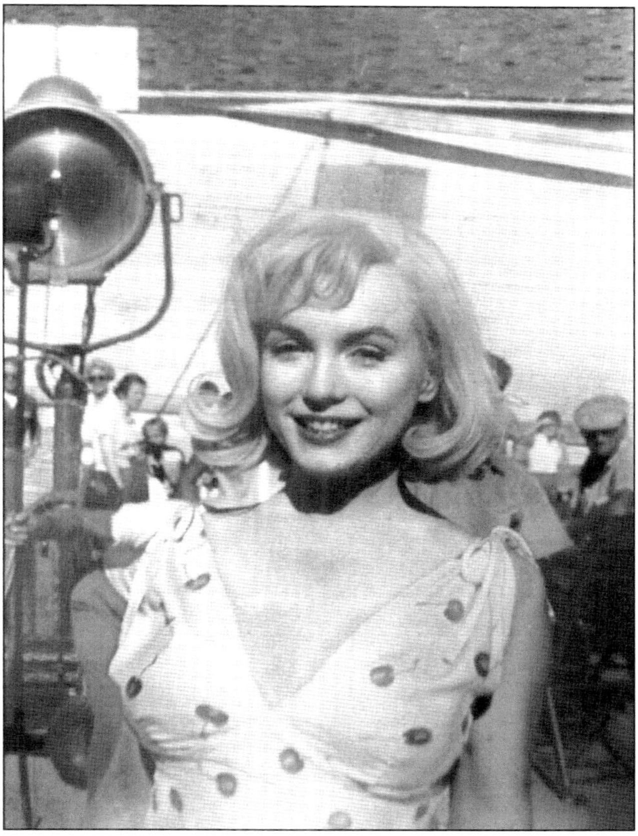

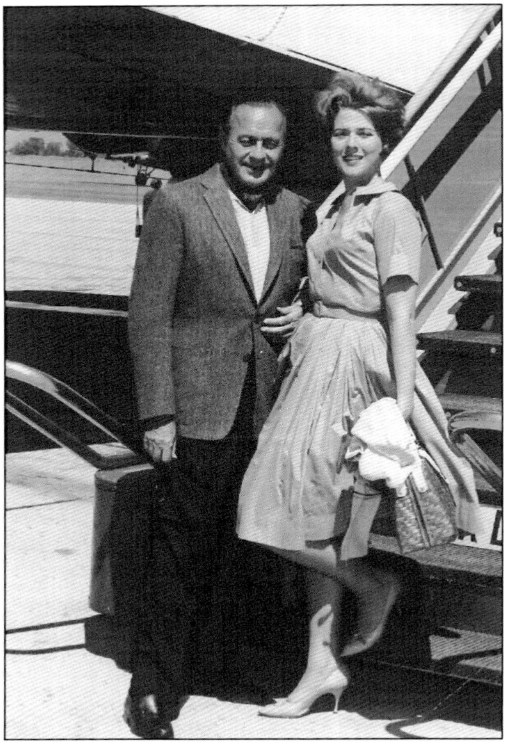

Comedian Jack Benny was a frequent and favorite performer at Harrah's and other Reno hotels during the 1950s and 1960s. In 1960, he and Diana Trask, an Australian singer and dancer who also performed on Benny's television show, touched down at the Reno airport for a Harrah's performance. (Photograph courtesy of the *Reno Gazette-Journal*.)

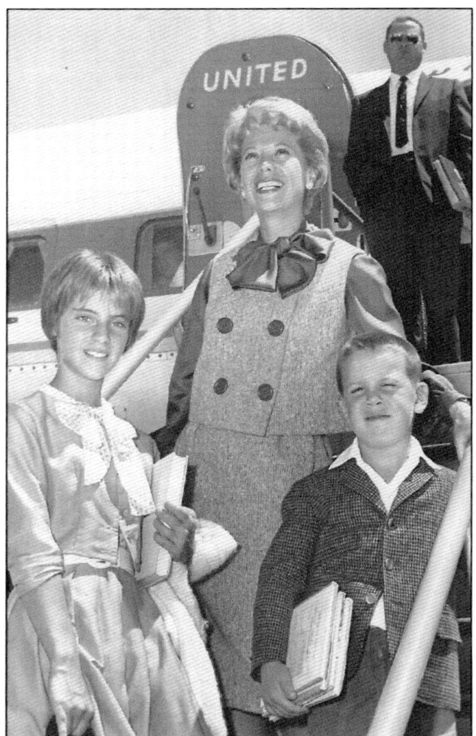

Television star Dinah Shore touched down at the Reno airport on June 23, 1961, with her children, Melissa, 13, and John, 7. Though she rarely performed at the clubs, Bill Harrah and his publicity men convinced Shore to sign on for a two-week performance at Harrah's South Shore Room. Her children had to bring their homework on the trip. (Photograph courtesy of the *Reno Gazette-Journal*.)

Legendary jazz musician Louis Armstrong, shown here with his wife, Lucille, and Harold Smith Jr. of Harolds Club, was a regular performer at the Fun Room at Harolds Club in the late 1960s. In December 1965, Armstrong dressed as Santa Claus and gave a performance for the orphans at the State Children's Home in Carson City. (Photograph courtesy of the *Reno Gazette-Journal*.)

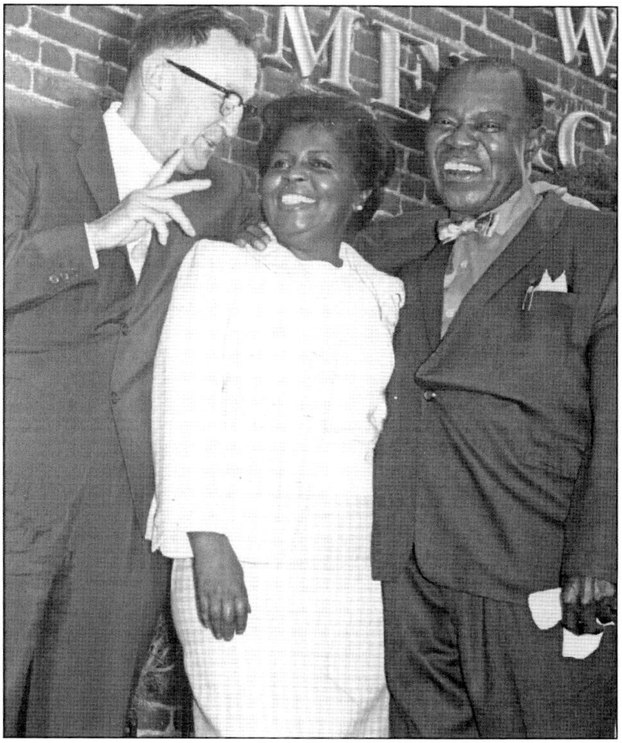

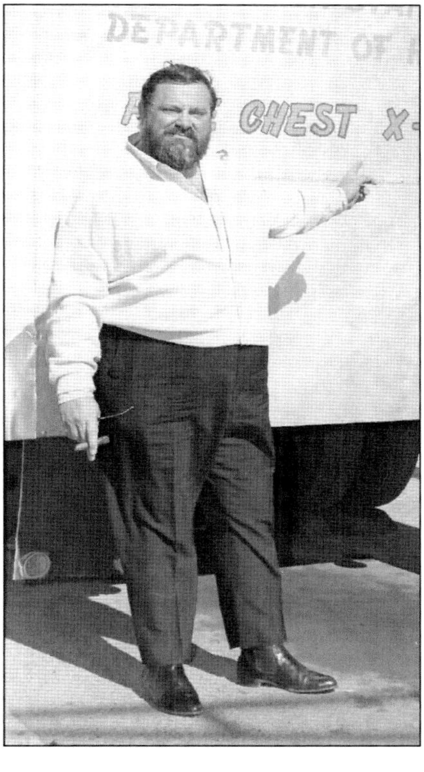

Famed trumpeter and band leader Al Hirt was a frequent headliner in Reno-area hotels in the 1960s and 1970s, including headlining stints at John Ascuaga's Nugget in Sparks. At the time, the New Orleans native was arguably the most popular trumpeter in the world; his 1963 album *Honey in the Horn* sold more than one million copies. (Photograph courtesy of the *Reno Gazette-Journal*.)

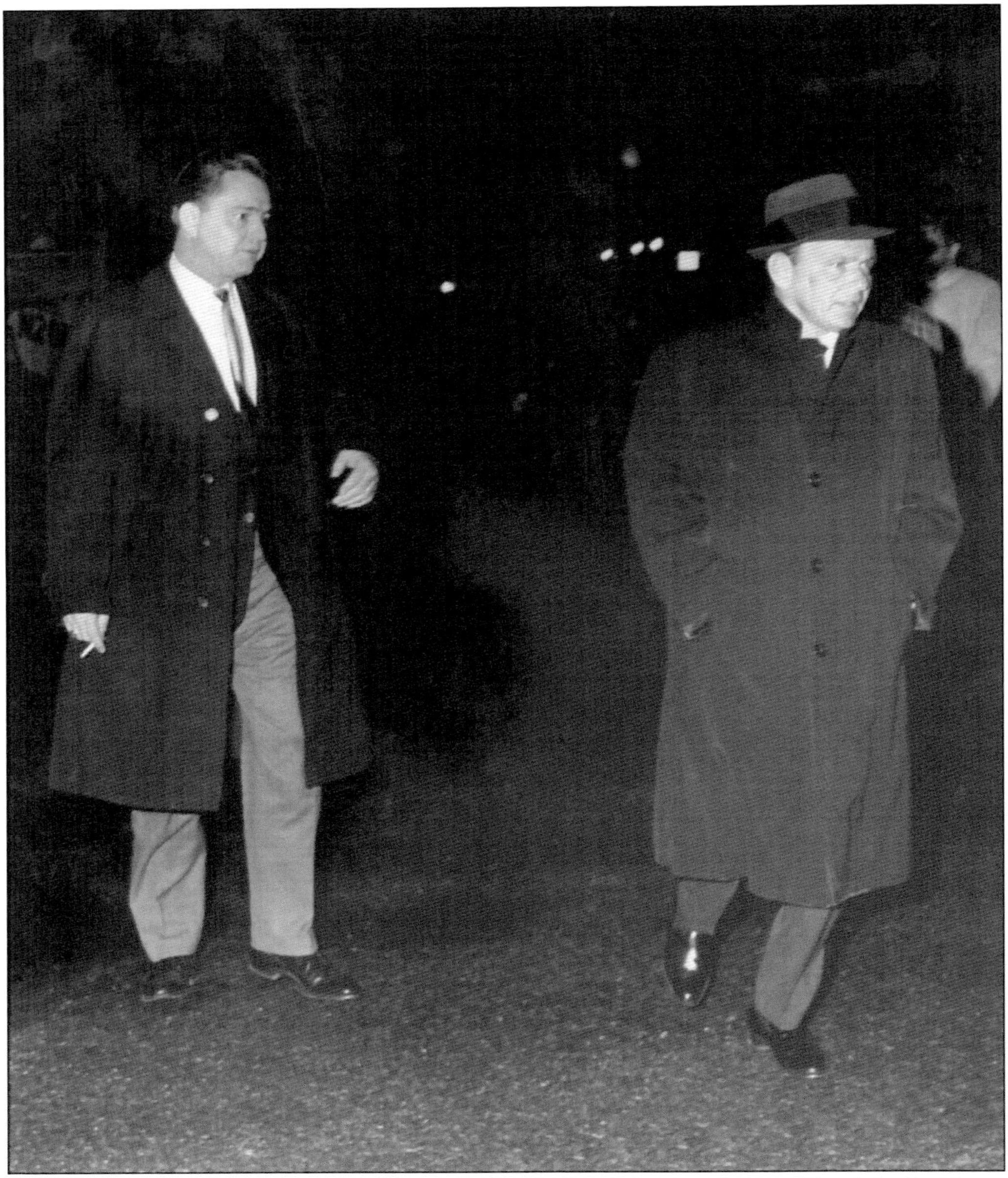

In December 1963, entertainer Frank Sinatra flew to Reno because his son, Frank Jr., had been kidnapped at Lake Tahoe. Meeting Sinatra at the Reno airport was Washoe County district attorney Bill Raggio. His son was freed after Sinatra paid the $240,000 ransom demanded by the kidnappers, who were later caught and imprisoned. The elder Sinatra and Raggio formed a lasting friendship. (Photograph courtesy of Bill Raggio Collection.)

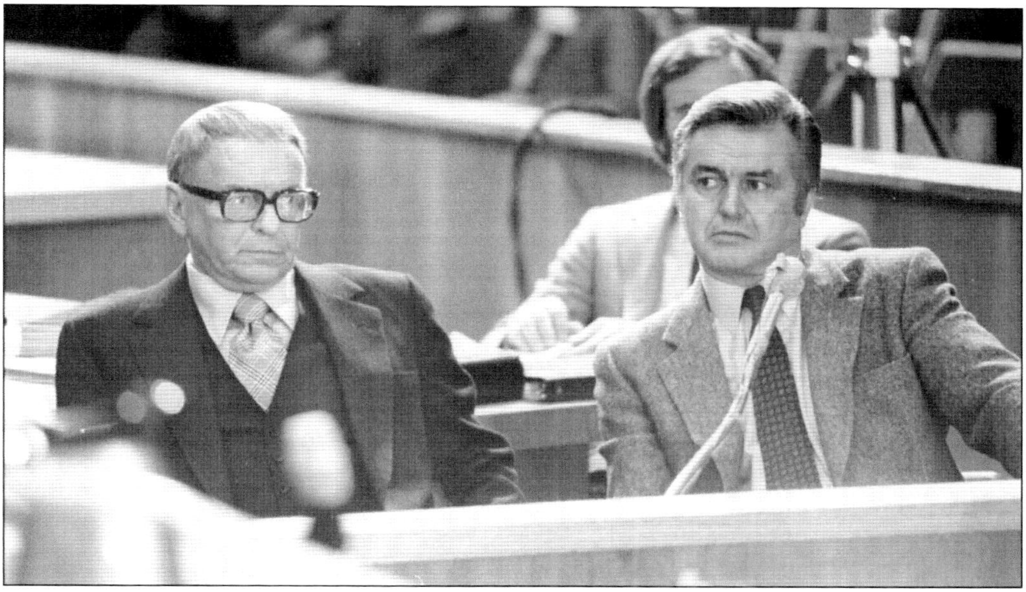

In 1981, Frank Sinatra applied for a gaming license in Nevada and called on his old friend Bill Raggio to represent him in front of the Nevada Gaming Control Board. The gaming license was granted. Appearing as character witnesses for Sinatra at the hearing were actors Gregory Peck and Kirk Douglas, who congratulated Raggio after the hearing. (Photographs courtesy of Bill Raggio Collection.)

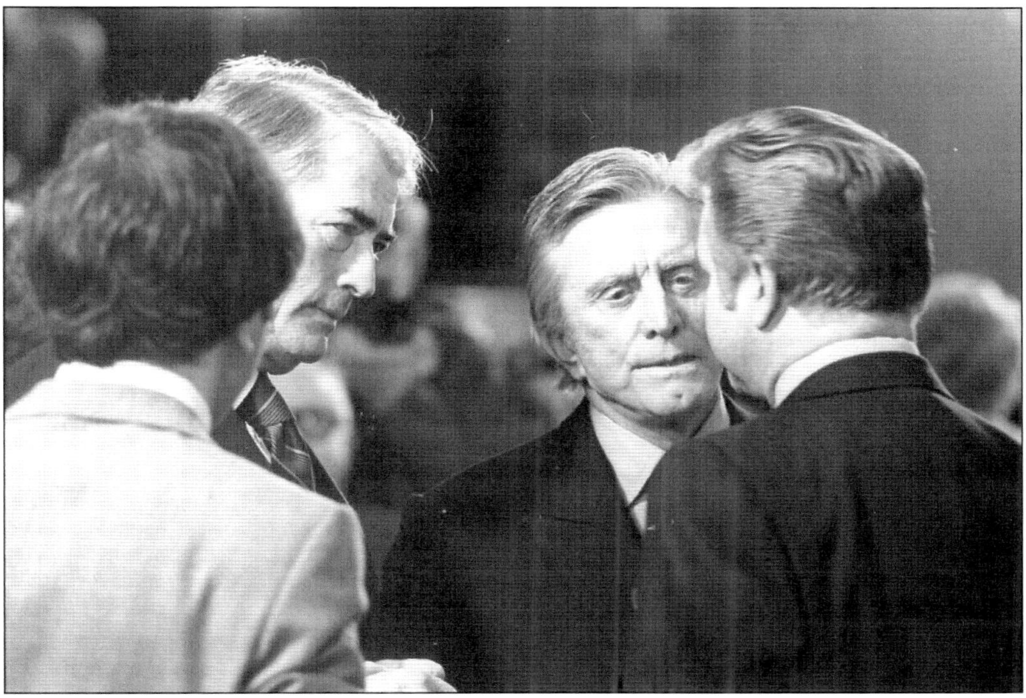

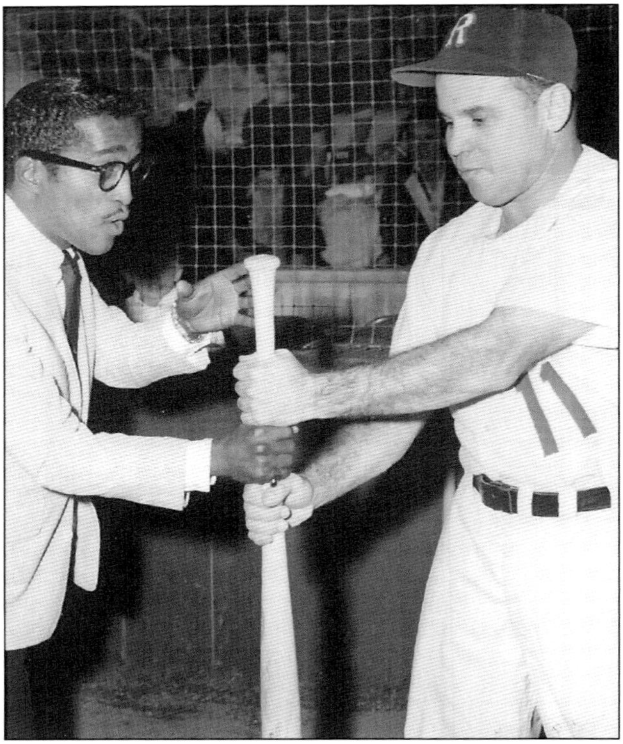

Through the 1950s, 1960s, and 1970s, Sammy Davis Jr., perhaps Reno's favorite entertainer, performed at the Mapes, Harrah's, and other area hotels. He also made appearances at other venues, including at Moana Stadium, where he clowned with Reno Silver Sox manager Ray Perry (left). In 1973, Davis and his son Mark, 13, toast each other at a luncheon at Harrah's Convention Center on May 20, 1973, on the occasion of Mark's bar mitzvah ceremony, which was held at Temple Sinai in Reno. (Photographs courtesy of the *Reno Gazette-Journal*.)

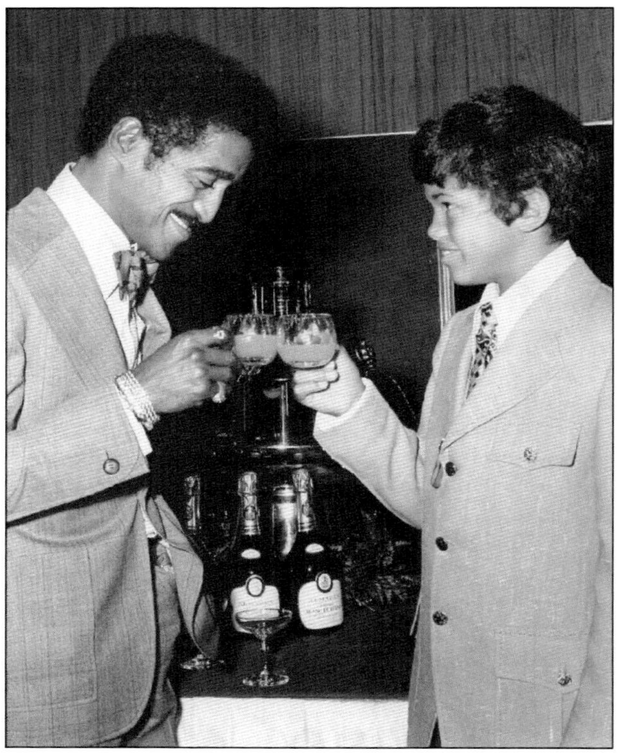

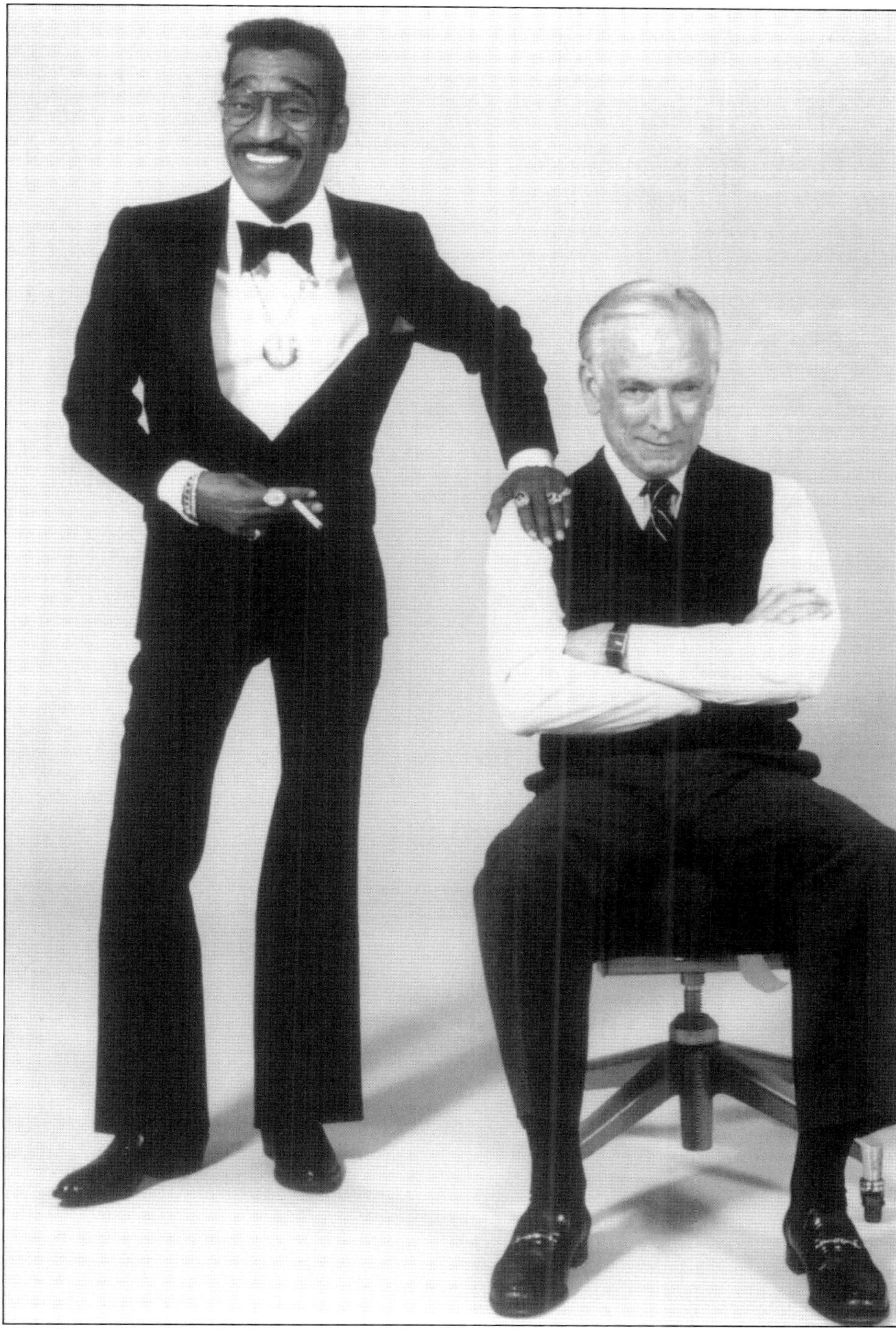

Sammy Davis Jr. was such a favorite of Harrah's founder Bill Harrah that the casino company renamed Harrah's showroom "Sammy's Showroom" in tribute to the entertainer after his death. The name remains in place today. Here, Davis poses for a photograph with Harrah's longtime publicity man Mark Curtis. (Photograph courtesy of the Mark Curtis Collection.)

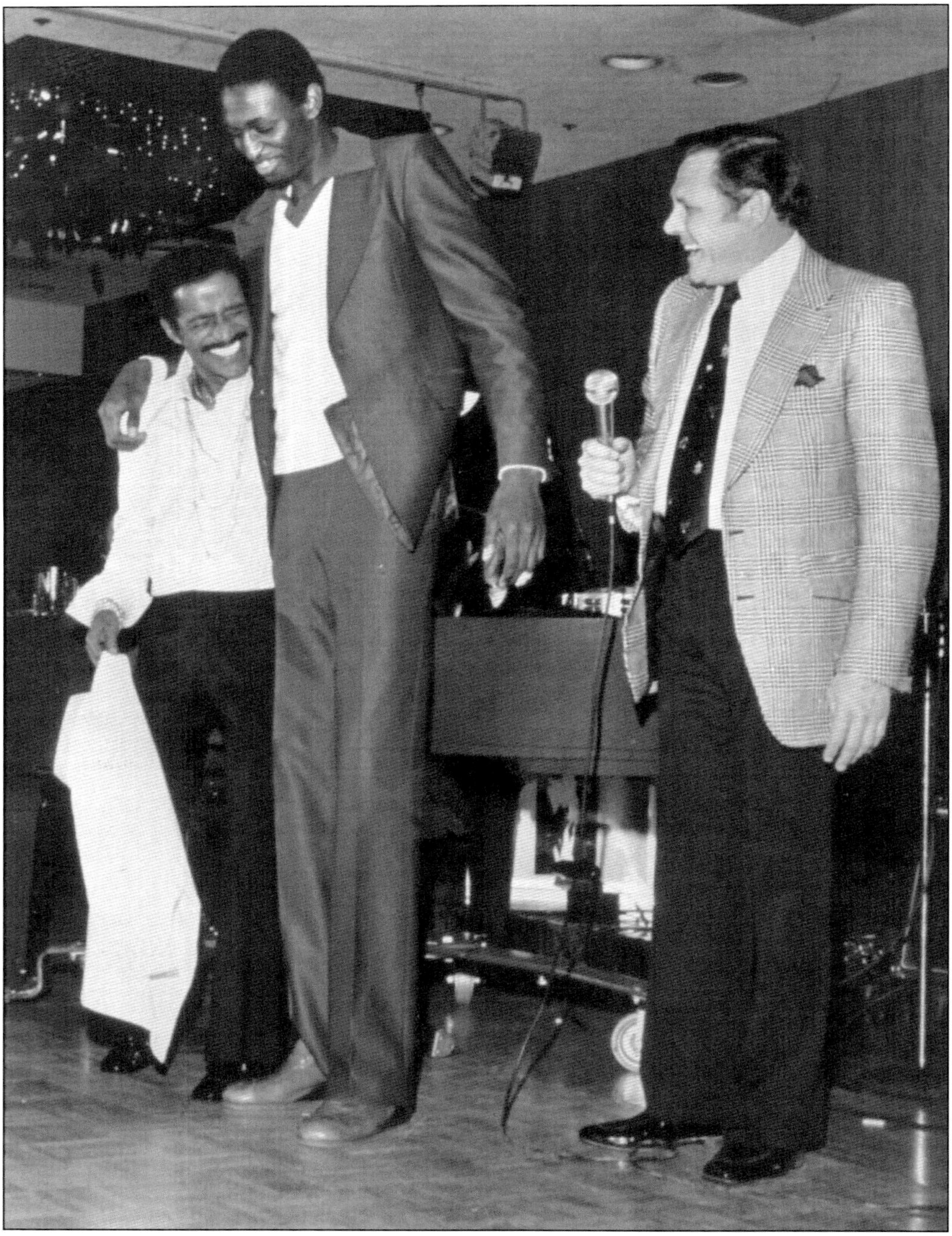

Sammy Davis Jr., at 5-foot-4, shares a laugh with 6-foot-11 University of Nevada basketball star Edgar Jones during a fundraiser for the University of Nevada athletics department. Jones was the university's all-time leading scorer and went on to play in the NBA for the Cleveland Cavaliers. Emceeing the fundraiser was Clayt Rabedeaux, the university's assistant athletics director. (Photograph courtesy of the *Reno Gazette-Journal*.)

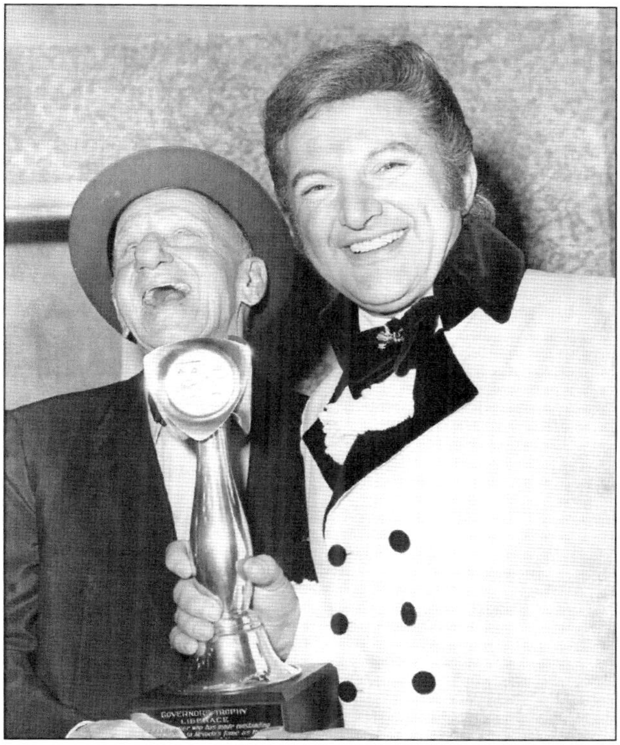

On June 24, 1969, legendary entertainers Liberace and Jimmy Durante took part in a Reno celebration honoring Liberace with the Governor's Trophy for his "outstanding contribution to Nevada's fame as the entertainment mecca of the world." Both Liberace and Durante were regular performers at Reno resorts and at John Ascuaga's Nugget in Sparks. (Photograph courtesy of the *Reno Gazette-Journal*.)

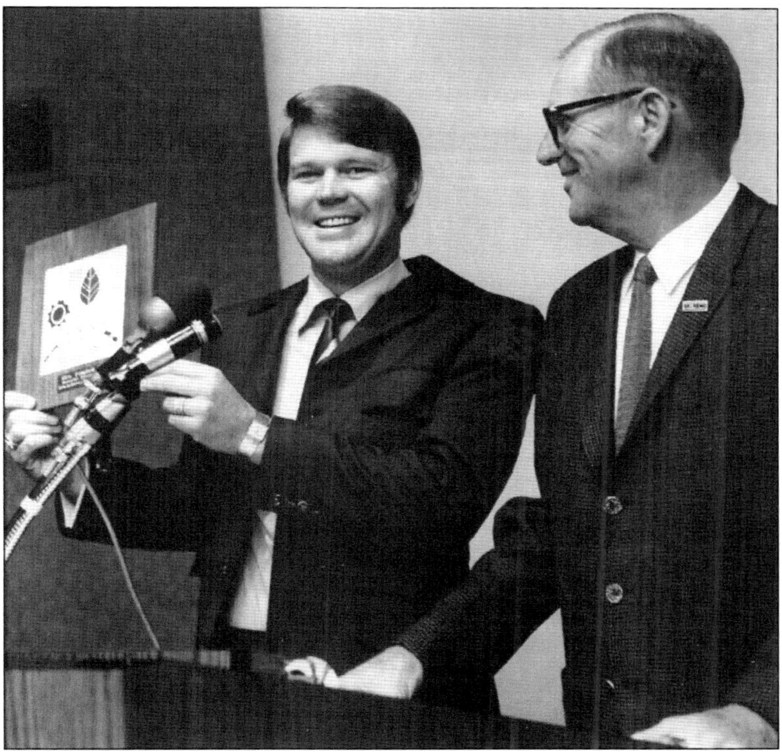

Glen Campbell holds a plaque declaring him an honorary citizen of Reno during a New Year's Eve, 1968, ceremony hosted by the Greater Reno Chamber of Commerce at Harrah's Reno. Chamber president Preston Q. Hale presented Campbell with the award. Campbell joined the likes of Petula Clark, Arthur Godfrey, and Jim Nabors in being presented with the award. (Photograph courtesy of the *Reno Gazette-Journal*.)

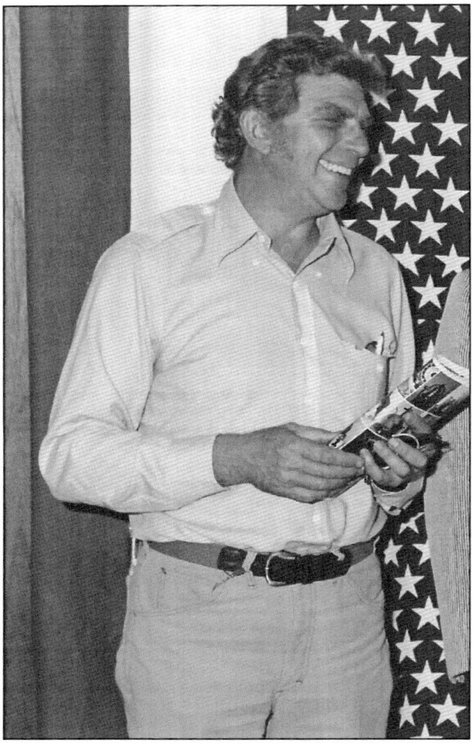

Andy Griffith, a 1960s and 1970s television icon, performed in Reno as a comedian and singer on a number of occasions, but he also came to town for other reasons. In June 1975, he came to Reno for the Harrah's Pony Express Museum Auction, an event selling memorabilia from the Pony Express mail service of the 1800s. Harrah's owner Bill Harrah established the museum and located it inside the National Automobile Museum while planning for a permanent home. Griffith's visit was part of the fundraising events for that effort. (Photograph courtesy of the *Reno Gazette-Journal.*)

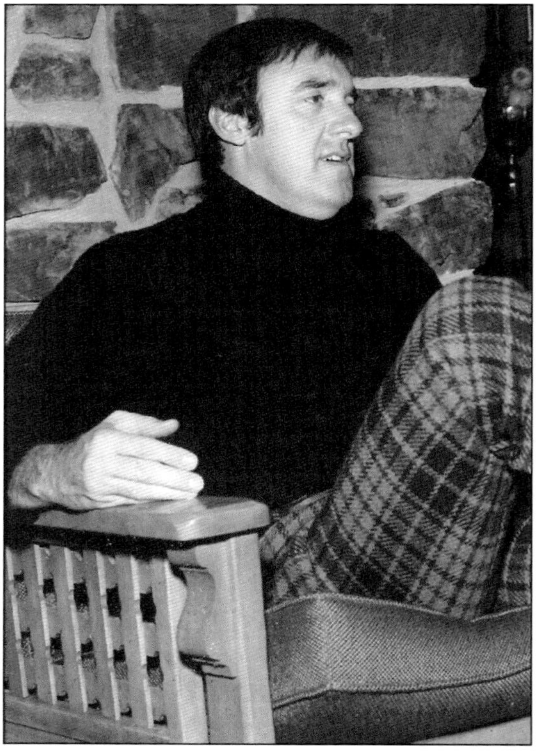

Actor and comedian Jim Nabors, who played Gomer Pyle on the *Andy Griffith Show* and the spinoff series *Gomer Pyle, USMC*, was also an accomplished singer and brought his popular act to Reno many times at the height of his career. In May 1967, Nabors volunteered as an official greeter at the Reno Police Department during National Police Week. (Photograph courtesy of the *Reno Gazette-Journal.*)

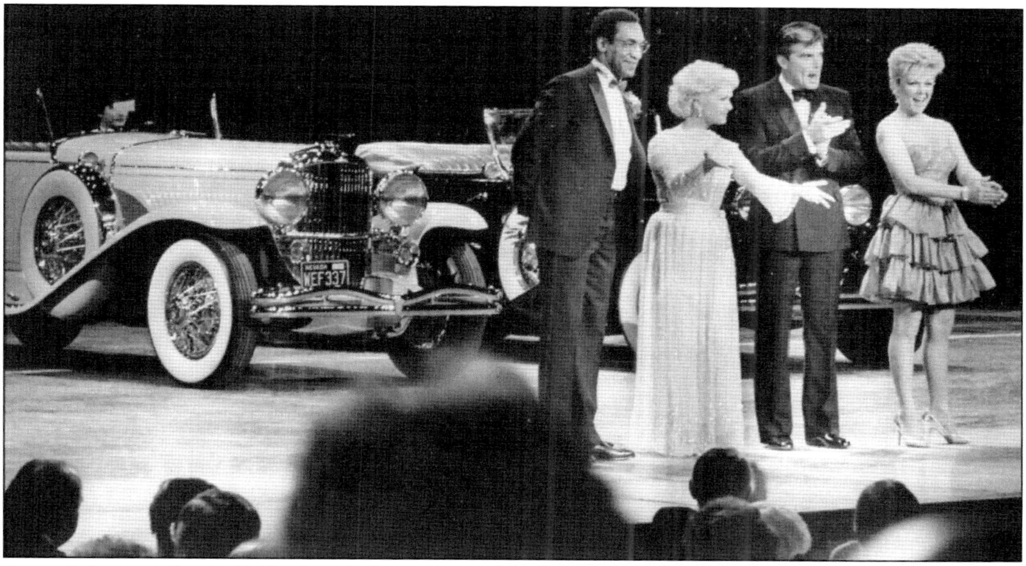

From left to right, Bill Cosby, Debbie Reynolds, John Davidson, and Lisa Hartman hosted a television special filmed at the MGM Grand Hotel in Reno to raise funds for the Harrah's National Automobile Museum. Cosby, Reynolds, and Davidson were all frequent performers at Harrahs in both Reno and Lake Tahoe from the 1960s through the 1980s. Cosby not only raised funds for the auto collection but also bought an indoor track for the University of Nevada, Reno. (Photograph by Marilyn Newton, courtesy of the *Reno Gazette-Journal*.)

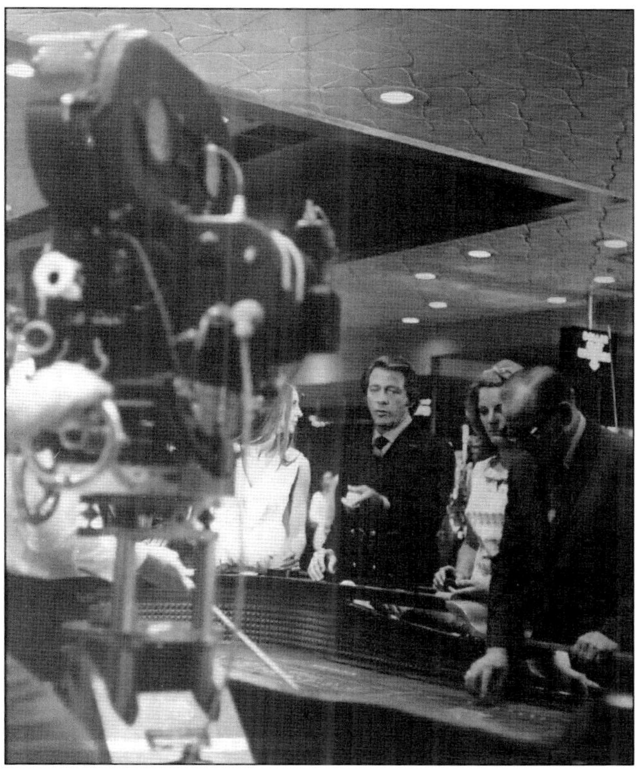

Actor Richard Crenna is filmed throwing dice at Harrah's Reno for the television movie *Thief* on June 25, 1971. The film, billed as "a love story about a man trying to find himself," starred Crenna, Angie Dickinson, and Cameron Mitchell. The cast also included 17 Harrah's employees who filled in as extras. (Photograph by Marilyn Newton, courtesy of the *Reno Gazette-Journal*.)

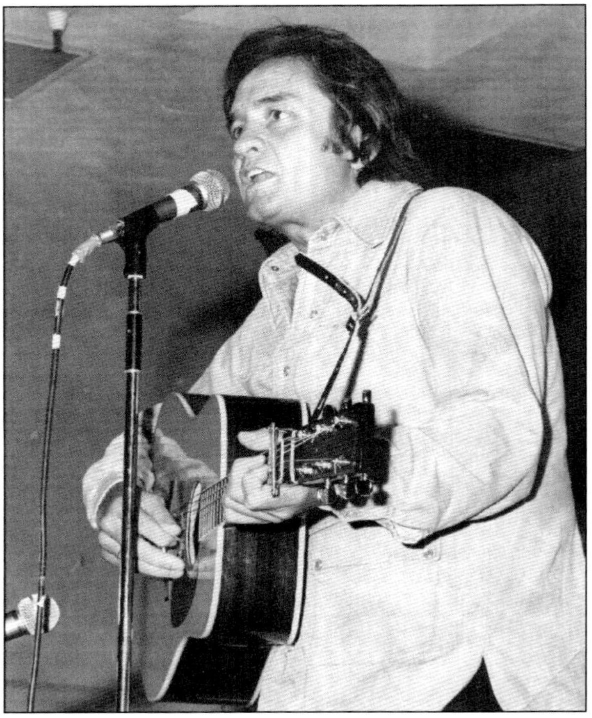

Legendary country singer Johnny Cash made a number of appearances in Reno, both as a solo artist and with fellow "Highwaymen" Waylon Jennings, Willie Nelson, and Kris Kristofferson. Cash's "Folsom Prison Blues," in which he sings "I shot a man in Reno / Just to watch him die," was a popular local hit. In 1973, Cash brought the song and a full concert to the inmates at Nevada State Prison. (Photograph courtesy of the *Reno Gazette-Journal.*)

Sisters Louise and Barbara Mandrell were not only popular country music singers and stars of their own television variety show, they also were boxing fans. In February 1982, the sisters had ringside seats to see Sugar Ray Leonard defeat Bruce Finch for the welterweight world championship at Reno's Centennial Coliseum. (Photograph by Marilyn Newton, courtesy of the *Reno Gazette-Journal.*)

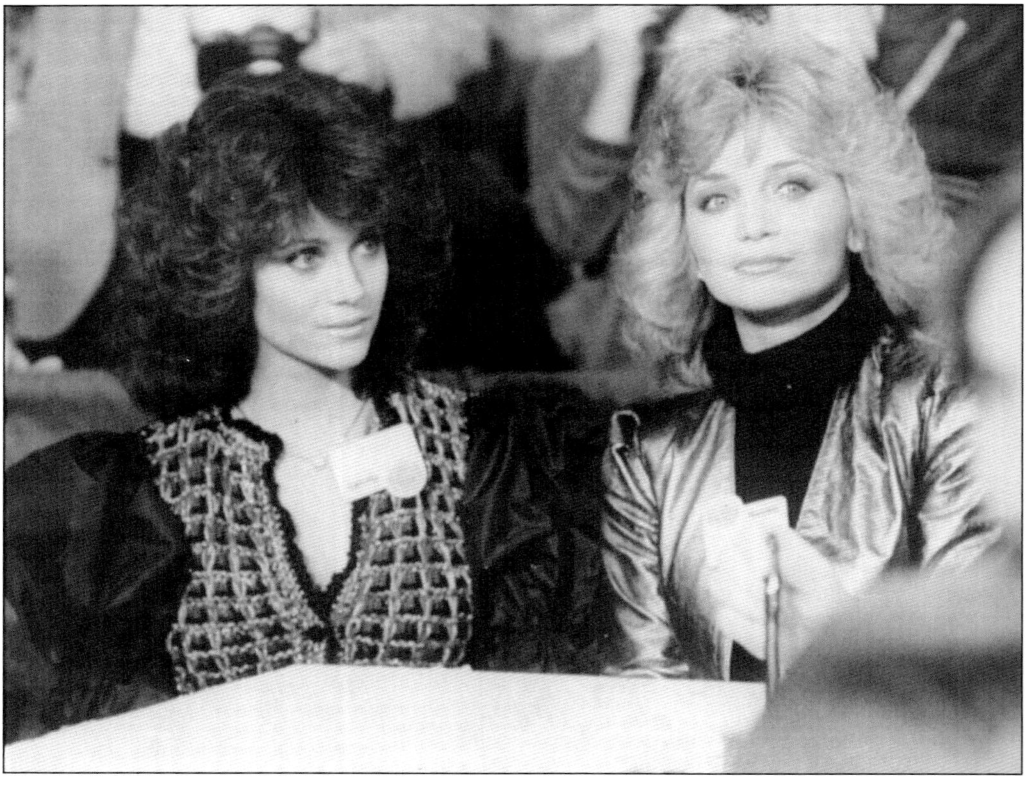

Tina Turner lit up the stage at Lawlor Events Center on the University of Nevada, Reno campus in 1984. Turner was on a concert tour to promote the release of her fifth solo album, *Private Dancer*. Her show packed the 11,000-seat arena, and this photograph graced the cover of the campus newspaper, *Sagebrush*. (Photograph by Laura DeSimone.)

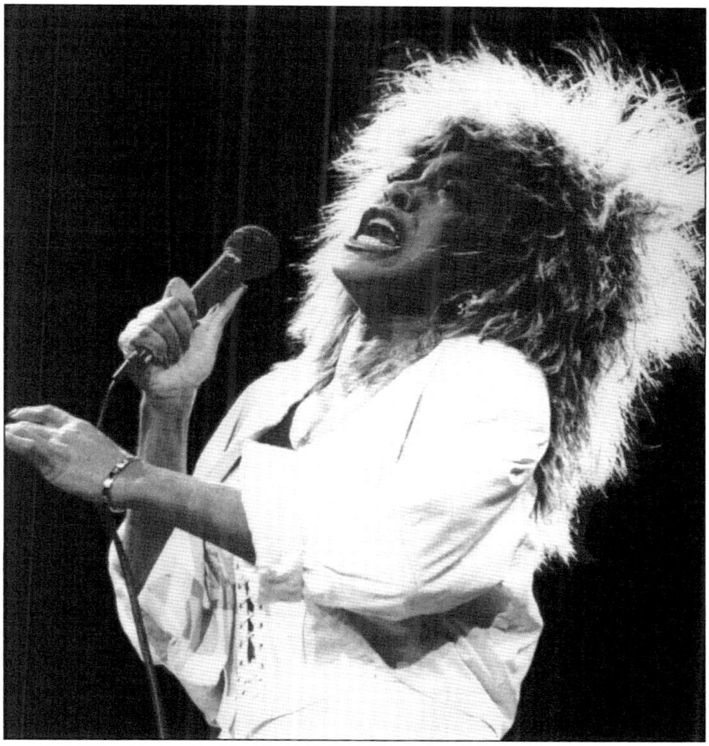

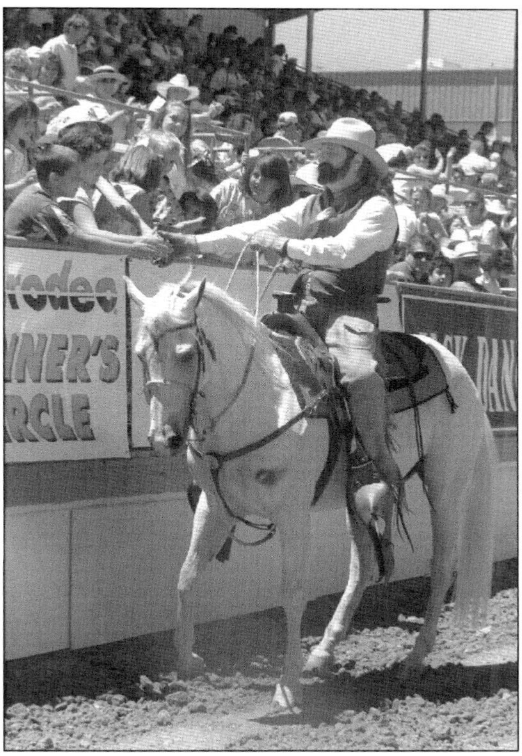

Country singer and cowboy Michael Martin Murphey performed at Reno resorts and was a frequent visitor to the annual Reno Rodeo. In June 1994, he headlined a concert at Mackay Stadium on the University of Nevada, Reno campus. He also twice served as grand marshal of the Reno Rodeo Parade, including in 1997. During a rodeo performance that weekend, he rode horseback into the arena and visited with fans. (Photograph by Marilyn Newton, courtesy of the *Reno Gazette-Journal*.)

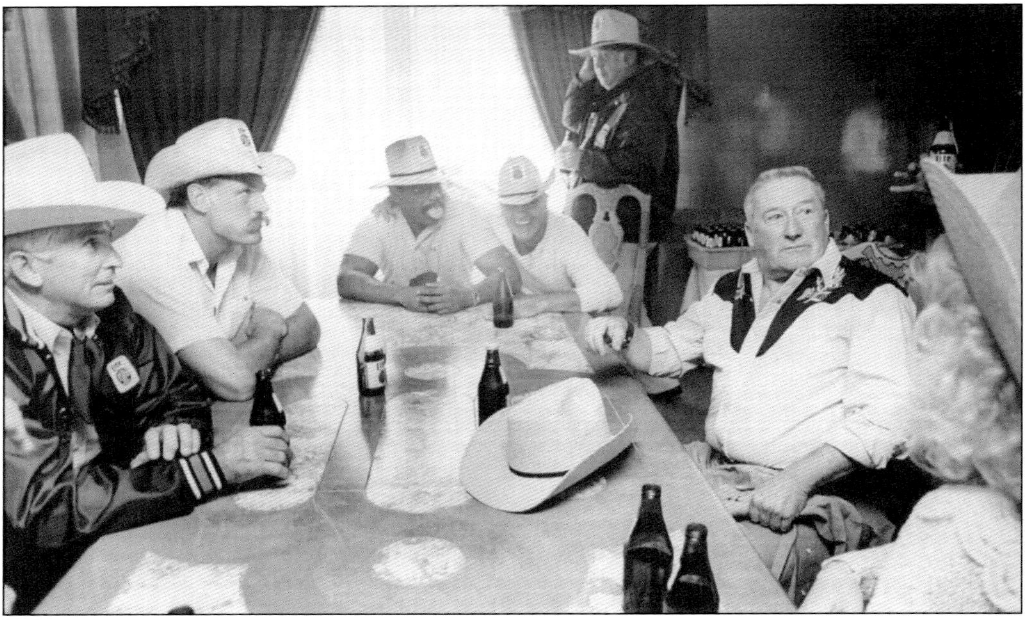

The Miller Lite All-Stars, including, from left to right, rodeo star Jim Shoulders, football stars Ben Davidson and Bubba Smith, hockey star Boom Boom Geoffrion, baseball star Marv Throneberry, and author Mickey Spilane, joke with each other during the filming of a Miller Lite beer commercial at the MGM Grand Hotel in Reno on October 4, 1981. Below, Smith, Throneberry, and Geoffrion laugh with actress Lee Meredith. (Photographs by Bob Dawson, courtesy of the *Reno Gazette-Journal*.)

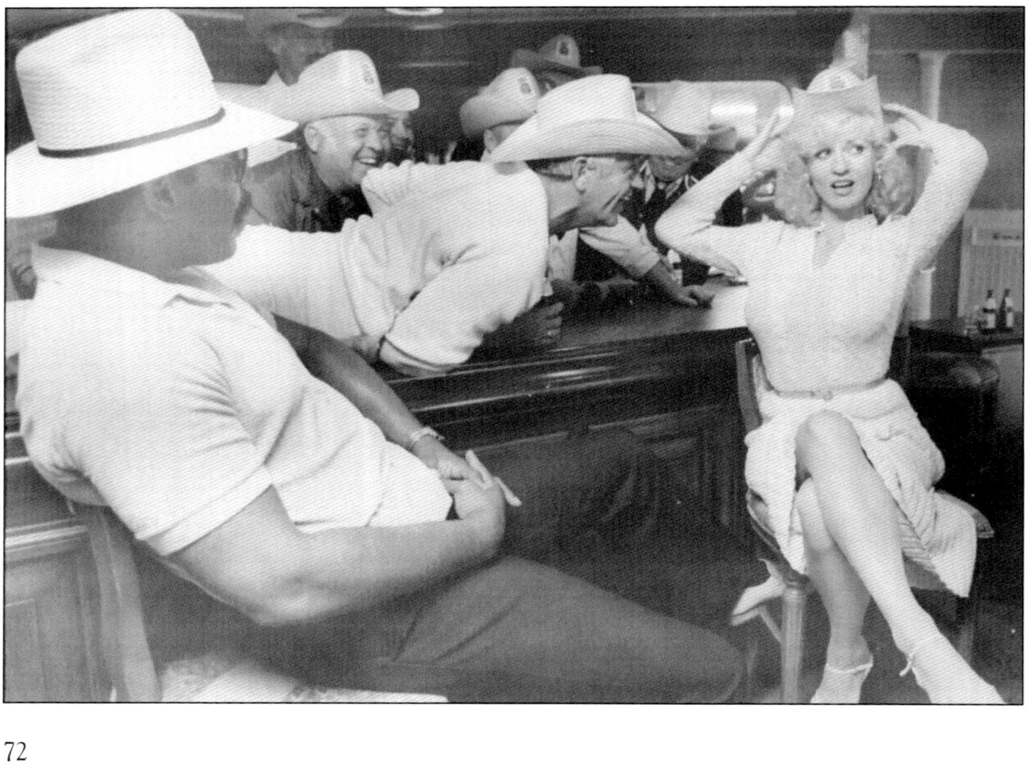

Conservative political icon Barry Goldwater traveled to Reno in 1974 to campaign on behalf of former Nevada governor Paul Laxalt in Laxalt's bid for a seat in the US senate. Laxalt's image is in the background as Goldwater addresses supporters. Laxalt won the election, defeating then–lieutenant governor Harry Reid in a close race. (Photograph by Marilyn Newton courtesy of the *Reno Gazette-Journal*.)

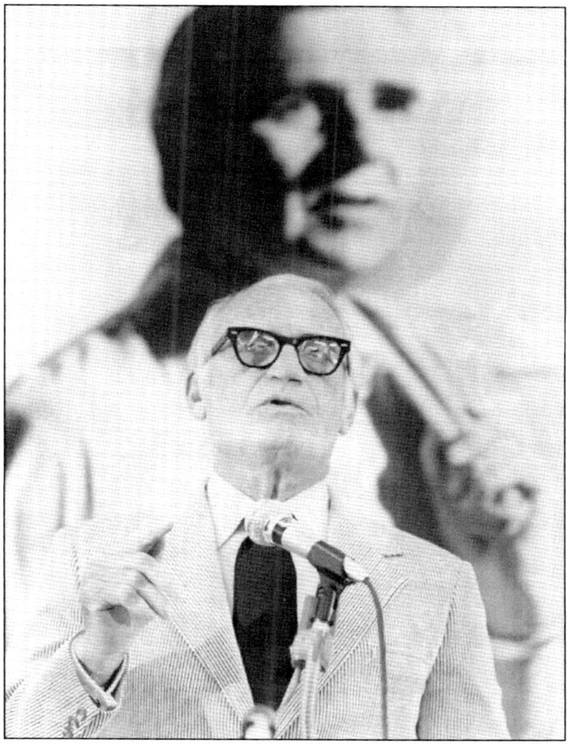

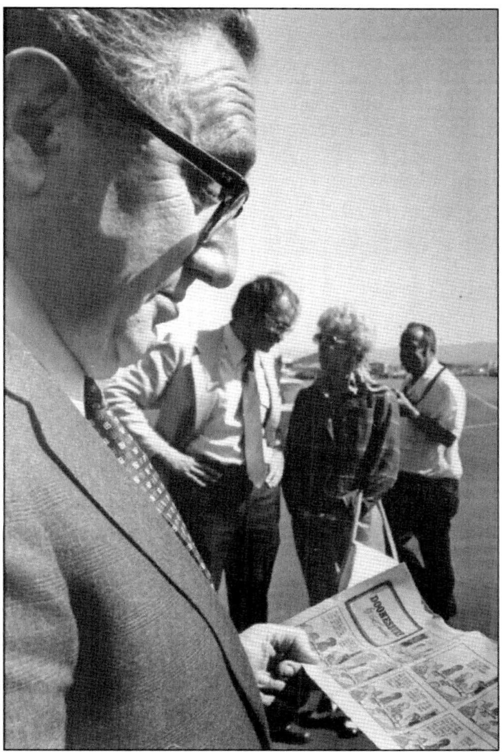

Henry Kissinger, the secretary of state under presidents Richard Nixon and Gerald Ford, was met by reporters and photographers at Reno-Tahoe International Airport in July 1979. A reporter handed Kissinger a copy of a "Doonesbury" Sunday cartoon from the *Nevada State Journal*. (Photograph courtesy of the *Reno Gazette-Journal*.)

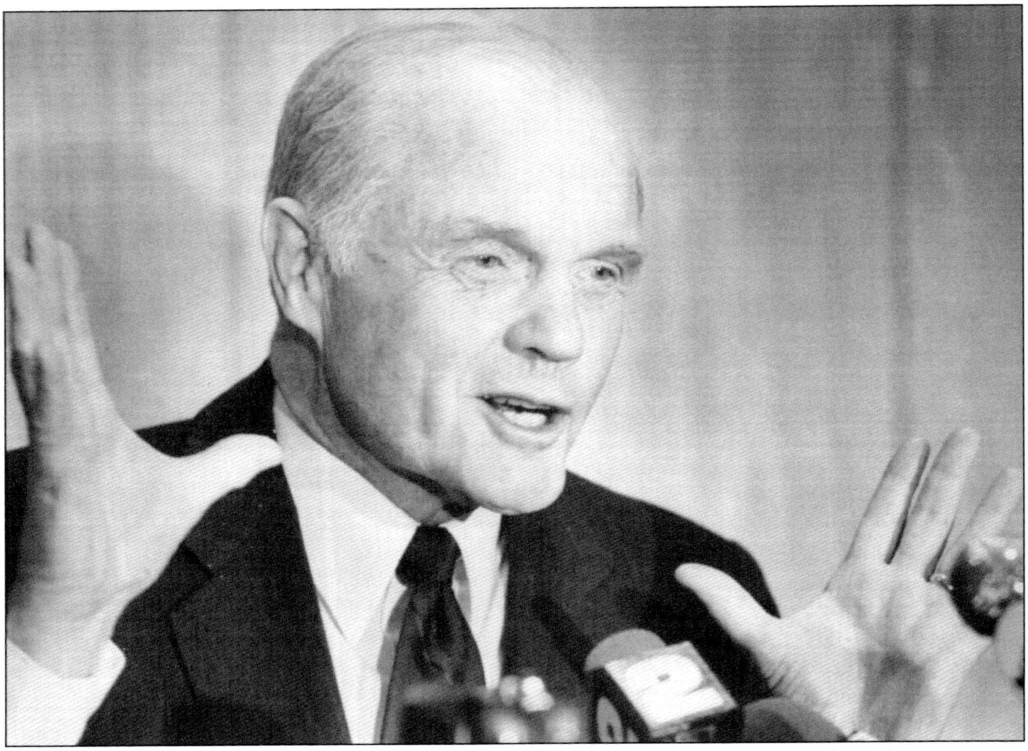

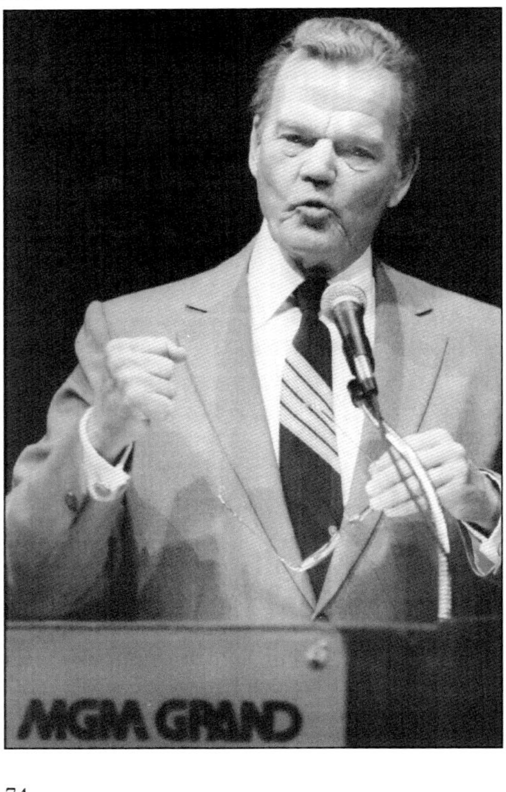

Former NASA astronaut John Glenn, the first American to orbit the earth, was running for president when he stopped in Reno on February 28, 1983. The Democratic senator from Ohio held a press conference at Harrah's Reno and visited with supporters throughout the day. He eventually lost the Democratic nomination to Walter Mondale. (Photograph by Mark Crosse, courtesy of the *Reno Gazette-Journal.*)

Conservative commentator Paul Harvey visited Reno and the MGM Grand Hotel on September 27, 1983, to address a convention of Big A Auto Parts dealers. Harvey's topic that day was "What's Wrong with America and What's Right with Reno." (Photograph by Lance Iverson, courtesy of the *Reno Gazette-Journal.*)

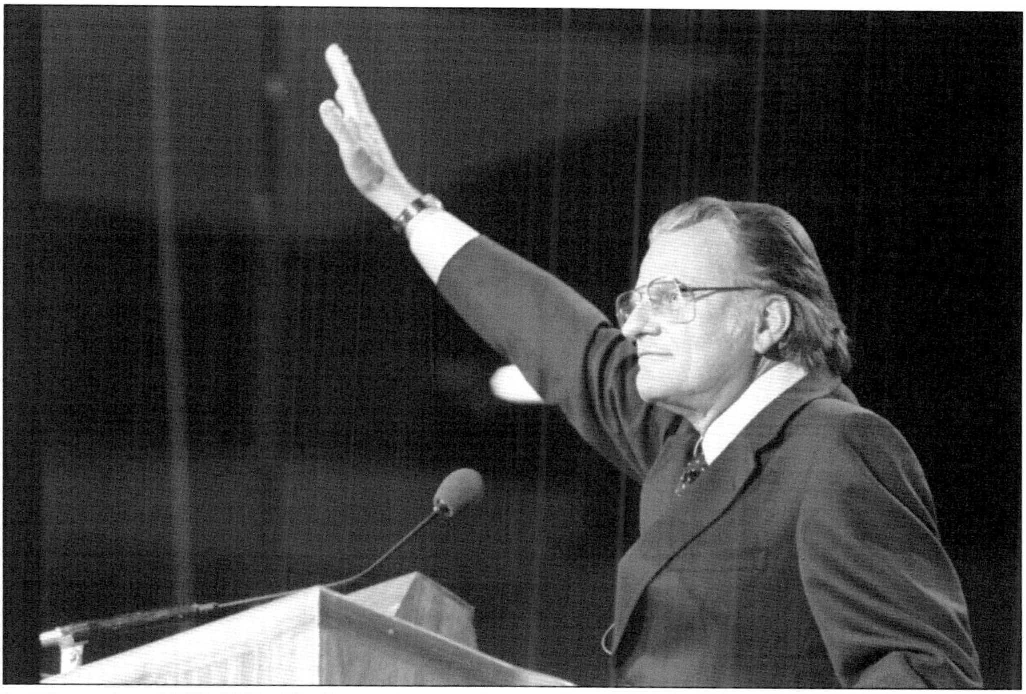

In November 1980, Billy Graham, America's preacher, brought his evangelical crusade to an overflow crowd at the Centennial Coliseum in Reno. At one point in the service, Graham asked for a show of hands of those who came from out of state and several hundred people raised their hands. Earlier in the day, Graham conducted a press conference with Nevada governor Robert List. (Photographs by Marilyn Newton, courtesy of the *Reno Gazette-Journal*.)

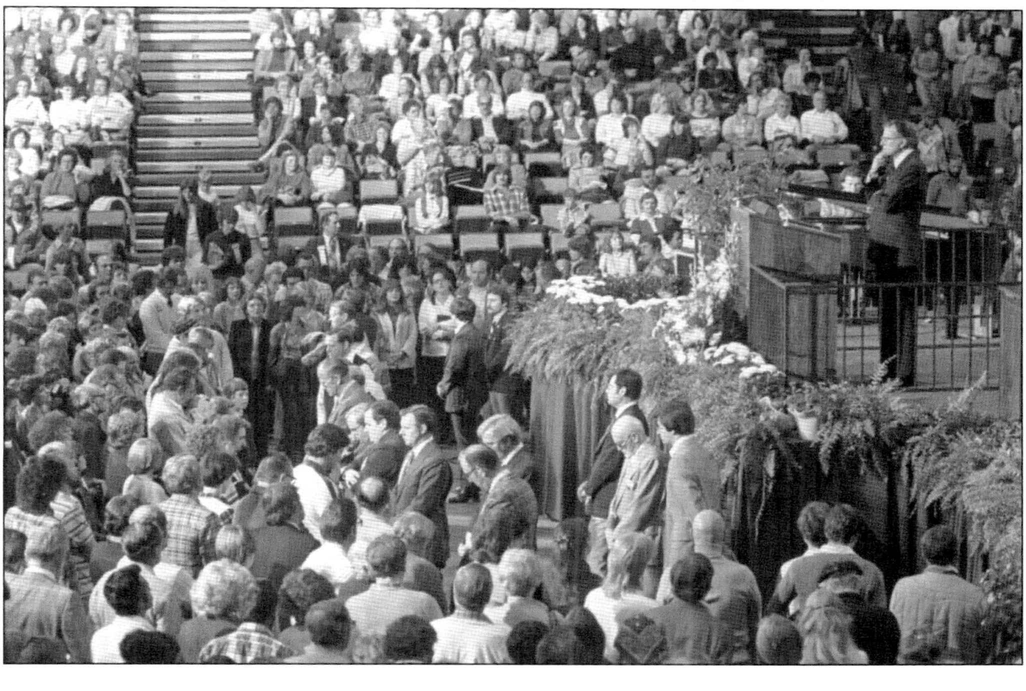

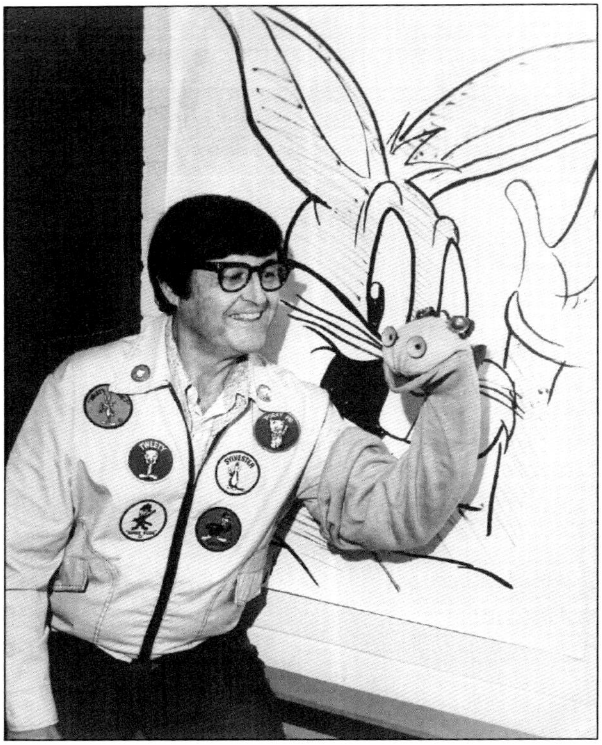

Bob Clampett, a famous illustrator and animator probably best known for his work on the *Looney Tunes* cartoons for Warner Brothers, was also a puppeteer, a producer, and a director. In his later years, he toured college campuses and lectured on the history of animation, which led him to the University of Nevada, Reno on December 10, 1974. (Photograph courtesy of the *Reno Gazette-Journal.*)

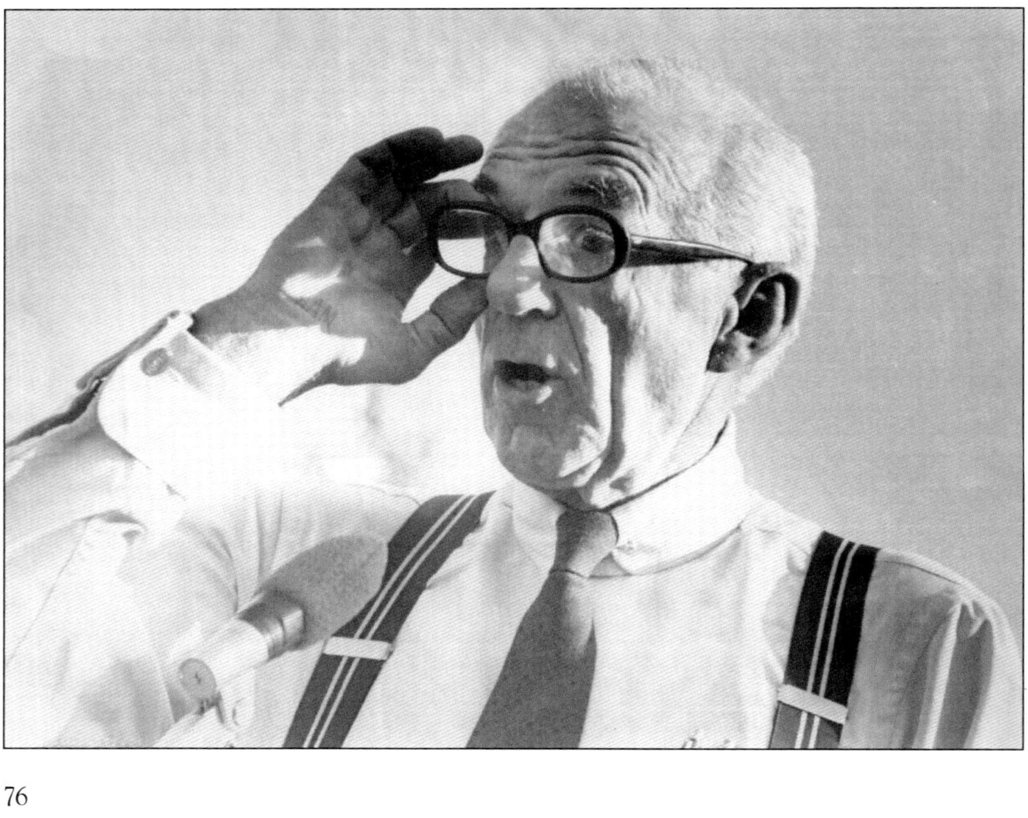

Dr. Benjamin Spock, a pediatrician best known for his 1946 book *Baby and Child Care*, visited the University of Nevada, Reno on March 8, 1972, to speak out against the Vietnam War on a tour of college campuses. Spock was also the People's Party candidate for president, challenging incumbent Richard Nixon. (Photograph courtesy of the *Reno Gazette-Journal.*)

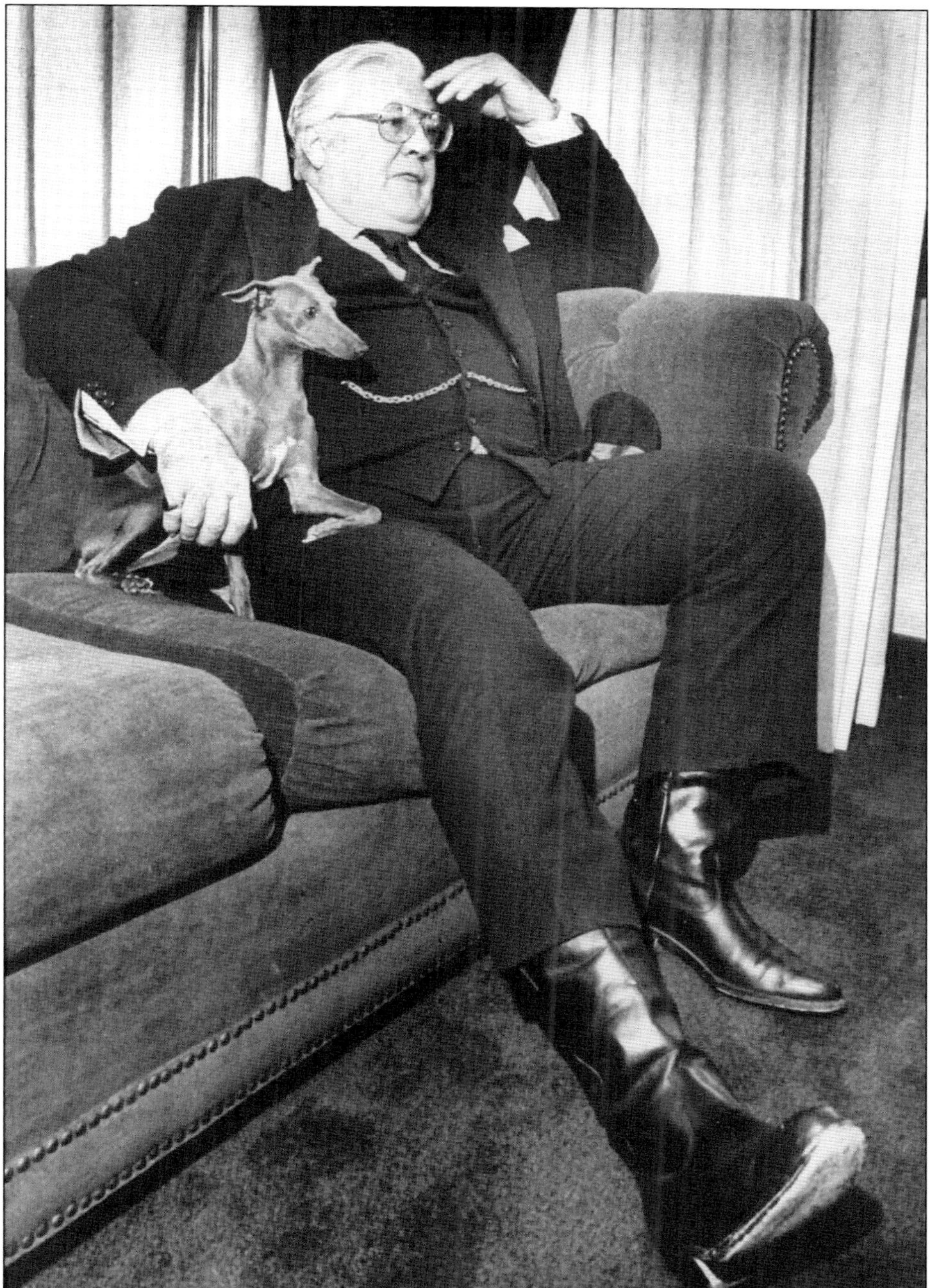

Attorney Melvin Belli, best known as Jack Ruby's defense lawyer after Ruby shot President Kennedy's assassin Lee Harvey Oswald, made regular trips to Reno in the 1960s and 1970s. "We generally come up once in the summer and once in the winter," he told the *Nevada State Journal*. "I love it up here. I've always liked Reno." In 1979, the 72-year-old Belli traveled to Reno with his wife, Lia, his daughter, Melia, and their dog, Wheldone Rumproast IV. (Photograph courtesy of the *Reno Gazette-Journal*.)

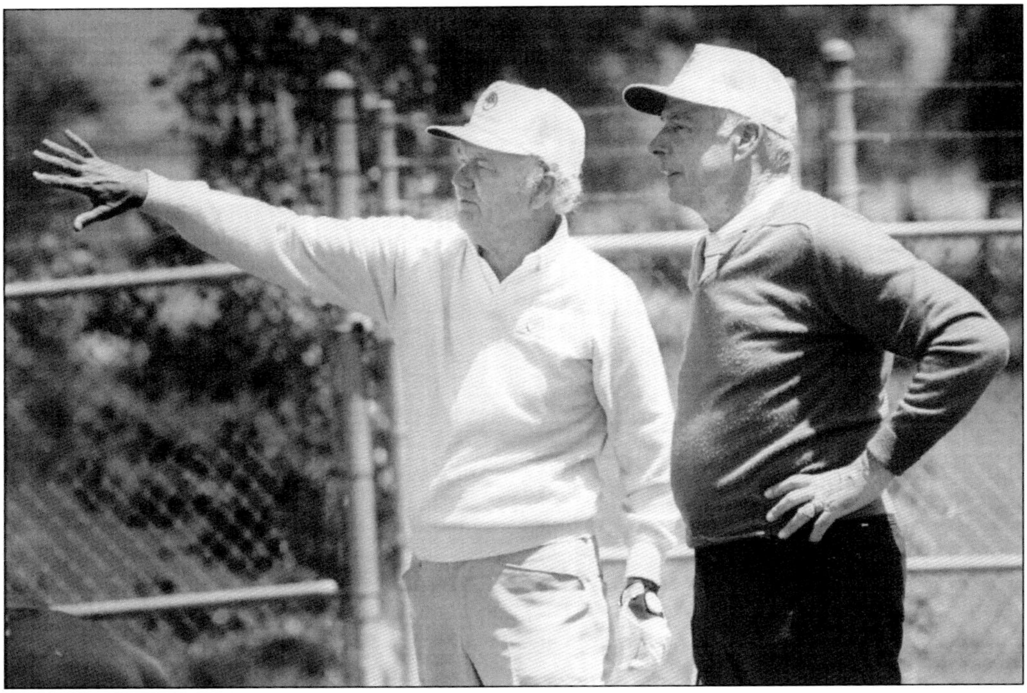

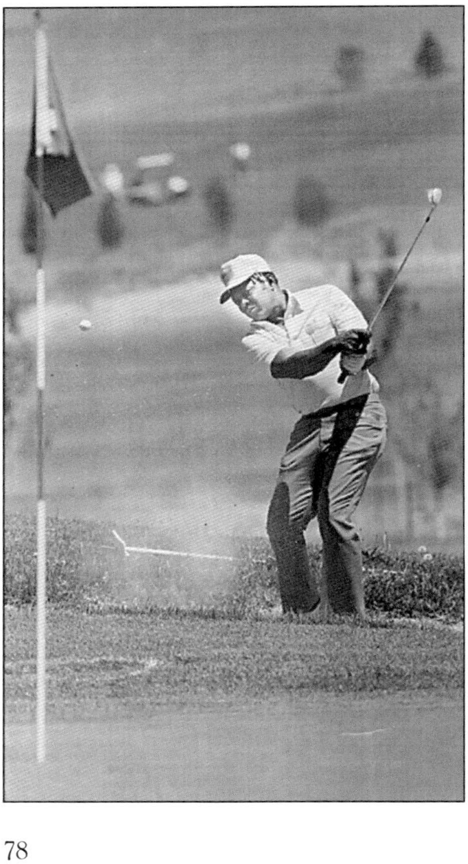

Baseball great Joe DiMaggio visited Reno dozens of times through the years, often participating in celebrity golf tournaments and pro-am events. In May 1984, DiMaggio was in town to play in the pro-am of the Gatlin Brothers Senior Golf Classic at Wildcreek Golf Course. Here, DiMaggio (right) discusses a shot with pro Bill Johnston. That night, DiMaggio attended a concert by the Gatlin Brothers on a fairway at the golf course. (Photograph by James Flenner, courtesy of the *Reno Gazette-Journal*.)

Baseball hall-of-famer Willie Mays blasts out of a bunker during a celebrity golf tournament in Reno in the 1970s. Like DiMaggio and a number of other baseball hall-of-famers, Mays often traveled to the Reno area for celebrity tournaments and other sporting events. In a 1970 tournament, one of Mays's playing partners, Harold Wilson, made a hole-in-one to win a new Ferrari. (Photograph courtesy of the *Reno Gazette-Journal*.)

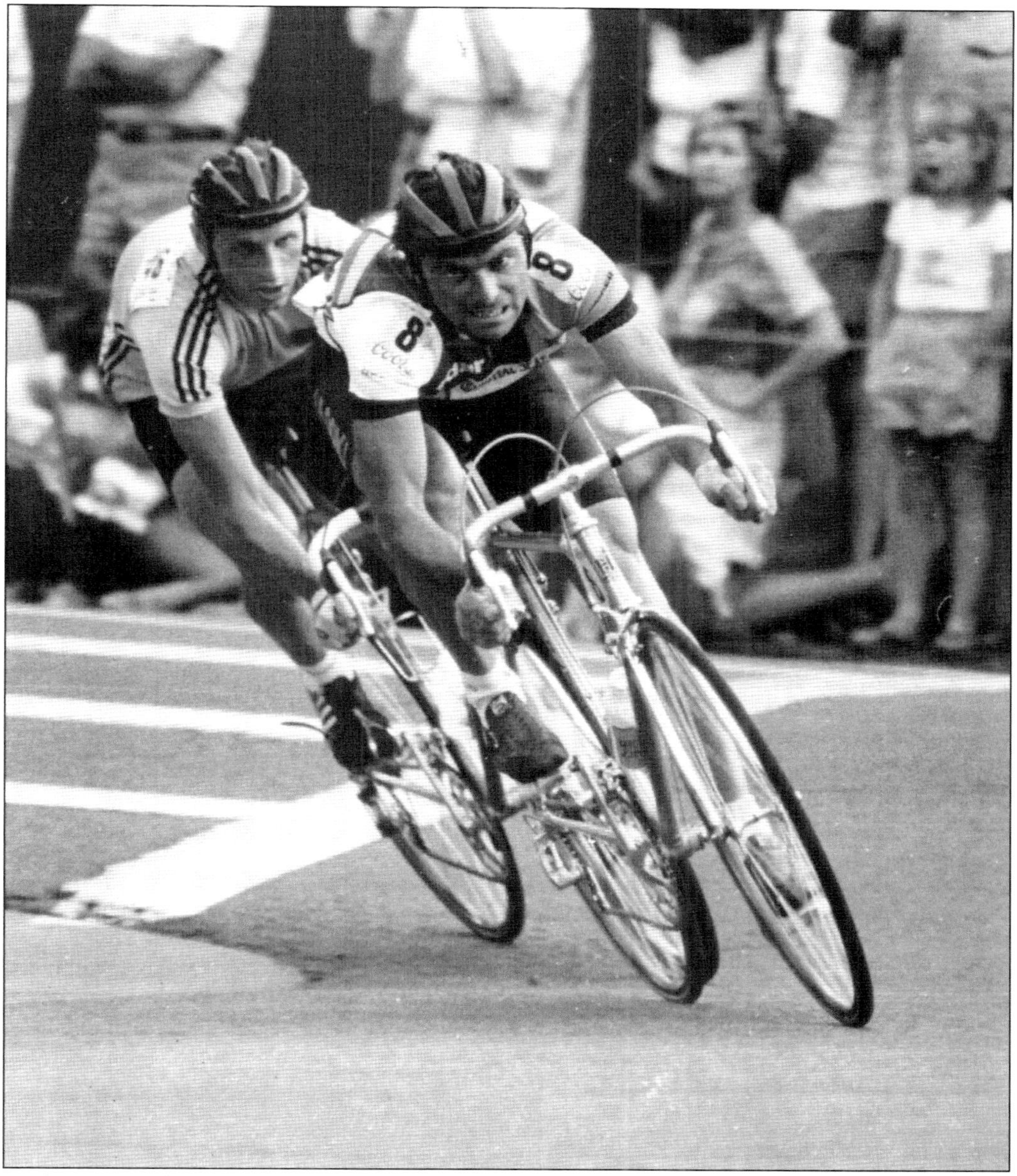

Cyclist Bernard Hinault, a five-time winner of the Tour de France, helped his teammate Greg LeMond of Reno spark a wave of cycling popularity in the United States in the 1980s. Hinault, LeMond, and the world's best cyclists passed through Reno in 1985 as part of the Coors Classic bicycle race. (Photograph courtesy of Chris Tumbusch.)

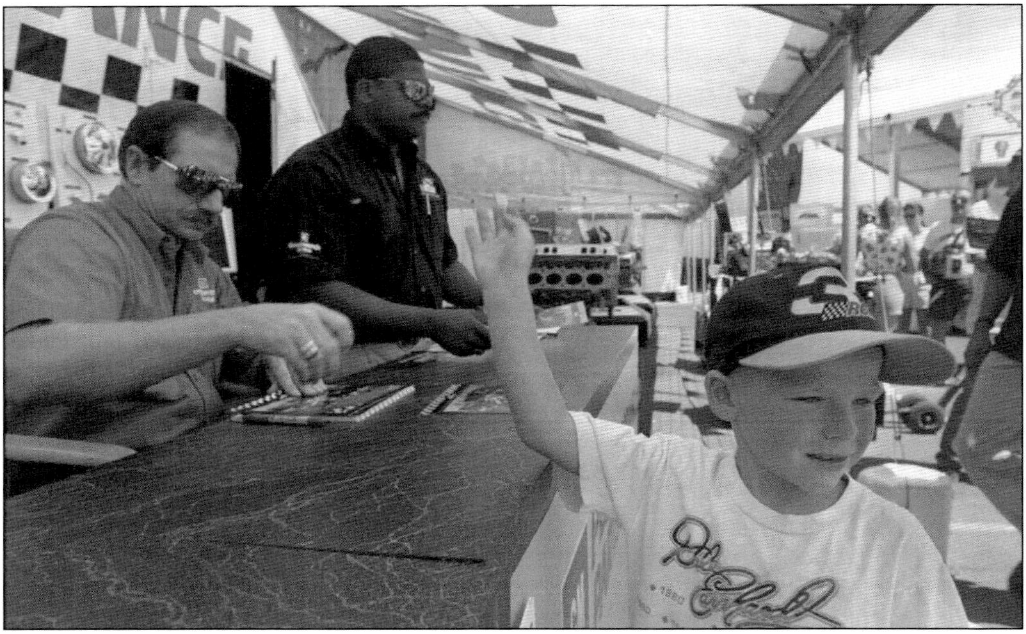

NASCAR driver Dale Earnhardt made seven-year-old Ryan Willaman of Reno one happy fan during Hot August Nights festivities in August 1997 at the Reno Hilton. Earnhardt was at the classic car festival signing autographs on behalf of General Motors, Goodwrench, and other sponsors. (Photograph by David B. Parker, courtesy of the *Reno Gazette-Journal*.)

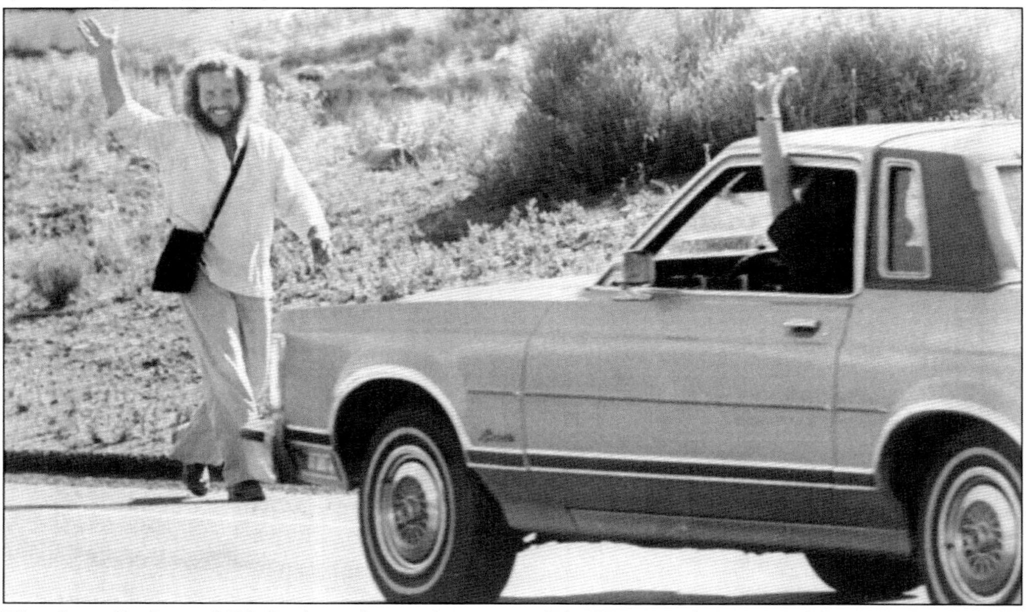

The friendly face of Ed Carlson, better known as "the Waver," has greeted Reno motorists for more than 40 years. Carlson, a native Iowan, said Reno is his home no matter where he travels, because he always finds himself returning. From the early 1970s through the 1990s, "the Waver" walked the 30 miles of highway between Reno and Carson City almost daily, waving to motorists. (Photograph by Marilyn Newton, courtesy of the *Reno Gazette-Journal*.)

Six

Silver Spurs

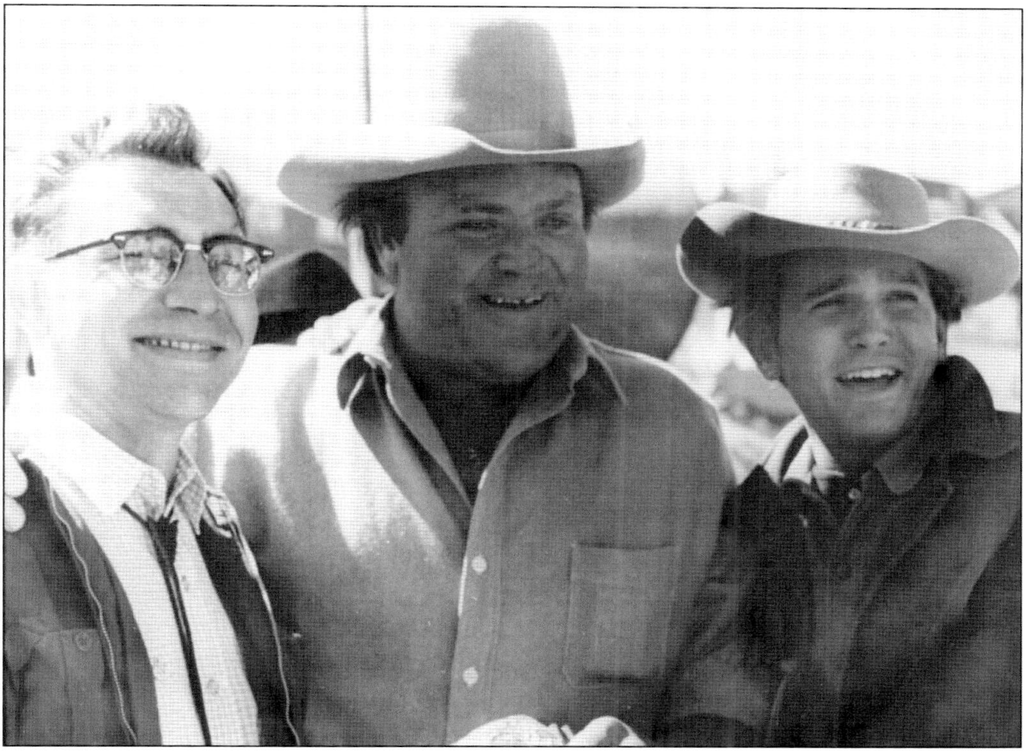

In 1950, the Greater Reno Chamber of Commerce, in order to generate publicity for the city, developed the Silver Spurs Award to be presented to an actor who best portrays the traditions of the West. Dan Blocker, famous as Hoss Cartwright in the television series *Bonanza*, was a two-time winner of the Silver Spurs Award, in 1962 and 1965. Nevada governor Grant Sawyer (left) made the presentation both times. Blocker's fellow *Bonanza* stars, including Michael Landon (right) attended the 1962 awards banquet. (Photograph courtesy of the Neal Cobb Collection.)

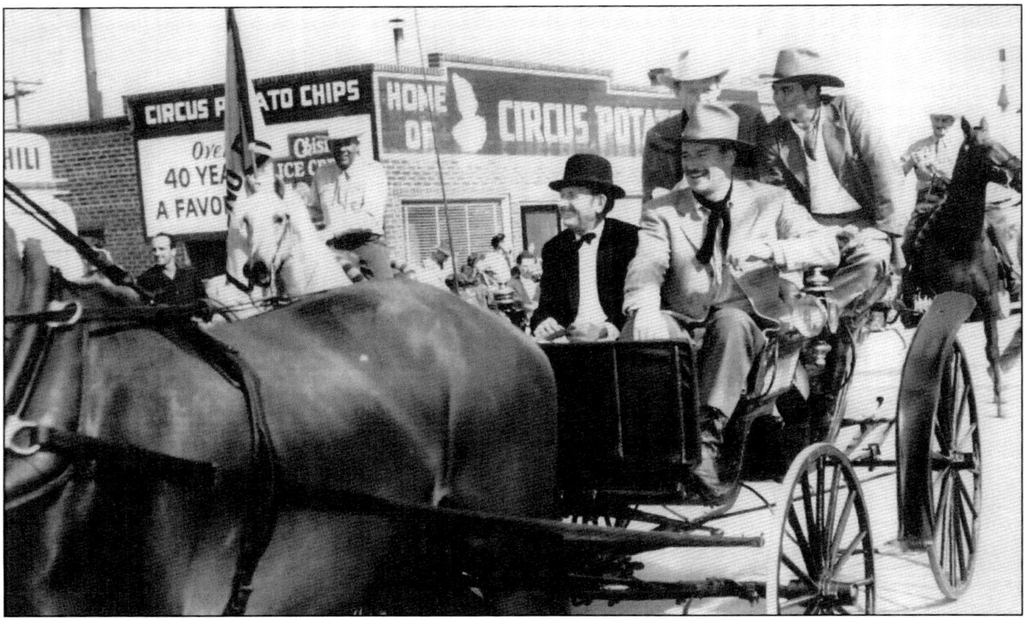

The first-ever recipients of the Silver Spurs Award were Western actor John Wayne and film director John Ford for their work in the film *She Wore a Yellow Ribbon*. Wayne and fellow Hollywood stars Ben Johnson and Harry Carey Jr. led a parade up Virginia Street escorted by the horsemen's group the Nevada White Hats, including Margaret and Robert Flick (below, with Wayne). The award was presented on May 13, 1950, by Gov. Vail Pittman in a banquet at the Mapes Hotel. (Photographs courtesy of the Neal Cobb Collection.)

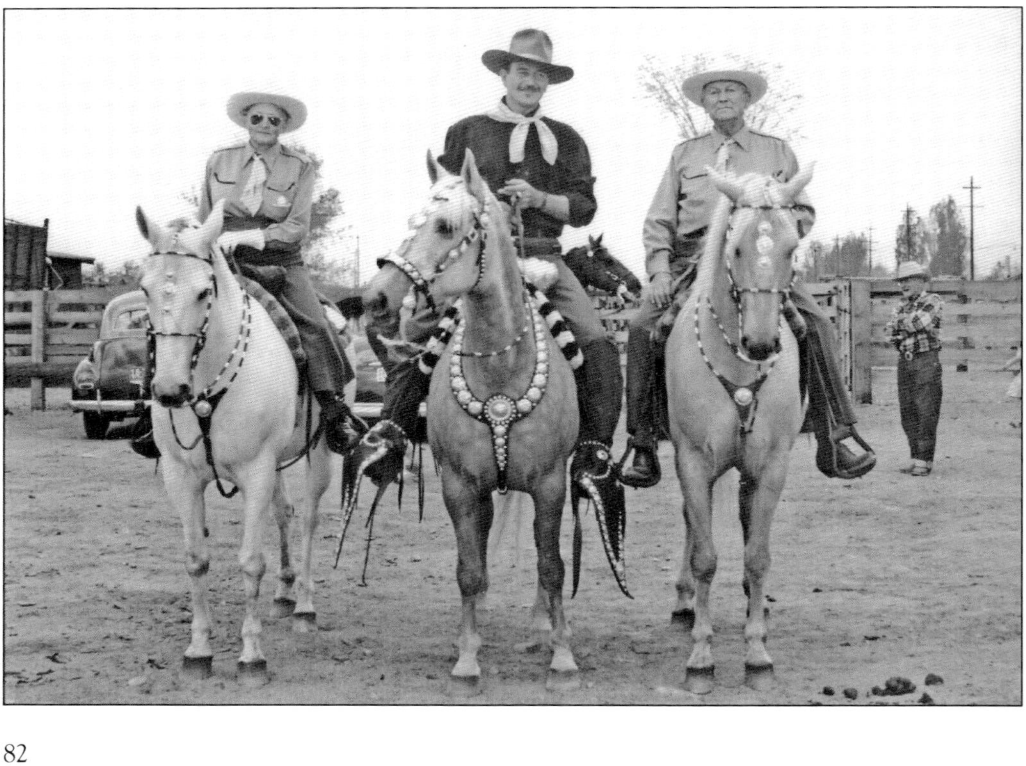

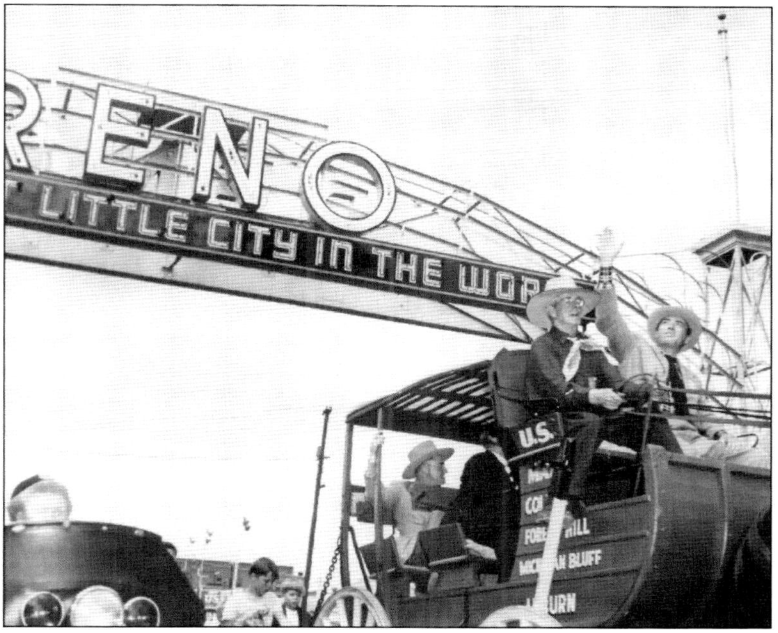

Gregory Peck received the Silver Spurs Award from the Greater Reno Chamber of Commerce on May 19, 1951, for his performance in *The Gunfighter*. The ceremony was held at the Riverside Hotel, and Peck was presented the award by Gov. Charles Russell. (Photograph courtesy of the *Reno Gazette-Journal*.)

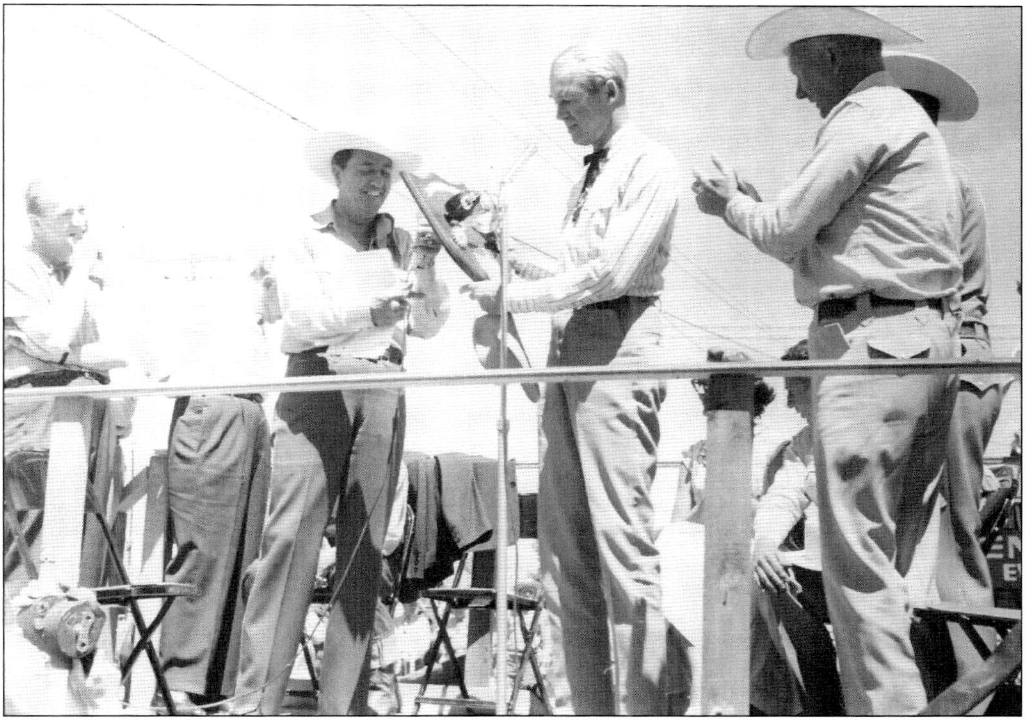

Veteran actor Jimmy Stewart was honored with the Silver Spurs Award in 1952 for his role in *The Man from Laramie*. His director, Anthony Mann, was also honored during the event. Stewart drove a Cadillac in the Reno Rodeo Parade and was presented with his award by Reno city councilman George Vargas. The Silver Spurs were made by Reno silversmith Hoot Newman. (Photograph courtesy of the *Reno Gazette-Journal*.)

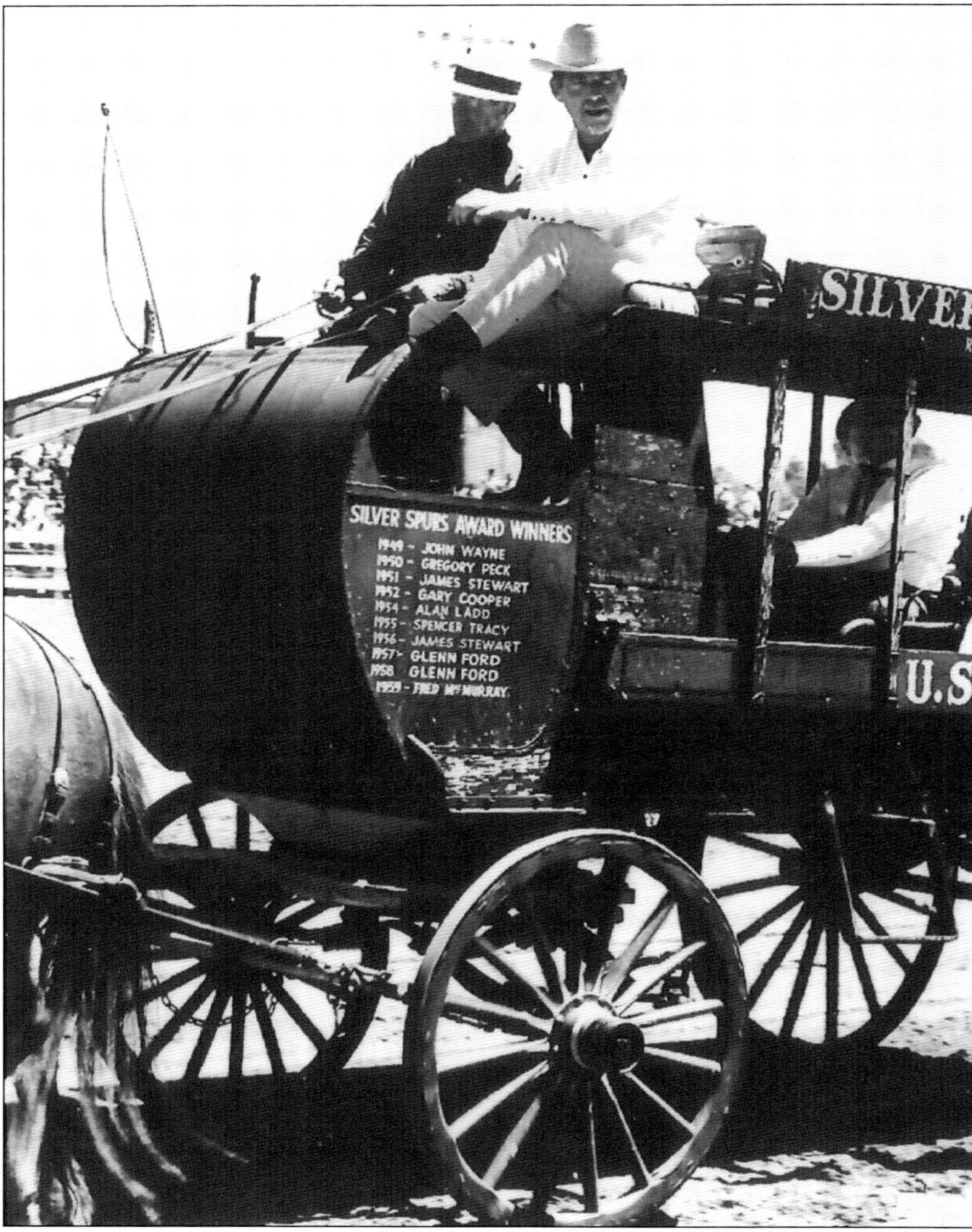

Fred MacMurray, atop the Silver Spurs Express stagecoach, was the 1959 winner of the Silver Spurs Award. Unfortunately, his last name was misspelled on the list of award winners. (Photograph courtesy of the Neal Cobb Collection.)

James Arness, who played Marshal Matt Dillon on the long-running television series *Gunsmoke*, was the first television actor to be honored with the Silver Spurs Award, in 1960. Arness was met at the Reno airport by Mayor Bud Baker and his wife, Dorothy. Below, Arness received the Silver Spurs Award from Nevada lieutenant governor Rex Bell, himself a former Hollywood Western actor, during a ceremony at the Mapes Hotel. (Photographs courtesy of the *Reno Gazette-Journal*.)

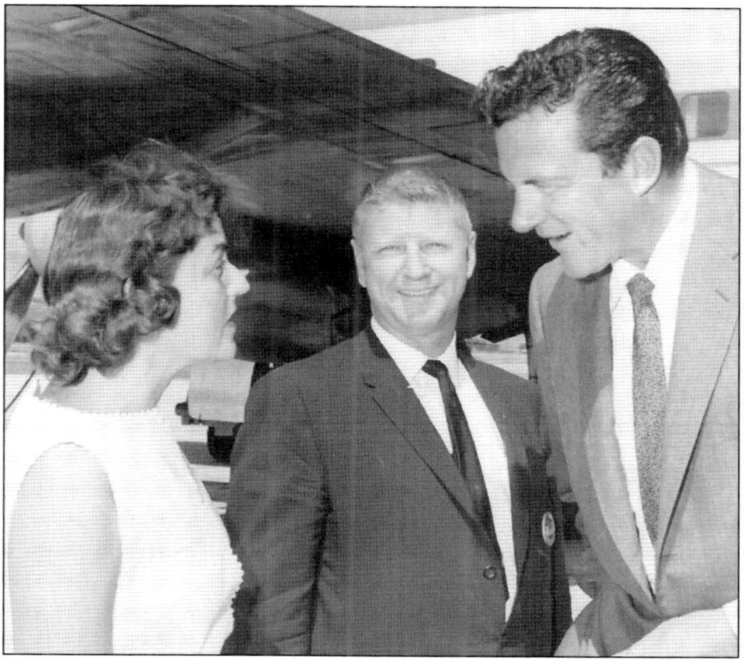

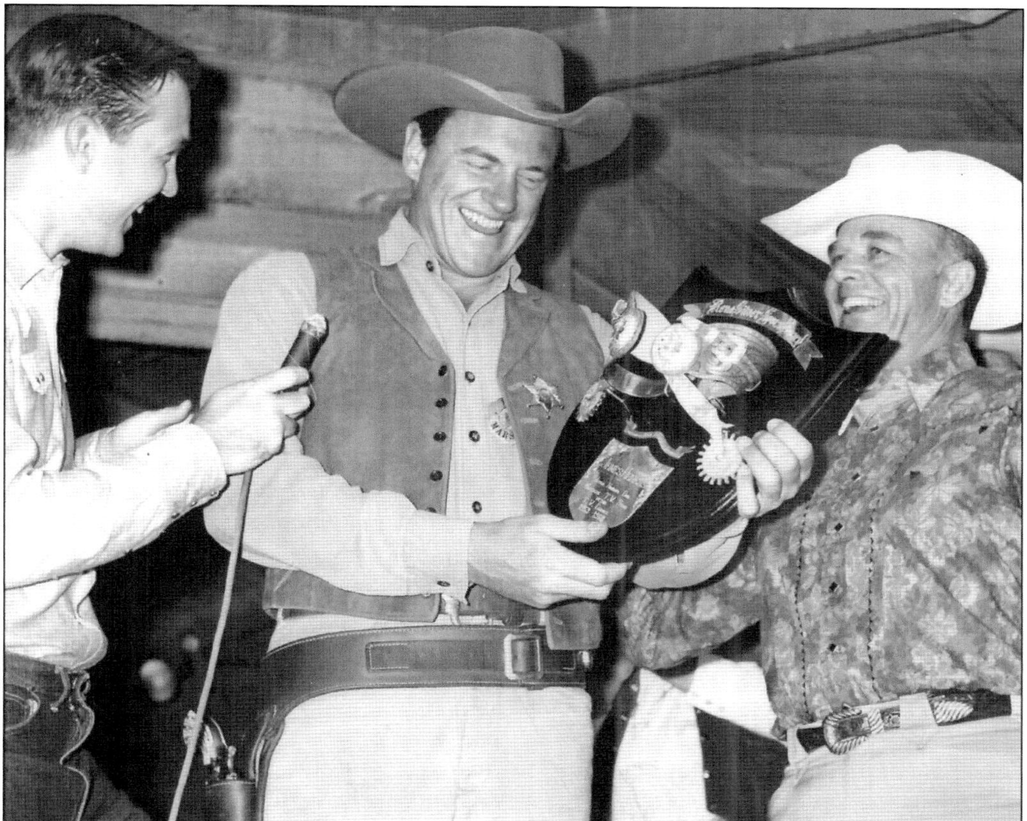

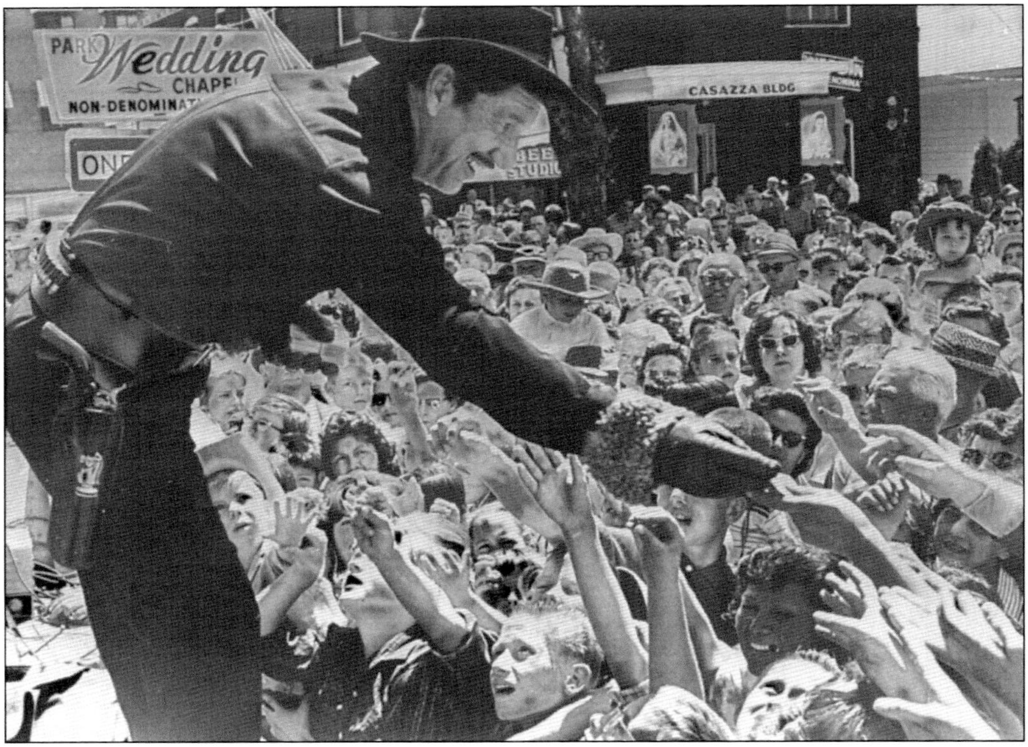

Richard Boone greets fans before receiving the Silver Spurs Award in 1961 for his role as Palladin in the television series *Have Gun, Will Travel.* Boone was feted with a downtown Reno parade and was also made an honorary chief of the Paiute Indian tribe. He was presented his Silver Spurs Award by chamber of commerce president Frank Bender. (Photographs by Marilyn Newton, courtesy of the *Reno Gazette-Journal.*)

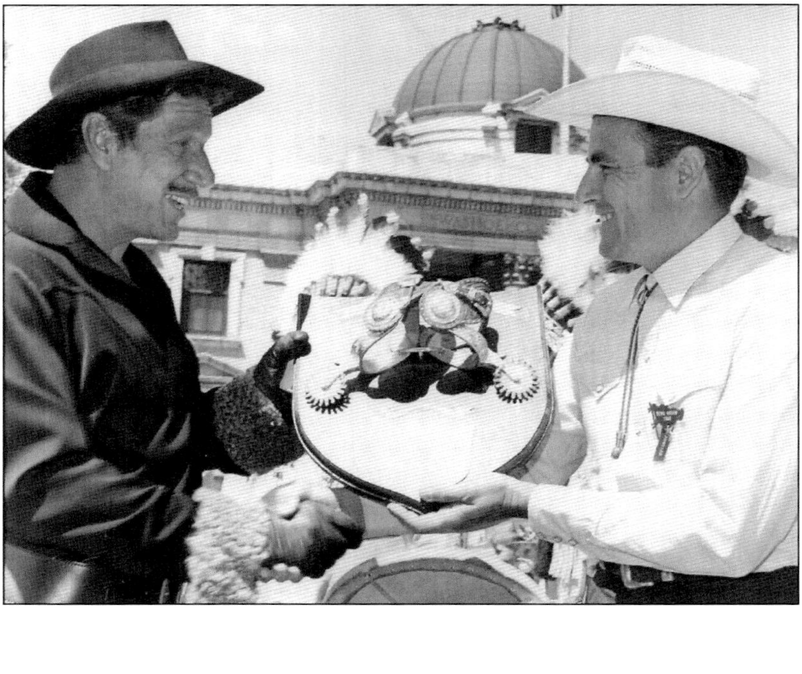

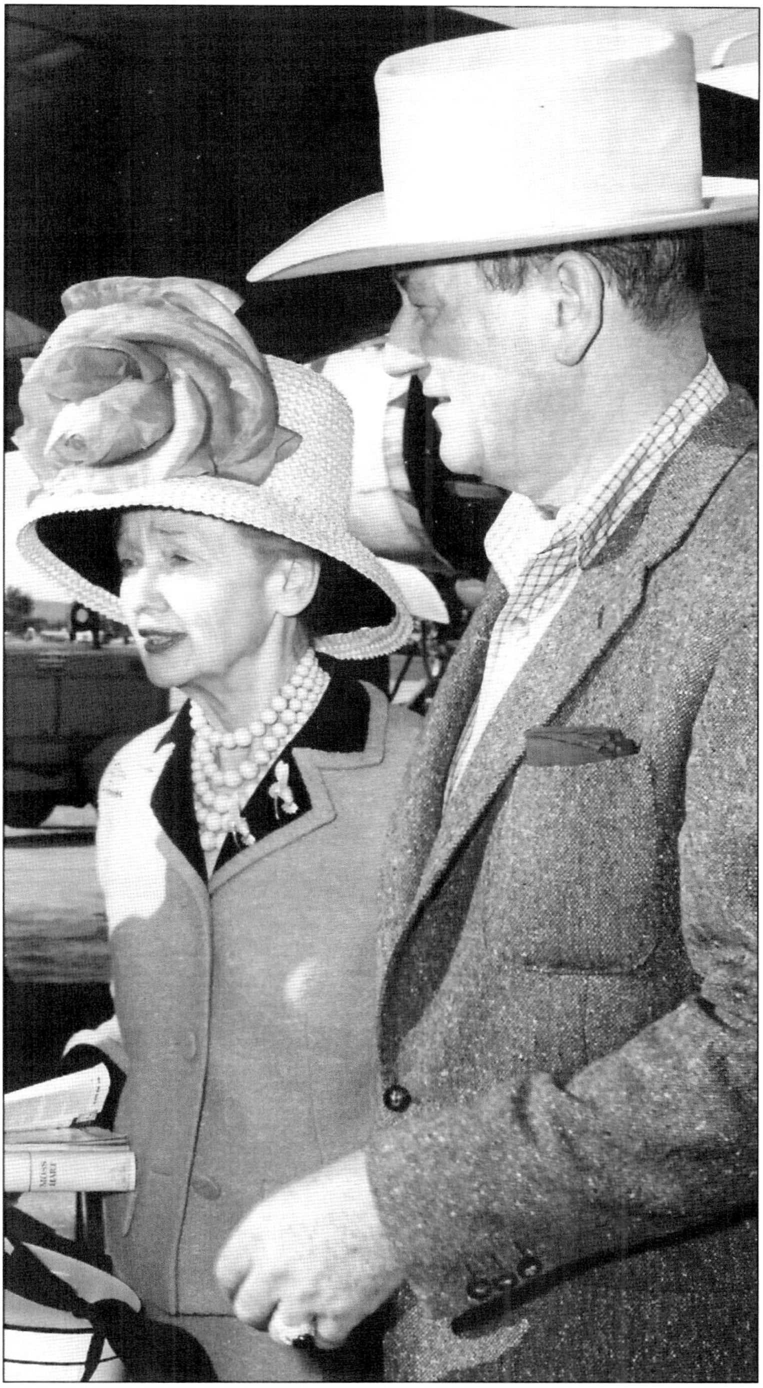

Famed Hollywood columnist Hedda Hopper, accompanied here by John Wayne, was honored in Reno in 1961 on the occasion of her 71st birthday. In addition to other activities around town, Hopper attended the Silver Spurs Award presentation to Richard Boone. (Photograph by Marilyn Newton, courtesy of the *Reno Gazette-Journal*.)

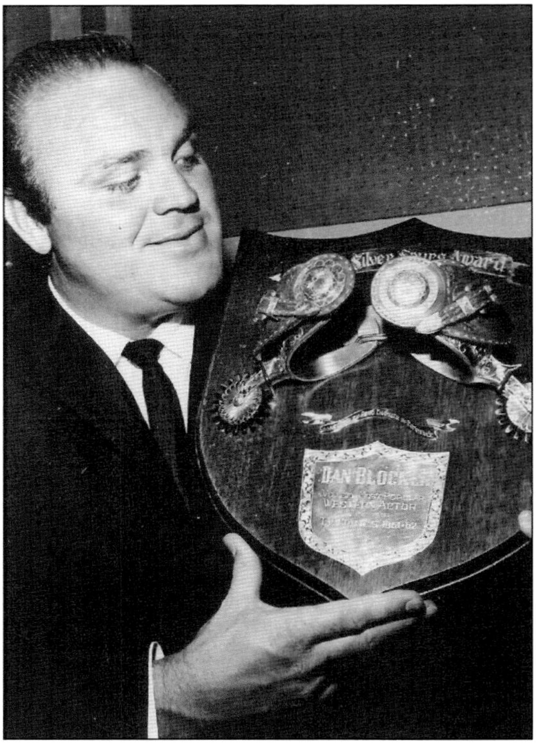

Dan Blocker, or Hoss Cartwright of *Bonanza* fame, started what the *Reno Evening Gazette* described as a "Bonanza monopoly" when he was presented the Silver Spurs Award in 1962. He was the only member of the Cartwright clan to win the award twice, taking it in 1965 after his TV family members Michael Landon and Lorne Greene won the award in 1963 and 1964, respectively. (Photograph by Marilyn Newton, courtesy of the *Reno Gazette-Journal.*)

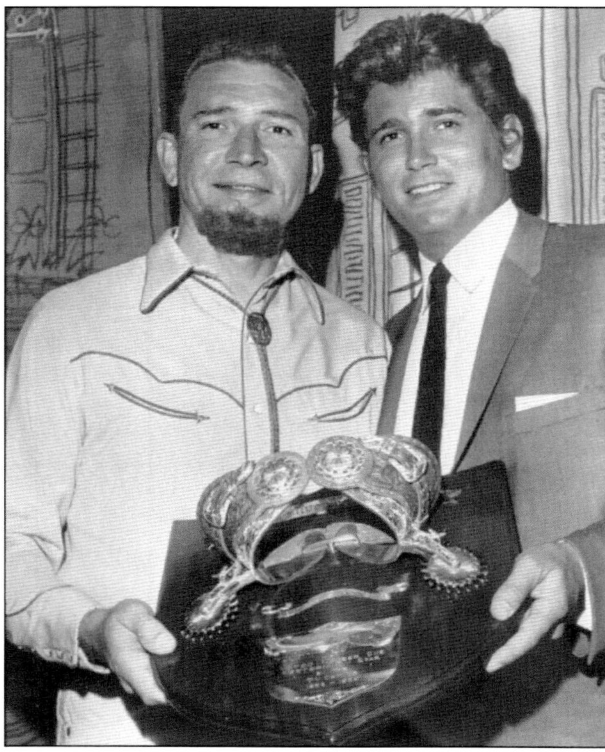

Michael Landon (right), who played Little Joe Cartwright on *Bonanza*, received the Silver Spurs Award from Nevada governor Grant Sawyer on May 16, 1964, in an event sponsored by the Greater Reno Chamber of Commerce. Landon also used the visit to Reno to reaffirm his marriage vows with his wife, Lynn, in a ceremony performed by Reno justice of the peace William Beemer. (Photograph by Marilyn Newton, courtesy of the *Reno Gazette-Journal.*)

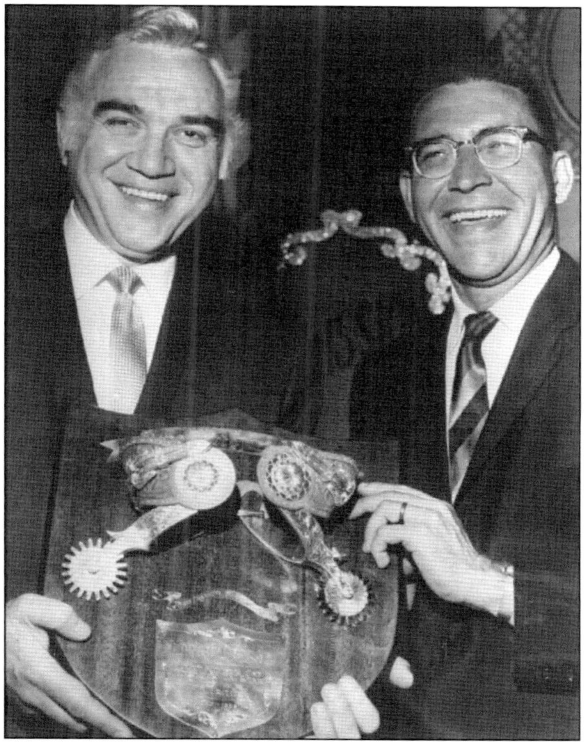

Lorne Greene (left), who portrayed patriarch Ben Cartwright on the television series *Bonanza*, received the Silver Spurs award from Gov. Grant Sawyer in a ceremony sponsored by the Greater Reno Chamber of Commerce on May 25, 1963. Greene told the crowd, "We at *Bonanza* are grateful for Nevada, Reno, Virginia City, and Lake Tahoe for providing a magnificent background." Below, Sawyer and his wife, Bette, greeted Greene and his wife, Nancy, at an event commemorating Nevada's centennial on October 31, 1964. (Photographs by Marilyn Newton, courtesy of the *Reno Gazette-Journal*.)

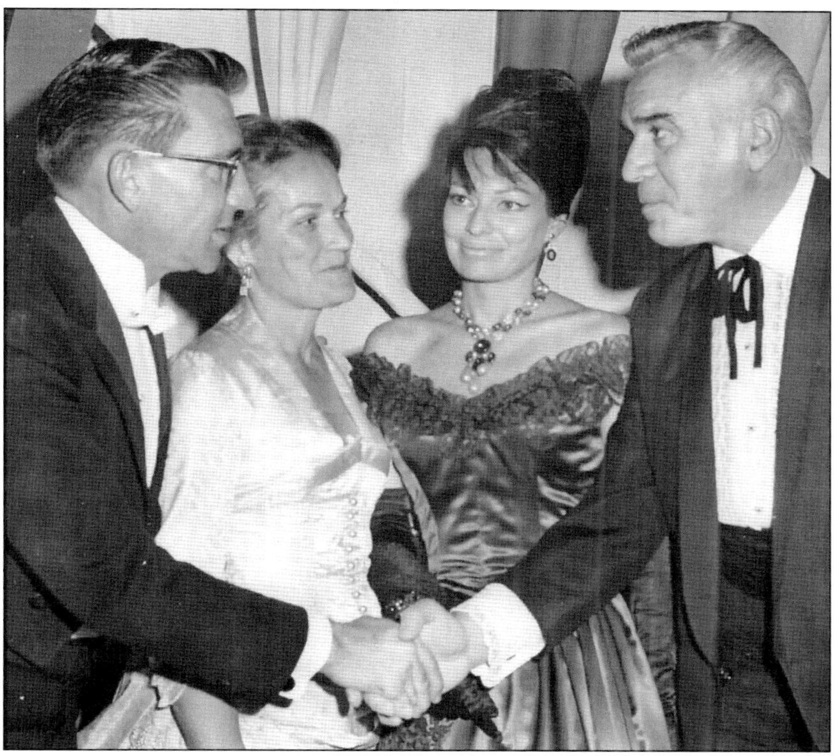

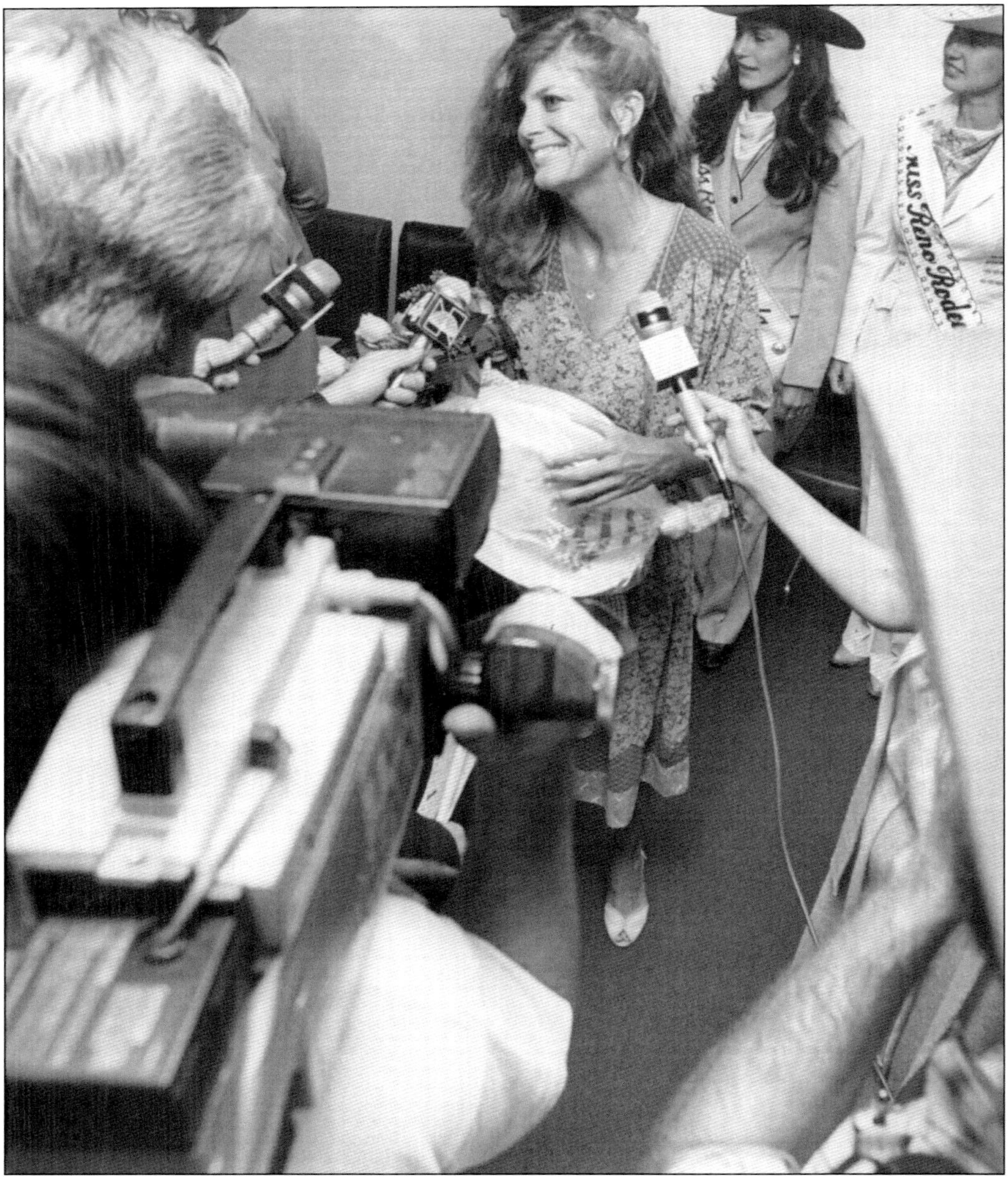

Katherine Ross became the first female winner in the history of the Silver Spurs Award in 1981 for her lead female role opposite Paul Newman and Robert Redford in the film *Butch Cassidy and the Sundance Kid*. Ross later starred in the film *The Sundance Woman*. (Photograph courtesy of the *Reno Gazette-Journal*.)

Seven

Reno Rodeo

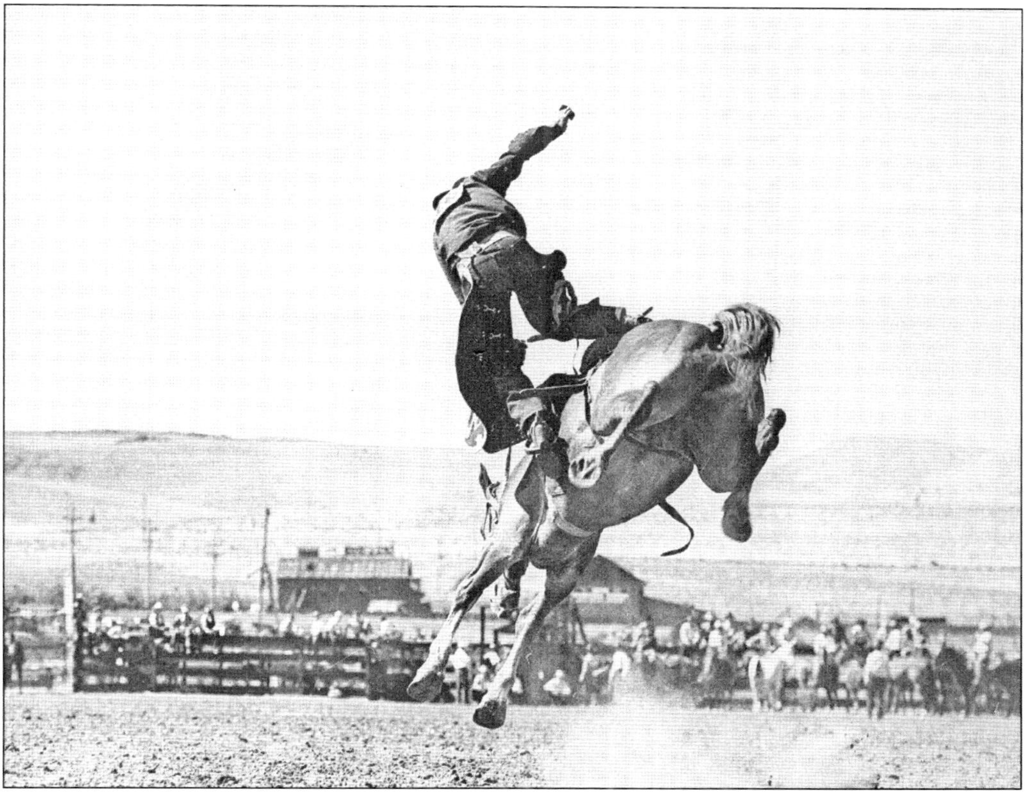

From its beginning in 1919, the Reno Rodeo has been a tradition in the city. And almost from the beginning, it was known as "The Wildest, Richest Rodeo in the West." Scenes like this from the 1930s helped put the "wild" into the rodeo. More than 90 years later, the event is one of the top professional rodeos in the country and the city's longest-running special event. (Photograph courtesy of the Reno Rodeo Association.)

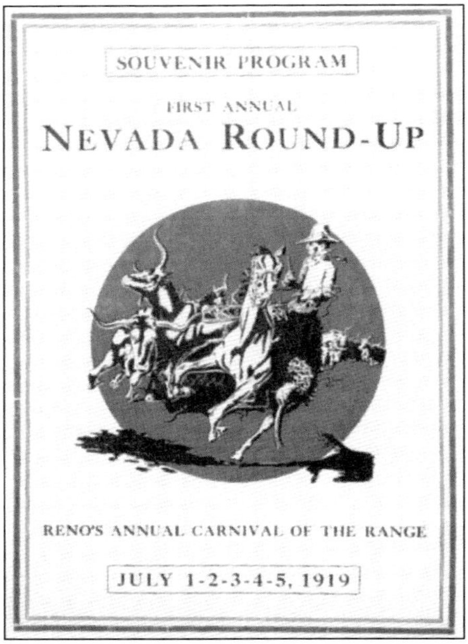

The program for the first Reno Rodeo, held over the Fourth of July weekend in 1919, included the artwork of a convicted cattle rustler named Will James. It was the first commercial piece of artwork for James, who was paid $20 for it. He became one of the country's best-known Western authors and artists, writing and illustrating 24 books. He married Reno girl Alice Conradt. (Courtesy of the Reno Rodeo Association.)

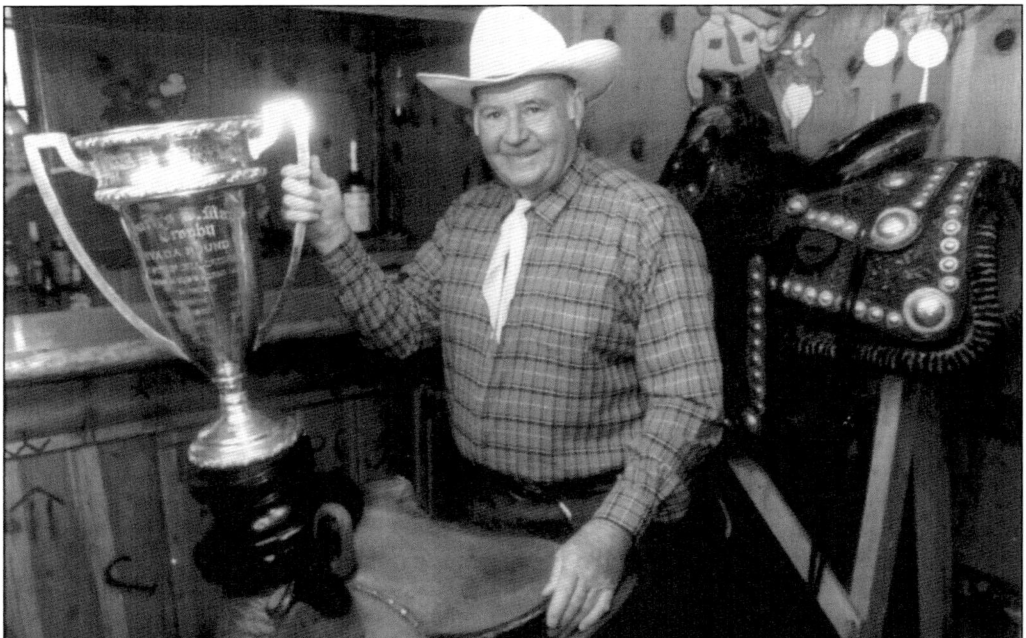

Beginning in 1920, a revolving silver cup known as the Charles W. Mapes Trophy recognized the bronc riding champion of the Reno Rodeo. The trophy was named for the Reno community leader and one of the founders of the rodeo. The revolving trophy would have the name of the winning rider engraved. Ben Dobbins was the first winner, in 1920. In later years, the award was revised to recognize the top Nevada saddle bronc rider. Today, the trophy is held by Charles W. Mapes Jr., who carried on his father's affection for the Reno Rodeo. (Courtesy of the *Reno Gazette-Journal*.)

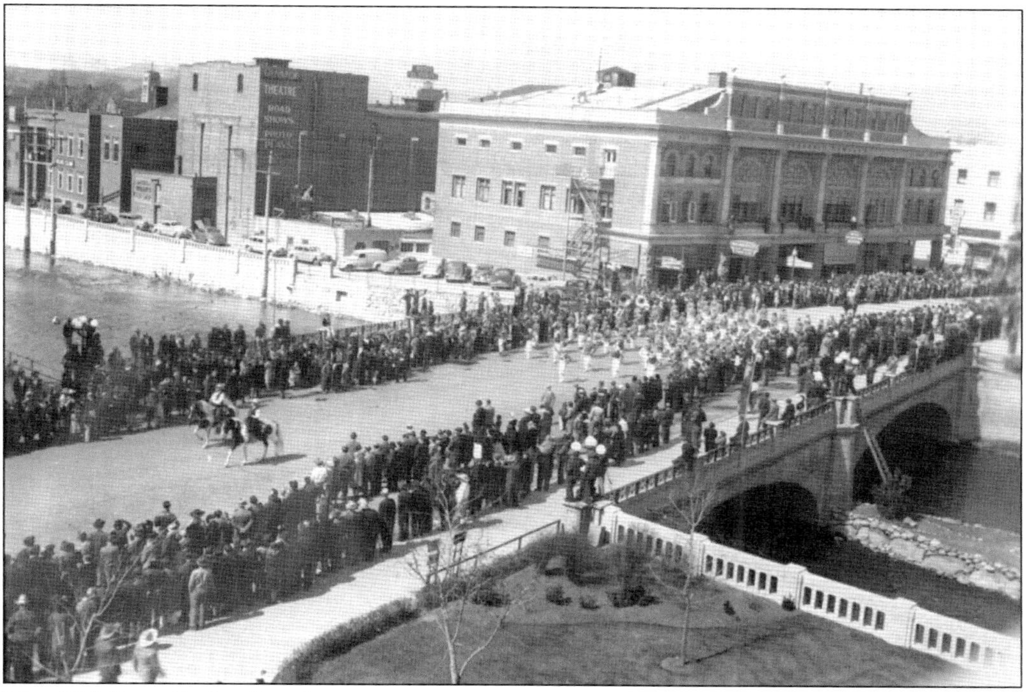

The 1932 Reno Rodeo Parade was billed by Reno newspapers as "the biggest parade Reno had ever seen." It stretched more than a mile in length and included dignitaries, celebrities, working cowboys, and Indians in tribal regalia, as well as clowns, divorcees, and cowboys from the dude ranches that became prominent with the liberalization of the divorce law in 1931. Leading the parade were Gov. Fred Balzar and Lt. Gov. Morley Griswold. (Courtesy of the Nevada Historical Society.)

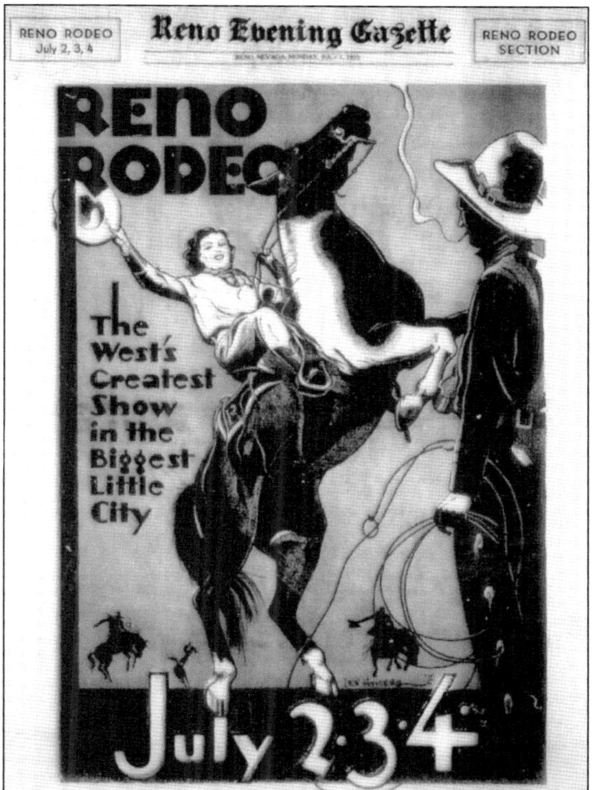

In 1935, the *Reno Evening Gazette* touted the Reno Rodeo as "The West's Greatest Show in the Biggest Little City" and took advantage of the skills of Reno artist Lew Hymers for the illustration of a cowgirl atop a raring bronc. It was a milestone year for the event, as the event officially took the name of Reno Rodeo and the Reno Rodeo Association was formed, made up of local businessmen who helped underwrite the event. (Courtesy of the *Reno Gazette-Journal*.)

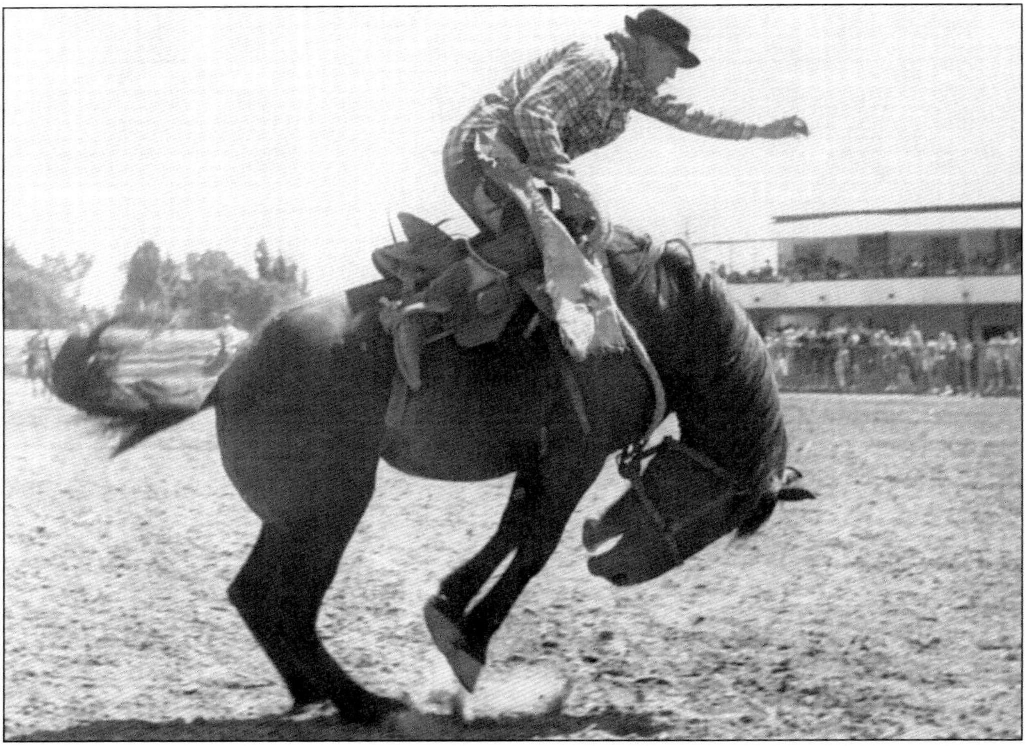

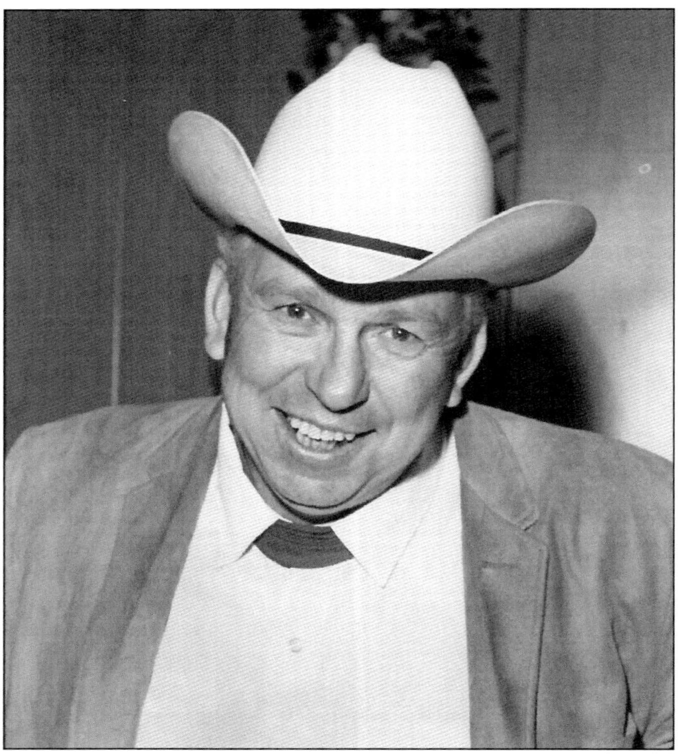

Slim Pickens was best known as a Hollywood actor in numerous Western films and as the man who rode an atomic bomb in the film *Dr. Strangelove*. But before his movie career began, Pickens, who was born Louis Bert Lindley Jr., was a rodeo cowboy, competing in saddle bronc riding at the Reno Rodeo in the early 1940s and also working the rodeo as a clown. Pickens attended the rodeo many times through the years and twice served as the grand marshal of the parade. (Above, photograph courtesy of the Ernie Mack Collection; left, photograph courtesy of the *Reno Gazette-Journal*.)

A highlight of the 1946 Reno Rodeo was the return of the women's bronc riding event, and the star of the show was Emma "Pee Wee" Burge. Born in 1919—the year of the first Reno Rodeo—Burge immigrated with her parents from Giswil, Switzerland, to California when she was nine. By age 17, she had embraced the Western way of life and began riding steers and broncs competitively. She was also an accomplished roper and trick rider. She stood only five feet tall and weighed less than 100 pounds, earning her the nickname "Pee Wee." She died in 2011 at age 92. (Courtesy of the Ernie Mack Collection.)

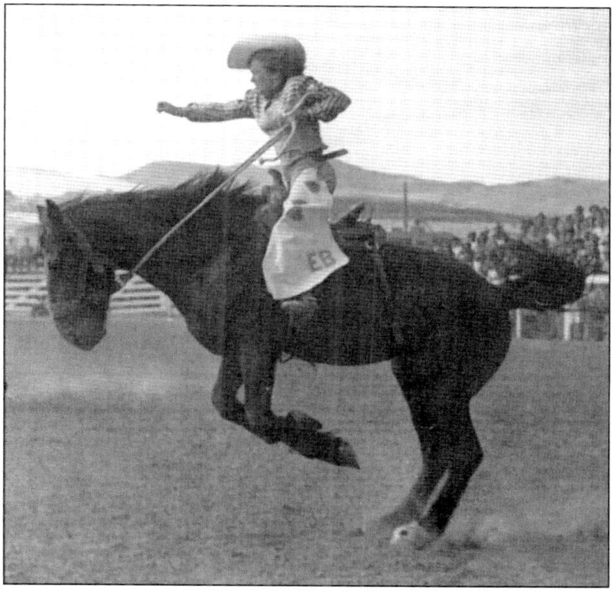

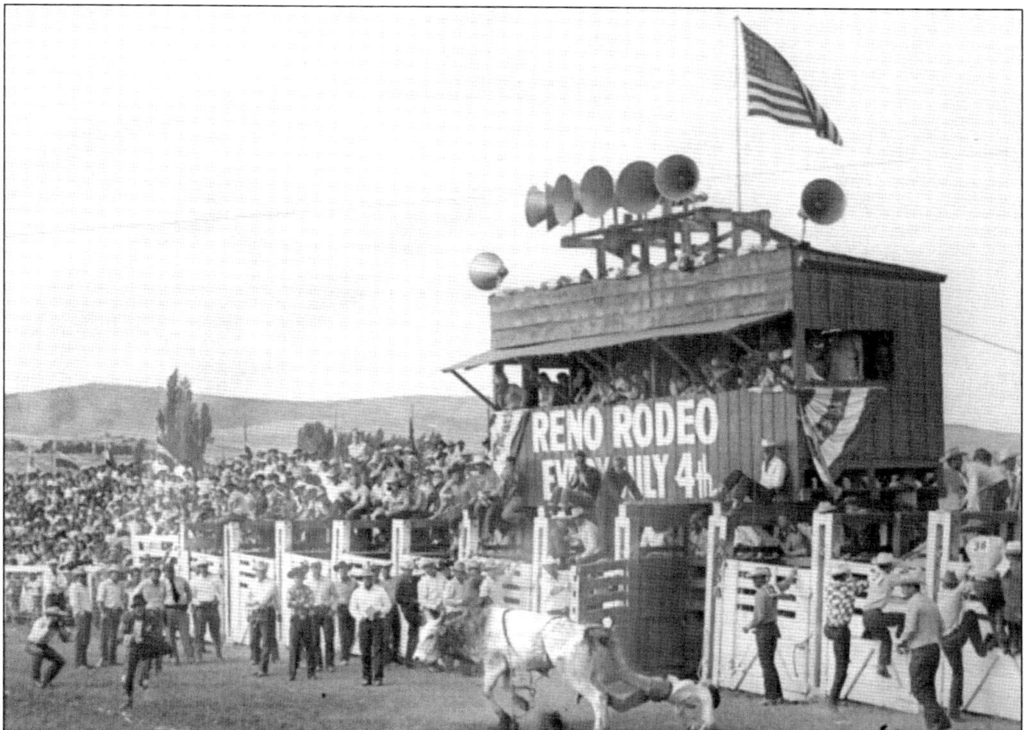

The Reno Rodeo established itself as one of the top events on the professional rodeo circuit in the 1940s, drawing the top cowboys from around the country and paying out more than $10,000 in prize money. In the 1940s, bull riding also became a standard event at the rodeo, adding an element of danger. The only fatality in the history of the rodeo came in 1947, when California cowboy Bill Brendler died after being stepped on by a bull. (Courtesy of the Ernie Mack Collection.)

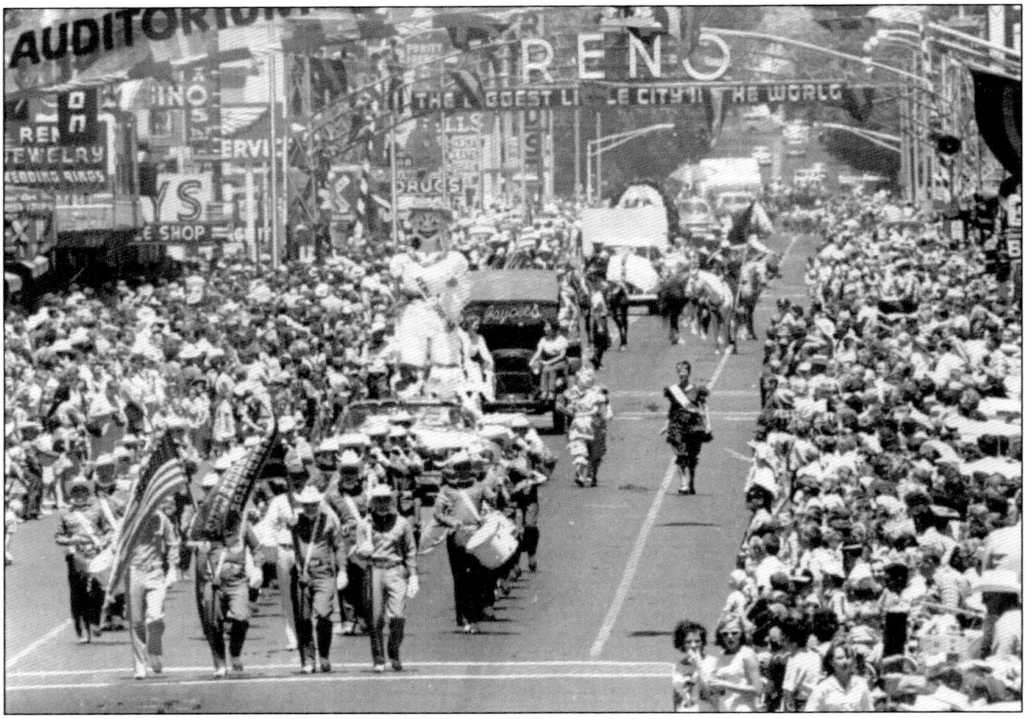

By the 1950s, the annual Reno Rodeo Parade was one of the most anticipated events of the summer, and thousands of onlookers packed downtown Reno to watch the hundreds of mounted participants, marching bands, and other entries. A highlight was seeing who was locked up in the "Black Mariah," a paddy wagon operated by the Reno Jaycees, who would "arrest" local officials and celebrities and hold them until a charity ransom was paid. (Photograph courtesy of the *Reno Gazette-Journal*.)

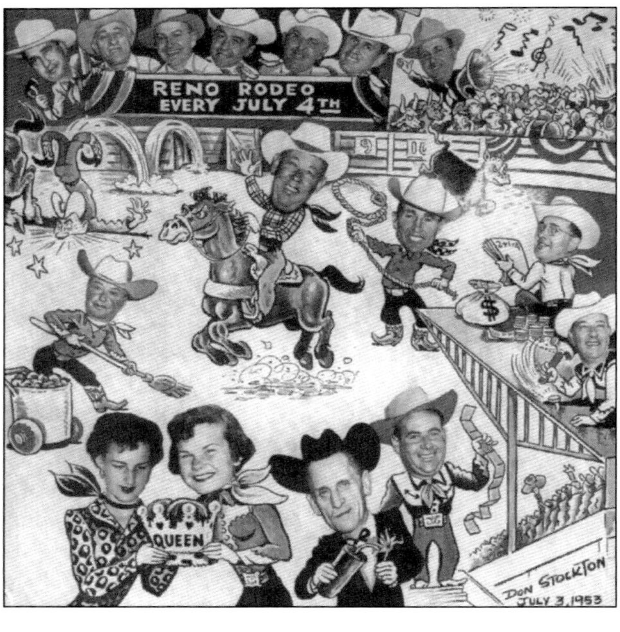

The board of directors of the 1953 Reno Rodeo Association included, from left to right, (first row, with unidentified queen candidates) Eddie Questa and Charles W. Mapes Jr.; (second row) Eck Holgate, Ray Peterson, Harry Frost, Larry Semenza, and Guy Lent; (third row) George Vargas, Gordon Harris, George Wingfield Jr., Link Piazzo, Roy Bankofier, Bill Stead, and Pat Sanford. (Photograph courtesy of Link Piazzo Collection.)

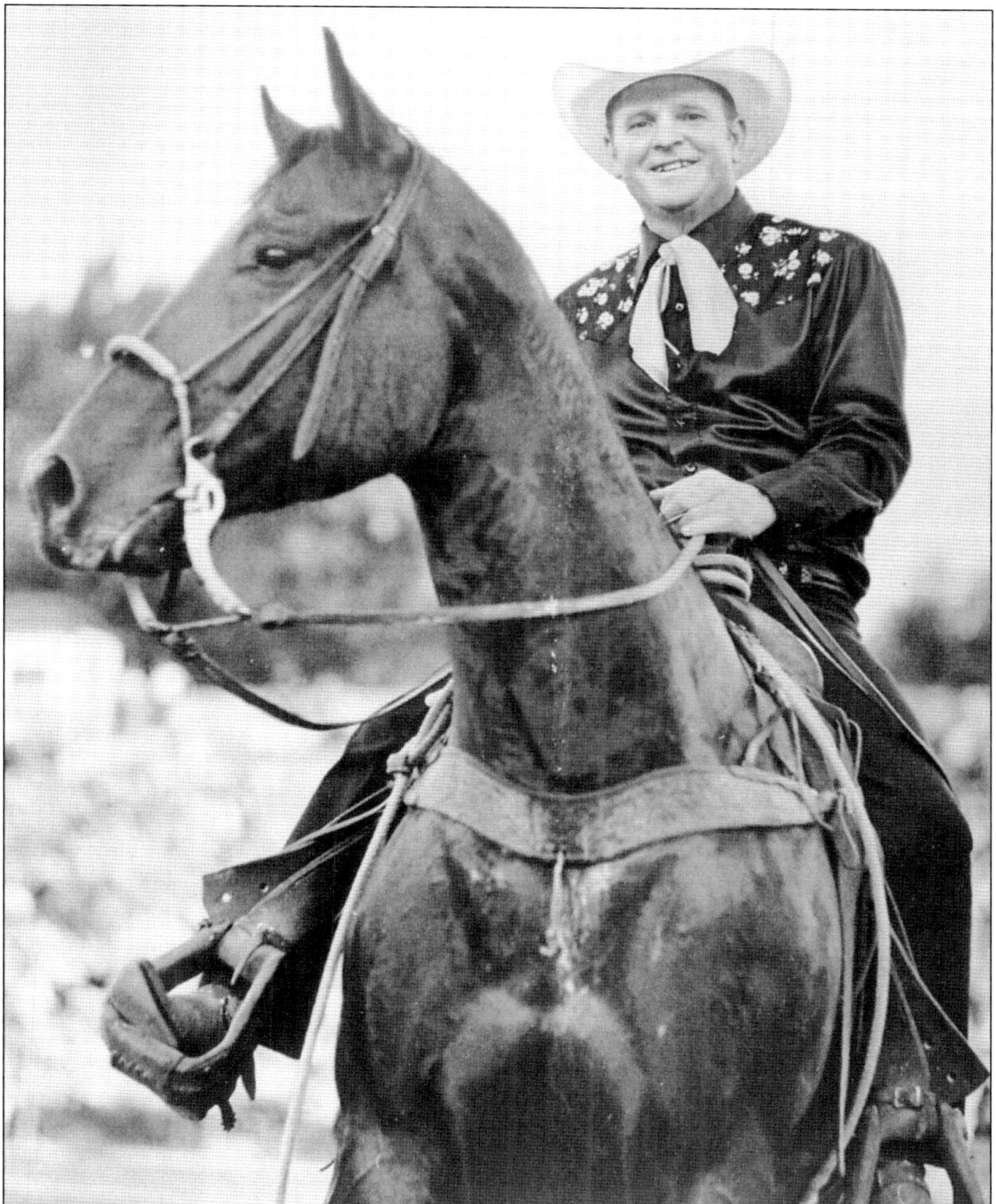

Cotton Rosser competed in his first Reno Rodeo in 1950, winning a $500 prize in saddle bronc riding. A ranching accident in 1955 ended his competitive career, and he turned instead to providing stock for rodeos, taking over the Flying U Rodeo Company. He and his family have been bringing stock to the Reno Rodeo for more than 50 years while also producing about 60 other rodeos throughout the West each year. Rosser has been inducted into the Pro Rodeo Hall of Fame and the National Cowboy Hall of Fame. (Photograph courtesy of the *Reno Gazette-Journal*.)

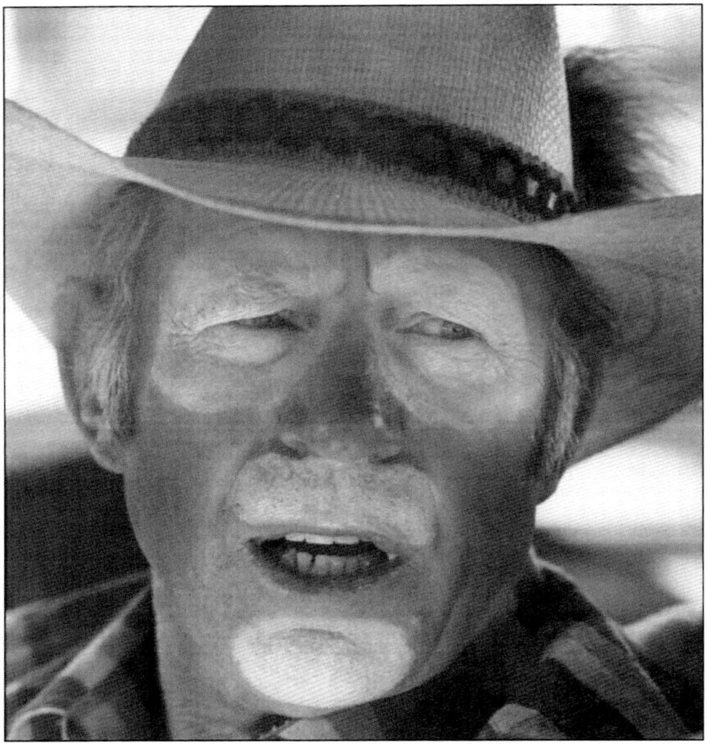

Wilbur Plaugher's rodeo career started as a competitor in the 1940s, but an offer to fill in as a rodeo clown and bullfighter in 1946 changed the course of his career and his life. He began appearing as the clown at the Reno Rodeo in the late 1940s and continued into the 1960s. He was considered one of the great rodeo clowns in the business, and his most popular act included trained ducks and dogs. Plaugher was inducted into the Pro Rodeo Hall of Fame in 1990. (Photograph by Marilyn Newton, courtesy of the *Reno Gazette-Journal*.)

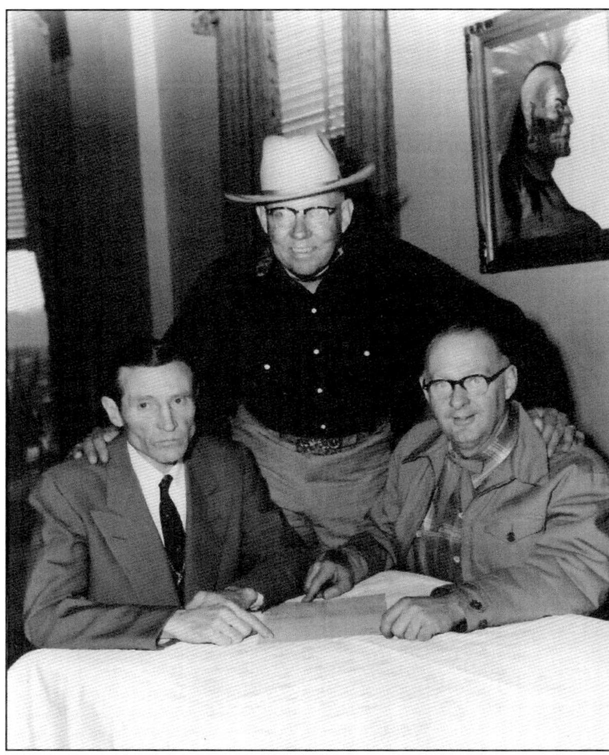

From left to right, the trio of Harry Frost, Ray Peterson, and George Southworth were part of the Reno Rodeo Association leadership for decades. The three Reno businessmen all served as president of the association. Peterson served as president from 1950 to 1962, before the association decided to install a new president each year. Frost succeeded him in 1963, and Southworth served as president in 1965. (Photograph courtesy of the *Reno Gazette-Journal*.)

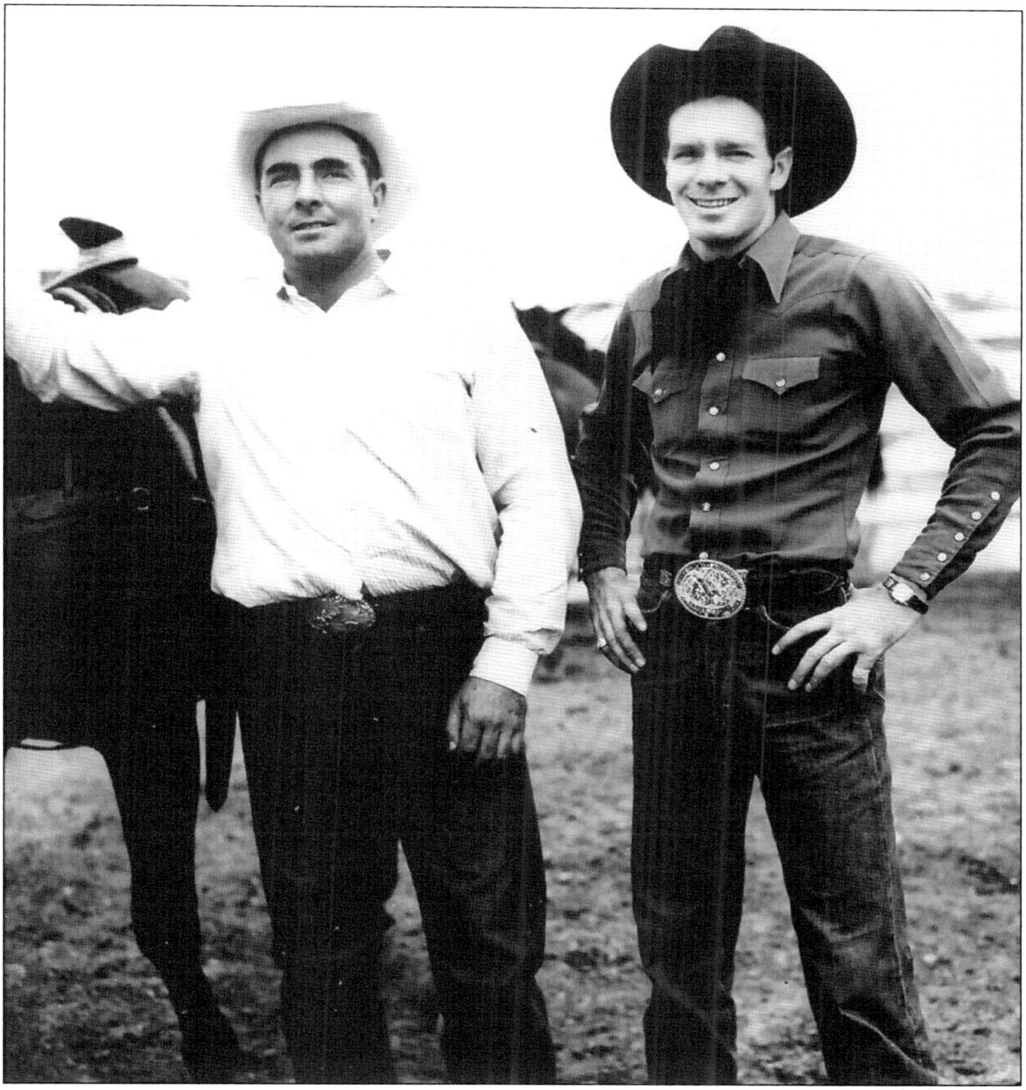

Two of the most successful cowboys in the history of the Reno Rodeo were also two of the greatest competitors in the sport. Harry Tompkins (left) and Casey Tibbs, both inaugural members of the Pro Rodeo Hall of Fame, dominated the Reno Rodeo in the 1950s. Tompkins won four Reno Rodeo titles, including an unprecedented three in the same year. In 1958, he won the all-around, bareback, and bull riding titles. Tibbs, meanwhile, won a record nine individual championships in Reno, including five saddle bronc titles, three all-around titles, and the bull riding title in 1953. (Photograph courtesy of the *Reno Gazette-Journal*.)

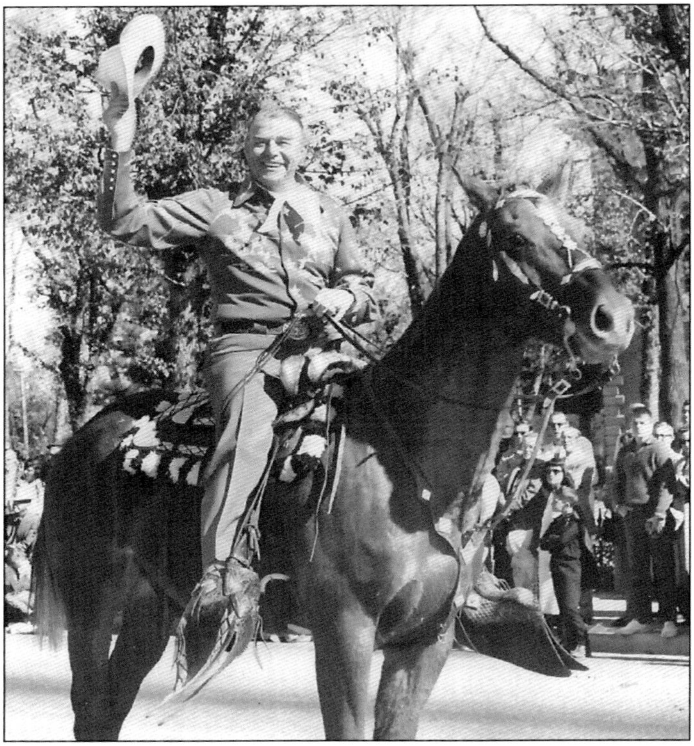

Rex Bell was a Hollywood Western film star in the 1920s, working alongside the likes of Tom Mix and Buck Jones in the silent-film era. In 1931, he married Clara Bow, Hollywood's "It Girl" and the most popular female star of the era. Bell had a lifelong love for the Reno Rodeo and especially its annual parade. He first rode in the parade in the 1930s, and after moving to Nevada and being elected lieutenant governor in 1954, he rode in the event annually, usually as the parade grand marshal. (Photograph courtesy of the *Reno Gazette-Journal.*)

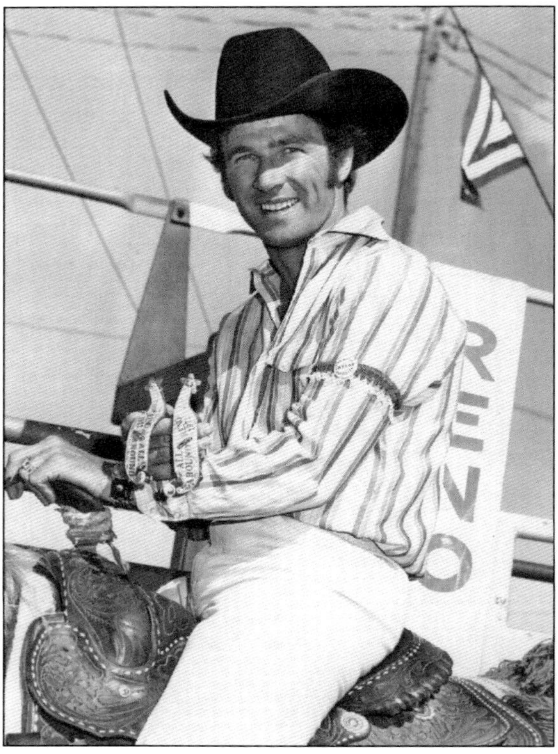

Larry Mahan first appeared at the Reno Rodeo in 1965 and won the bull riding title on his way to winning his first world championship in the event. Over the next 10 years, Mahan established himself as rodeo's biggest star, winning a then-record six world all-around championships and two world titles in bull riding. In 1971, he captured the all-around title at the Reno Rodeo, holding the set of trophy silver spurs given to each event champion. He also won the saddle bronc riding in 1973. (Photograph courtesy of the *Reno Gazette-Journal.*)

In 1976, Bob Tallman, a Winnemucca native and former college student at the University of Nevada, Reno, was hired to announce the Reno Rodeo. For more than 40 years, Tallman has returned annually to announce the event, one of dozens of events he announces throughout the year. Inducted into the Pro Rodeo Hall of Fame in 2004, Tallman is often called "The Voice of Rodeo." He has been named the Professional Rodeo Cowboys Association announcer of the year multiple times and has announced the Wrangler National Finals Rodeo a record 20 times. (Photograph courtesy of the *Reno Gazette-Journal.*)

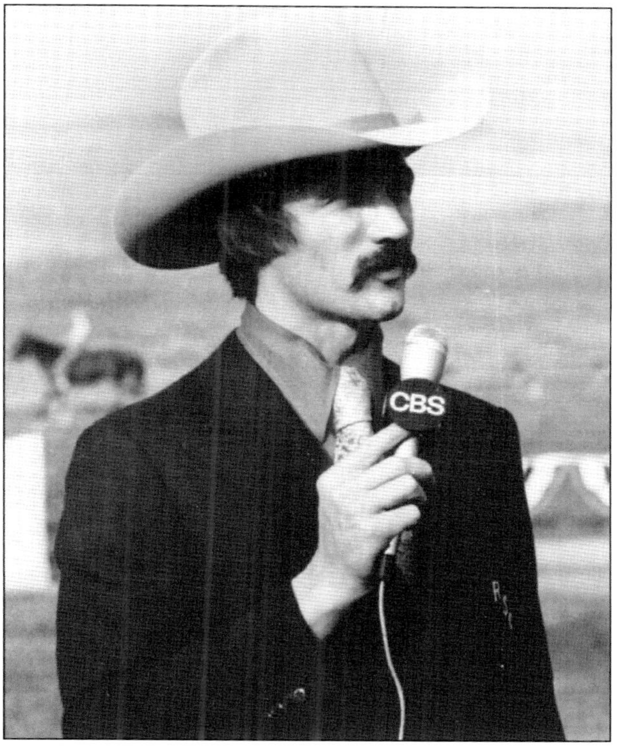

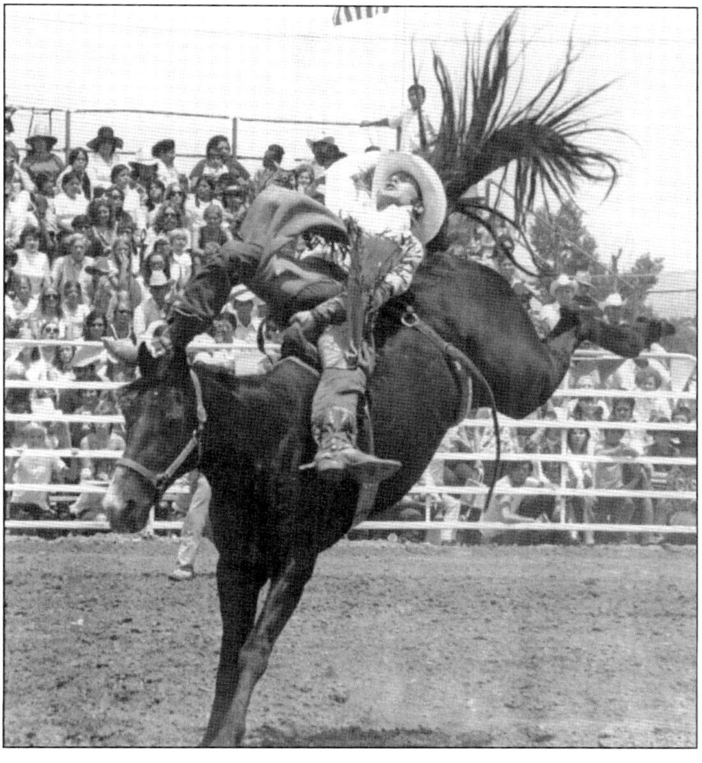

Chris LeDoux competes in the 1976 Reno Rodeo on his way to becoming the world champion bareback rider. While LeDoux never won the Reno Rodeo, he became a popular figure at the event in his second career as an entertainer. A country singer who wrote songs about cowboys and rodeos, LeDoux headlined concerts that preceded the Reno Rodeo, including in 1994, when he appeared at Mackay Stadium on the University of Nevada, Reno campus with Michael Martin Murphey, Toby Keith, Doug Supernaw, Asleep at the Wheel, and cowboy poet Waddie Mitchell. (Photograph courtesy of the *Reno Gazette-Journal.*)

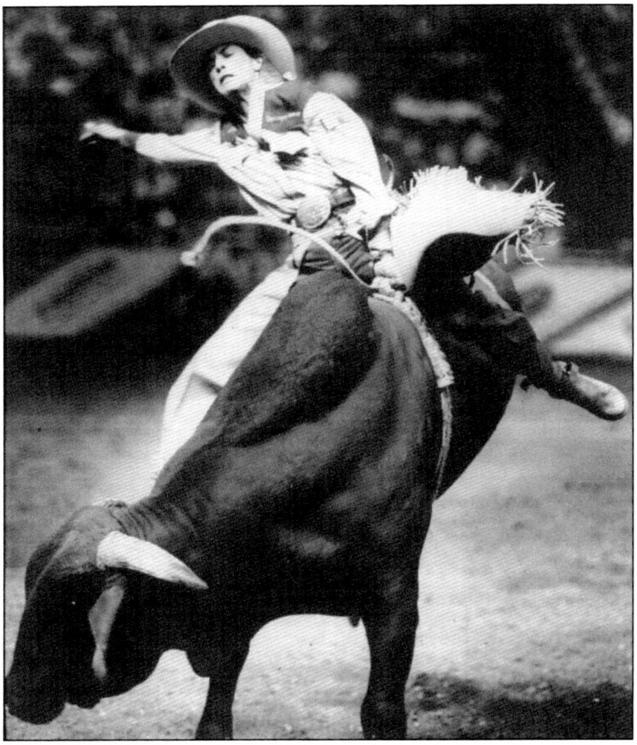

Always smiling, always friendly Lane Frost, shown here riding in the 1985 Reno Rodeo, was one of rodeo's most popular stars. After winning the world championship in 1987, he competed in a nationally televised series of events against the previously un-ridden bucking bull Red Rock, riding the bull four out of seven times. Frost was tragically killed in a bull riding accident at Cheyenne Frontier Days in 1989. His story was later told in the film *Eight Seconds*, starring Luke Perry. (Photograph courtesy of the *Reno Gazette-Journal*.)

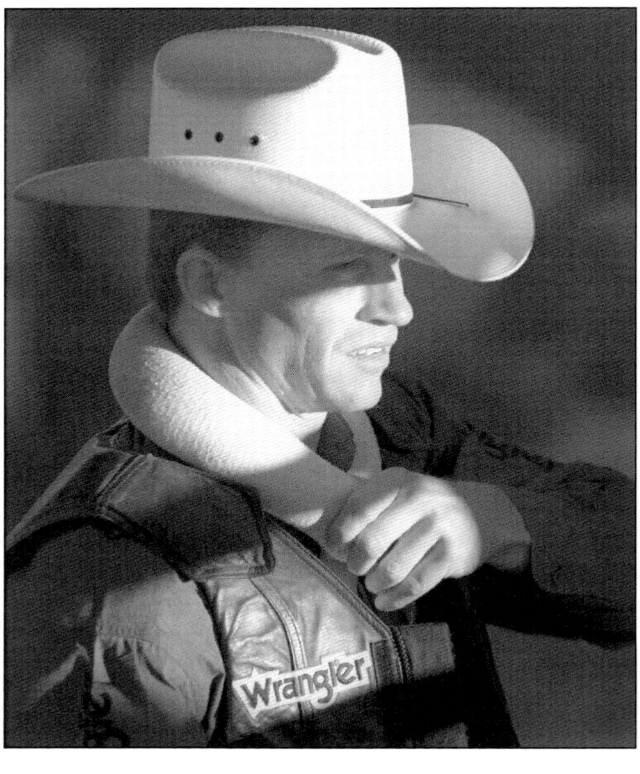

Ty Murray, widely considered the greatest rodeo cowboy of all time, dominated the sport in the 1990s, winning a record seven world all-around championships and two world titles in bull riding while setting records for single-season and career earnings. He also had great success at the Reno Rodeo, winning four titles, including three all-around championships and the saddle bronc championship in 1990. Murray was inducted into the Pro Rodeo Hall of Fame in 2000 and remains a great ambassador for rodeo and bull riding. (Photograph by Jean Dixon, courtesy of the *Reno Gazette-Journal*.)

Eight

The Champs

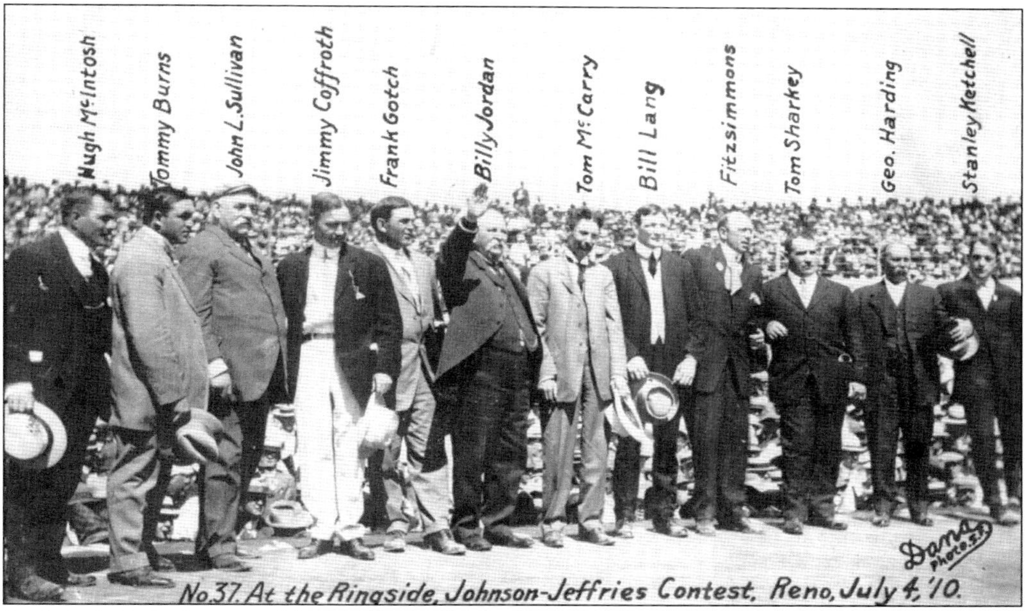

On July 4, 1910, the eyes of the world were focused on Reno—at the time a small, bustling railroad town of 17,000—for a boxing match pitting Jack Johnson, the black heavyweight champion, against the white former champion Jim Jeffries in what writers billed as "The Fight of the Century." More than 20,000 people descended on Reno, including the greatest turnout of boxing champions in the sport's history. The lineup in the specially constructed arena included past heavyweight champions Tommy Burns, John L. Sullivan, and Bob Fitzsimmons. (Photograph courtesy of Jack Bacon Collection.)

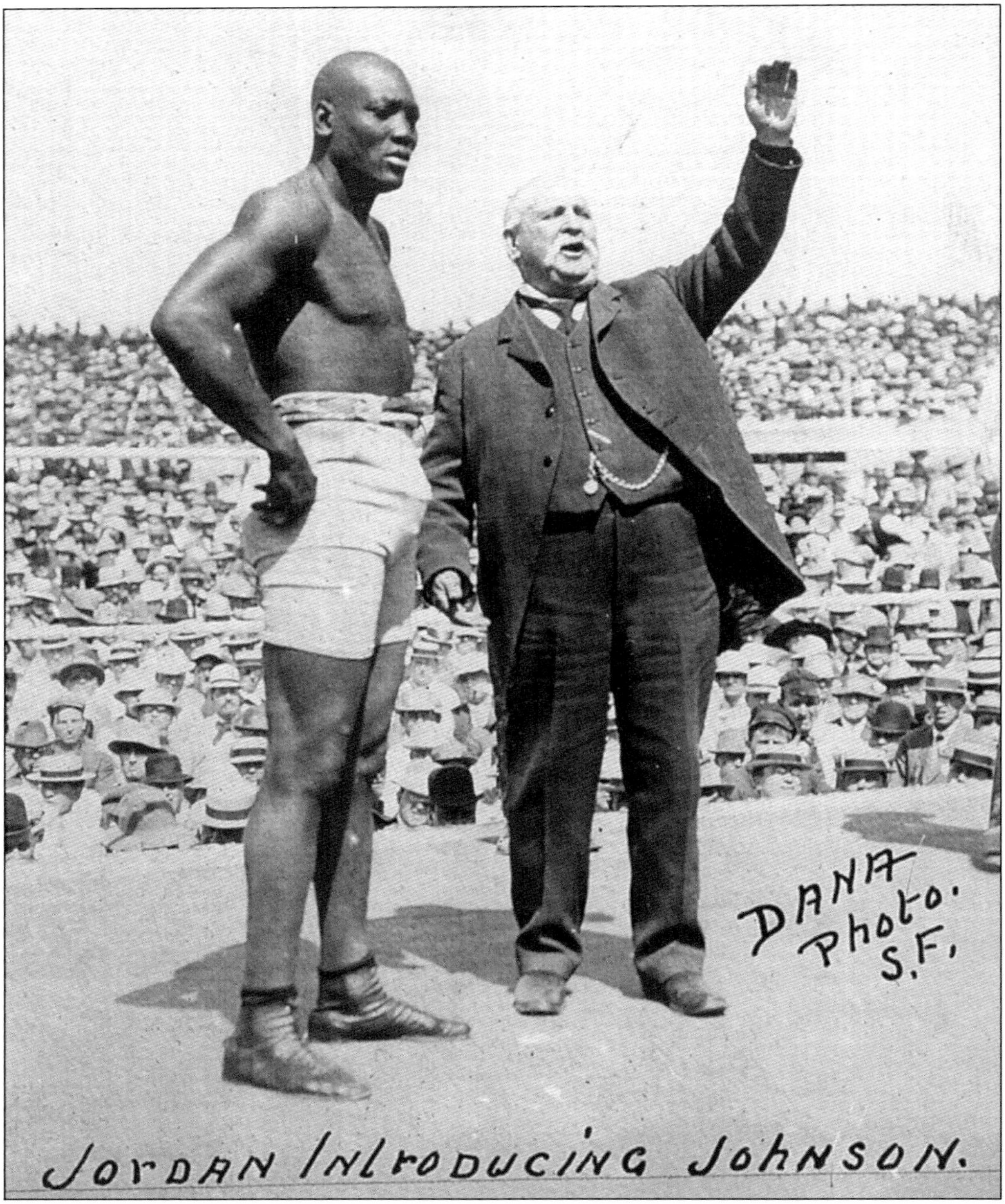

Jack Johnson, being introduced by announcer Billy Jordan before his July 4, 1910, fight against former champion Jim Jeffries in Reno, held the heavyweight championship from 1908 to 1915. The first African American to hold the title, Johnson was reviled by much of white America. He answered the hatred with a flamboyant lifestyle and by beating every "Great White Hope" that boxing promoters put in front of him, including Jeffries, the former champion. (Photograph courtesy of Jack Bacon Collection.)

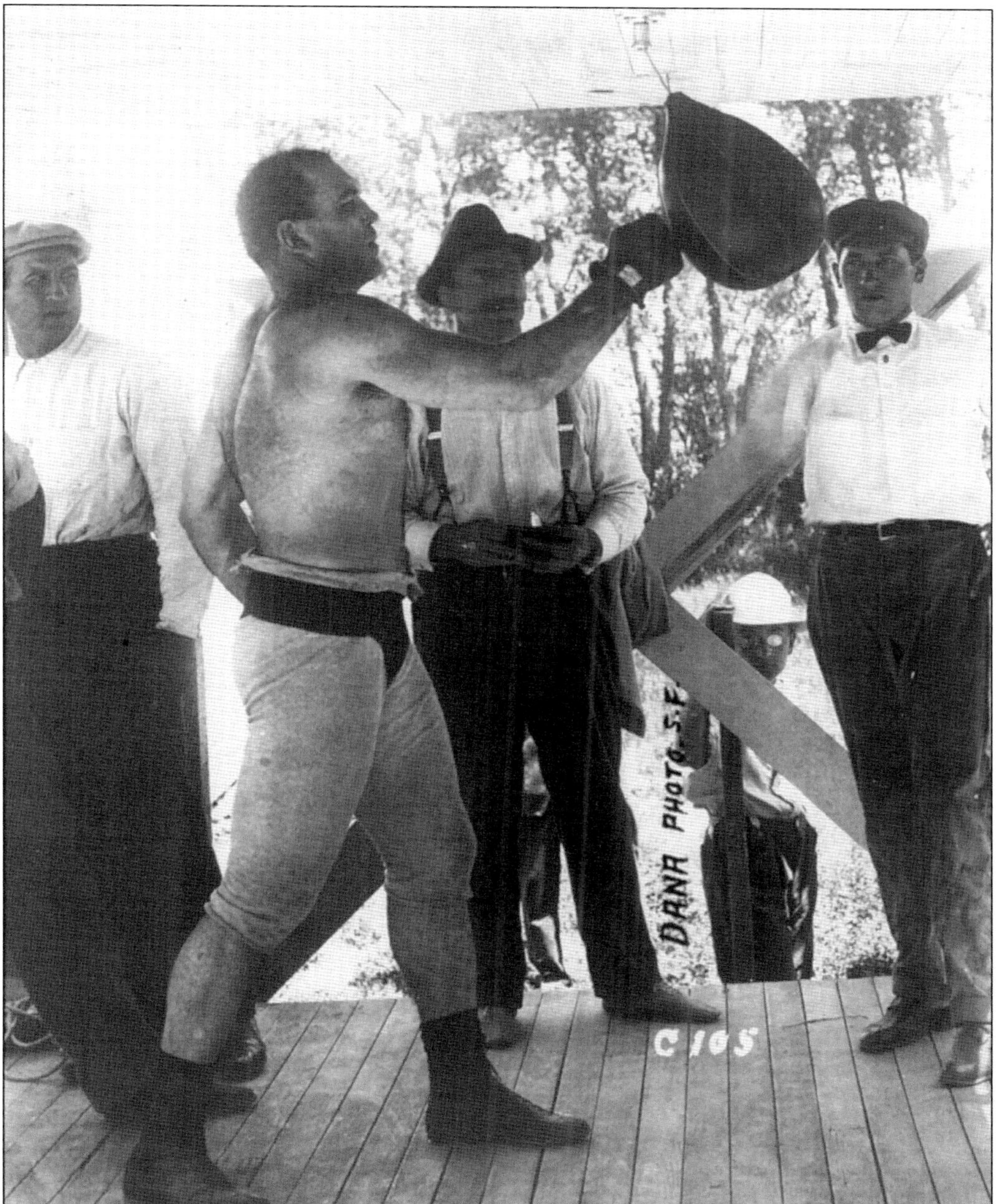

Jim Jeffries, the world's heavyweight champion from 1899 to 1904, was never beaten and never knocked down during his championship career. He retired undefeated in 1904, saying he had run out of challengers. He was reluctantly lured out of retirement in 1909 by those who wanted a white champion to retake the world heavyweight title from champion Jack Johnson. Jeffries, who had retired to his alfalfa farm in Southern California, had to lose more than 100 pounds to prepare for the fight. He trained in Reno at Moana Springs resort. (Photograph courtesy of Jack Bacon Collection.)

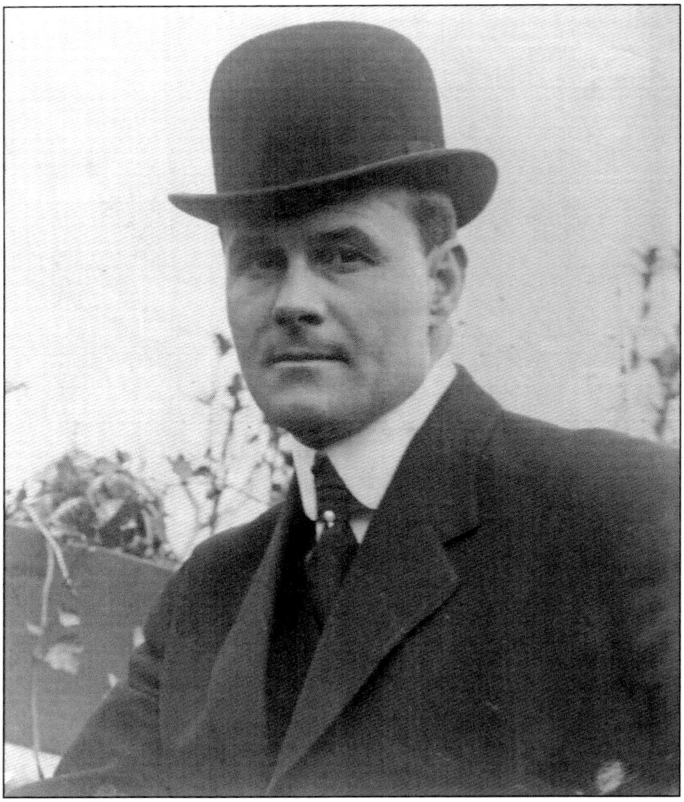

Tex Rickard was a saloon owner in Ely in eastern Nevada in 1909 when he shocked the boxing world by winning the rights to promote the Johnson-Jeffries fight. His previous boxing experience had been promoting the Joe Gans–Battling Nelson fight in Goldfield in 1906, but it was considered more of a publicity stunt for the central Nevada gold mining town. Rickard wanted to hold the Johnson-Jeffries fight in the population center of San Francisco, but when California governor James Gillett prohibited it, Rickard quickly moved it to Reno. (Photograph courtesy of Gary Schultz Collection.)

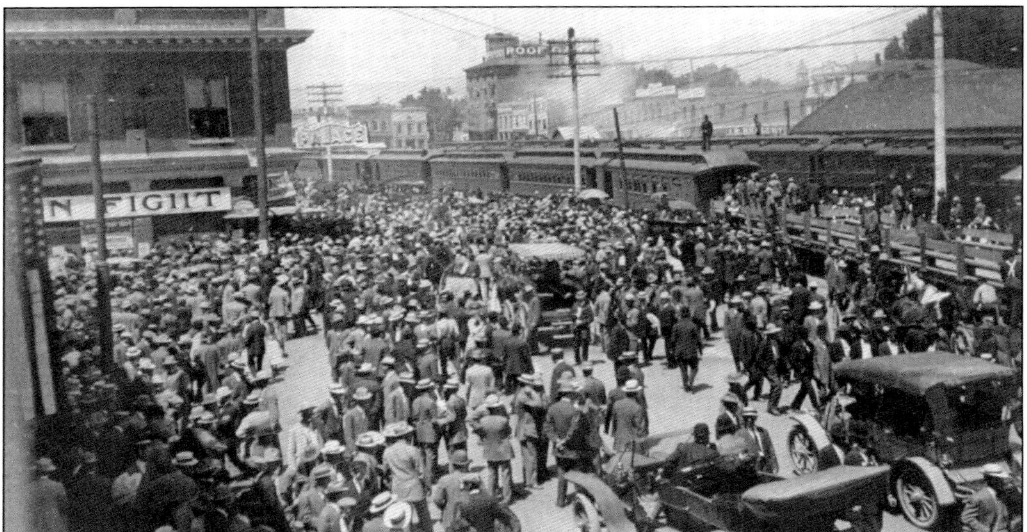

Reno's population more than doubled as fight fans from across the country packed the city for the Johnson-Jeffries fight. Hotels and restaurants overflowed, and special railcars were brought in to be used as sleeping quarters because there were no rooms left. In restaurants, according to newspaper reports, the demand was so great that "dishwashing was replaced by dish scraping." (Photograph courtesy of Jack Bacon Collection.)

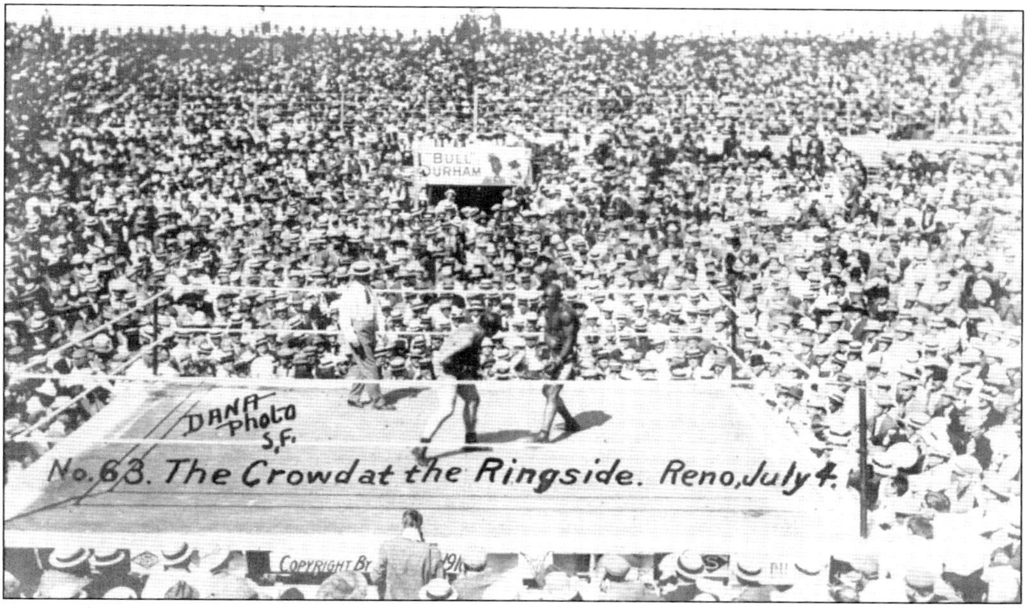

A crowd of more than 20,000 people, the vast majority of them cheering for former champion Jim Jeffries, packed the arena off East Fourth Street for what was billed as "The Fight of the Century" between Jeffries and reigning heavyweight champion Jack Johnson. Promoter Tex Rickard also served as the referee in the bout. (Photograph courtesy of Nevada Historical Society.)

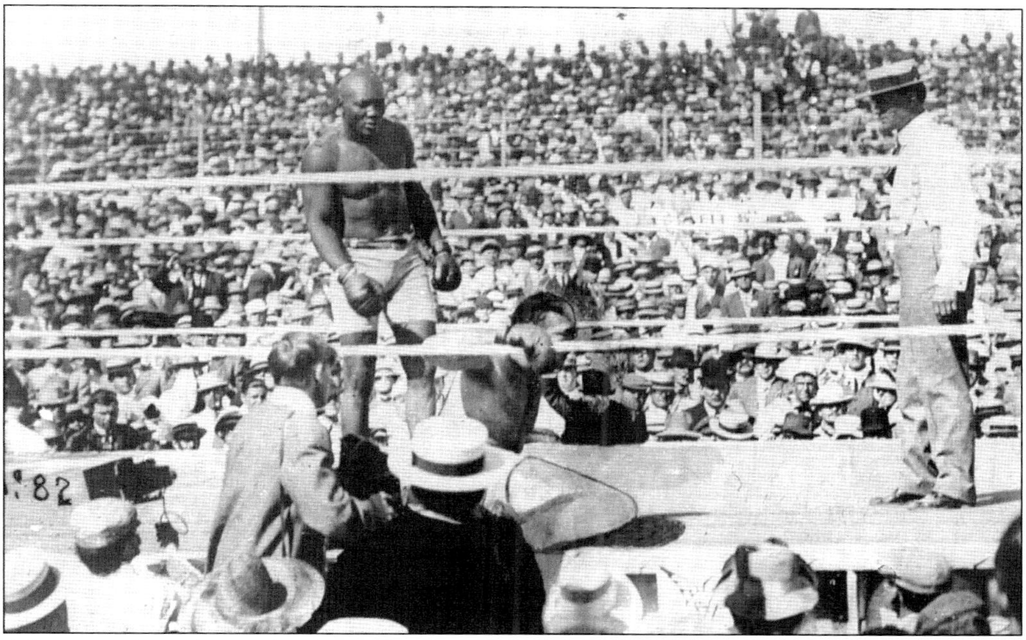

After punishing former heavyweight champion Jim Jeffries for 15 rounds, Jack Johnson put Jeffries on the mat for the first time in his career with a relentless flurry of punches. Jeffries rose but was sent quickly to the mat again and then a third and final time before referee Tex Rickard stopped the bout and awarded the victory to Johnson, sending Jeffries into permanent retirement. (Photograph courtesy of Jack Bacon Collection.)

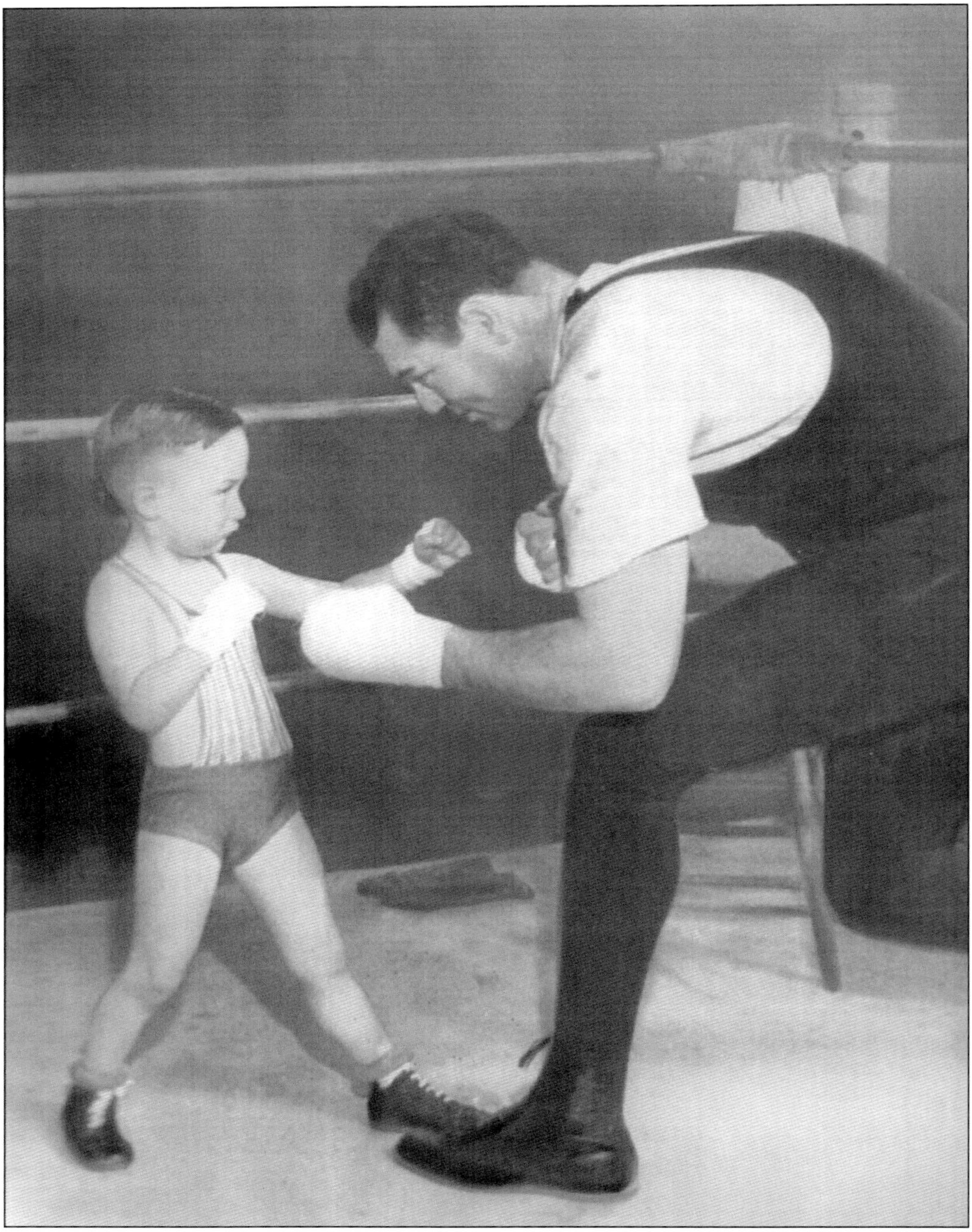

Jack Dempsey, the heavyweight champion from 1919 to 1926, arrived in Reno in April 1931 to take advantage of Nevada's new divorce law, which required only six weeks of residency to obtain a divorce. He rented a house in the mansion district of California Avenue for $1,000 per month and was immediately a popular figure around town. Dempsey was especially beloved by children, who would follow the champion everywhere he went. In this photograph, Dempsey clowns with four-year-old Buddy Garfinkle of Reno, whose father, Imey, operated the Chestnut Street Arena, where Dempsey trained for a comeback. (Photograph courtesy of Buddy Garfinkle Collection.)

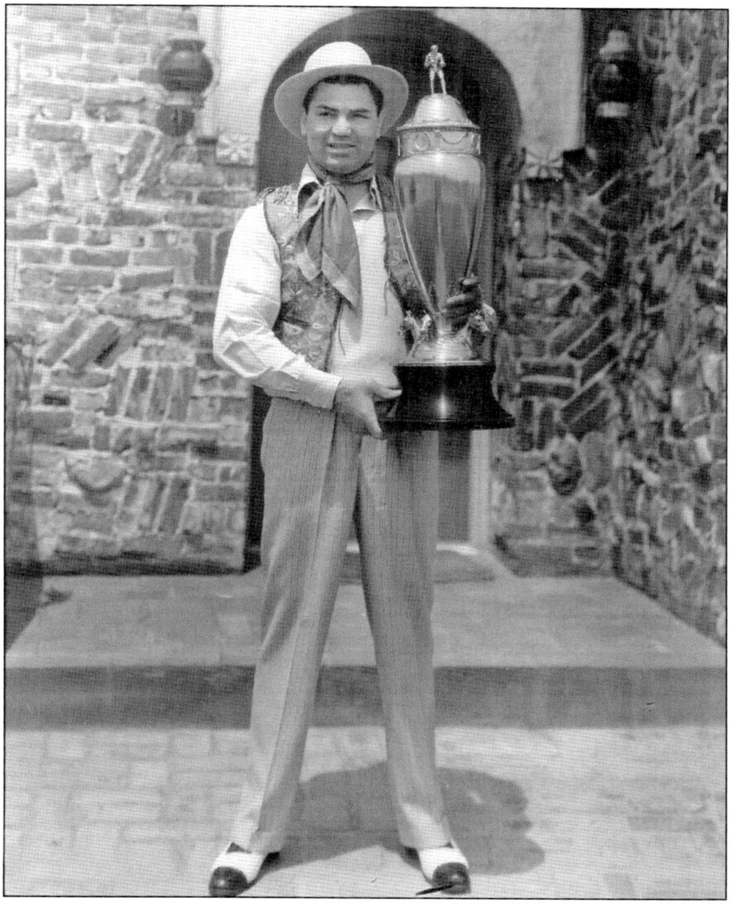

Jack Dempsey found Reno much to his liking in 1931—so much so that he purchased a home on San Joaquin Miller Avenue. After barnstorming the country in exhibition boxing matches in the summer of 1931, a tired Dempsey returned to Reno and told reporters, "It's good to be home." In 1932, Dempsey sponsored the saddle bronc riding at the annual Reno Rodeo and awarded the trophy, called the "Jack Dempsey Trophy," to the winner, Pete Knight of Canada. (Photograph courtesy of Bill Griswold Collection.)

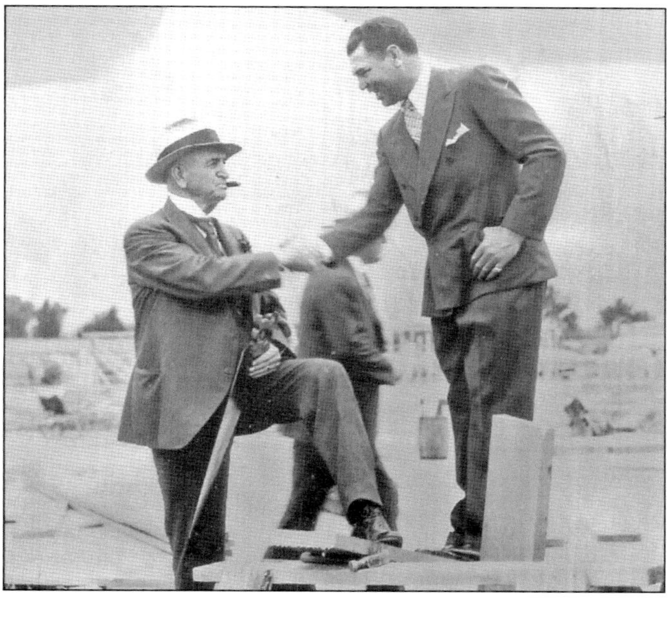

After moving to Reno in April 1931, Jack Dempsey (right) and Reno businessmen and city leaders, including Mayor E.E. Roberts (left), began planning a heavyweight boxing match for the Fourth of July in 1931. Plans were made for a 15,000-seat arena, and ground was broken in May 1931 with a handshake between Dempsey and Roberts. The match was made between heavyweights Max Baer and Paolino Uzcudun, with Dempsey acting as the promoter and referee. (Photograph courtesy of Colleen Rosencrantz Collection.)

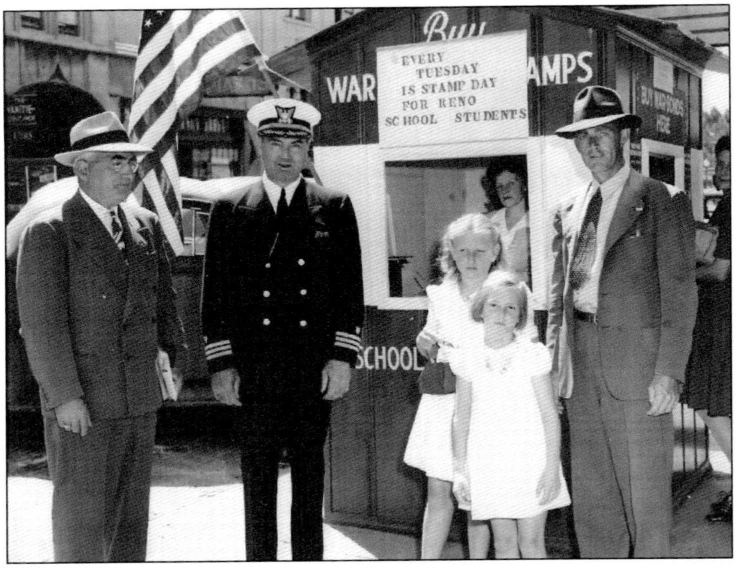

As an officer with the US Coast Guard during World War II, Jack Dempsey returned to his former hometown of Reno on July 3, 1944, to sell War Bonds. In just a few hours, set up on Virginia Street in downtown Reno, Dempsey raised $456,000. To the left of Dempsey is Glen Myers, and to the right is bond drive chairman Ernest Brooks. (Author's collection.)

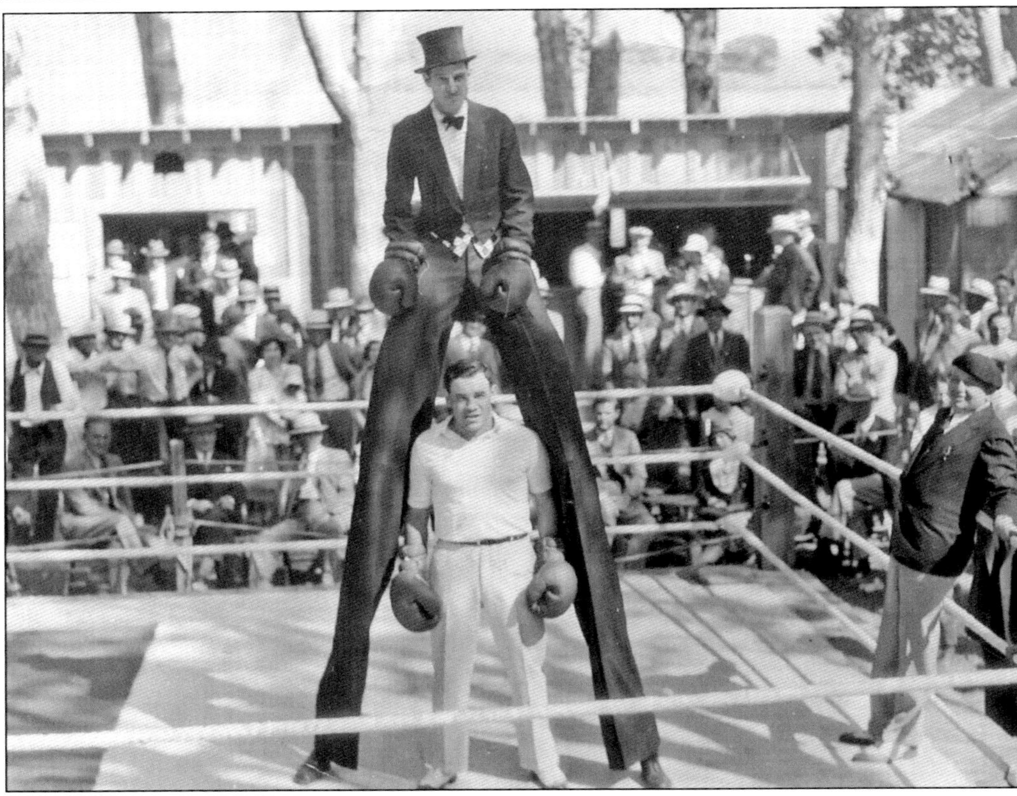

Paulino Uzcudun, a European heavyweight champion from the Basque country in Spain, was a popular figure in Reno in 1931 when he was matched against Max Baer in a heavyweight bout promoted by Jack Dempsey. Thousands of Basques arrived in Reno to cheer for Uzcudun, nicknamed "The Basque Woodchopper," who defeated Baer in a 20-round bout on a blistering Fourth of July 1931. (Author's collection.)

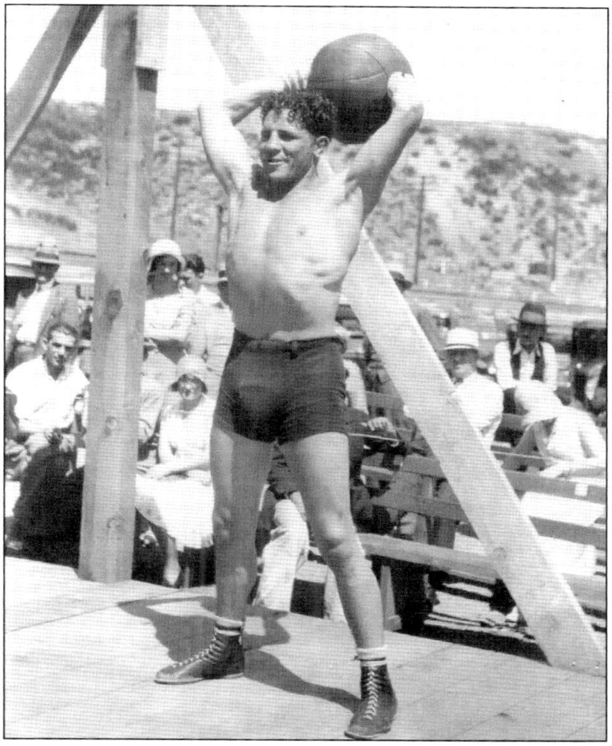

Max Baer, who won the world heavyweight championship in 1934 and held it for a year, was a frequent and popular visitor in Reno. He first appeared in 1931, dropping a unanimous decision to Paolino Uzcudun in a fight promoted by Jack Dempsey. Baer married actress Dorothy Dunbar in Reno a few days after the fight. He divorced her a year later in Reno as he arrived to battle King Levinsky in another Dempsey-promoted bout. Below, Baer deals a hand of blackjack to Swede Oleson (left) and Nick Abelman at Abelman's Riverside Hotel in the 1940s. (Right, photograph courtesy of Colleen Rosencrantz Collection; below, photograph courtesy of Bill Pettite Collection.)

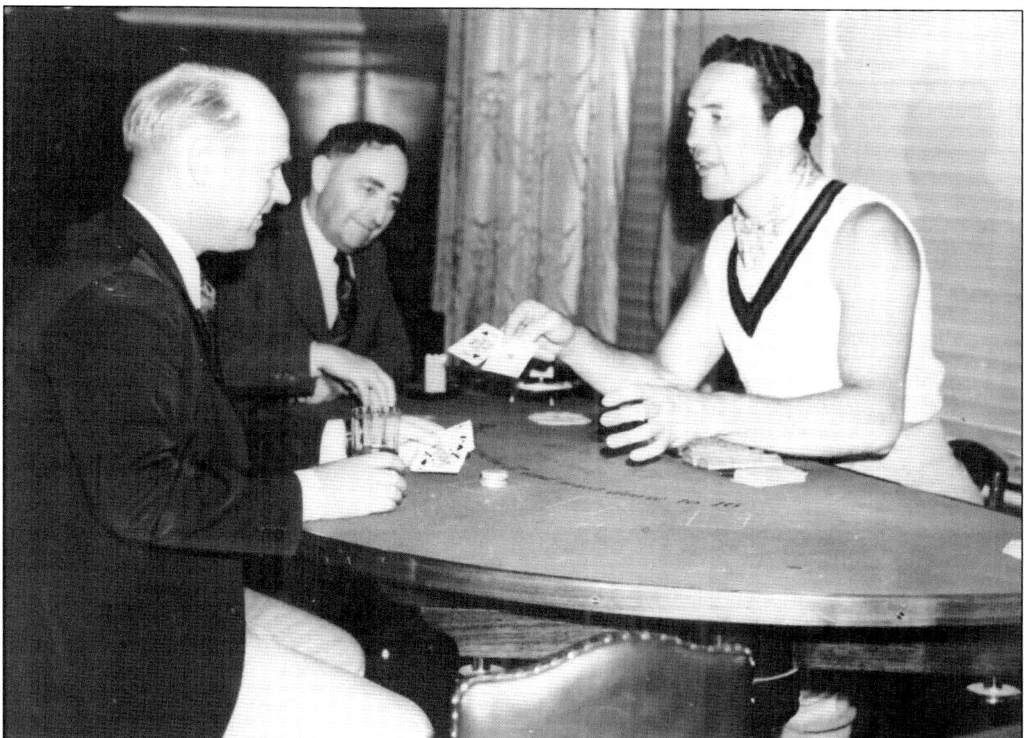

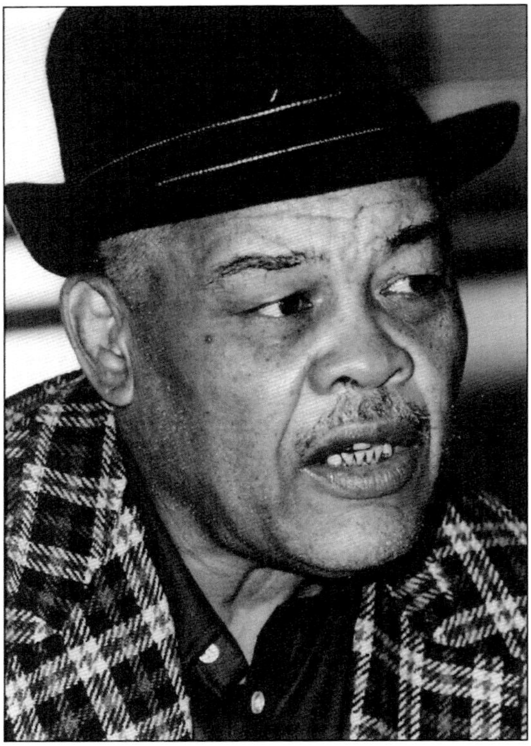

Joe Louis, "The Brown Bomber," the heavyweight champion from 1937 to 1949, wanted to talk about anything but his own career when he arrived at the Reno airport while on his way to Carson City for an event honoring Rocky Marciano. Louis was quick to offer his opinion on then–heavyweight champion Muhammad Ali compared to champions of the past, saying Jack Dempsey would have dominated Ali. (Photograph courtesy of the *Reno Gazette-Journal.*)

Rocky Marciano, heavyweight champion from 1952 to 1956 and the only heavyweight champion to leave the sport with an undefeated record, at 49-0, was preparing for a broadcasting career when he visited Reno in 1962. Marciano was the master of ceremonies for the Holiday Hotel's annual Mug Hunt Golf Tournament and participated in the event as well. (Photograph courtesy of the *Reno Gazette-Journal.*)

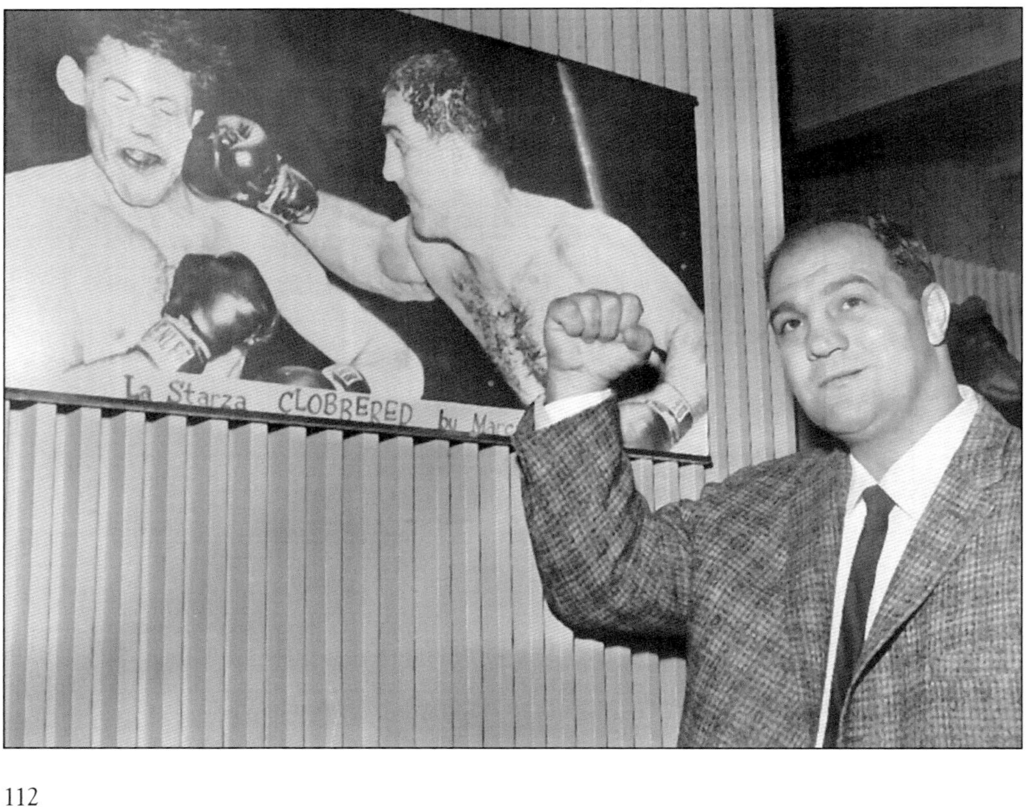

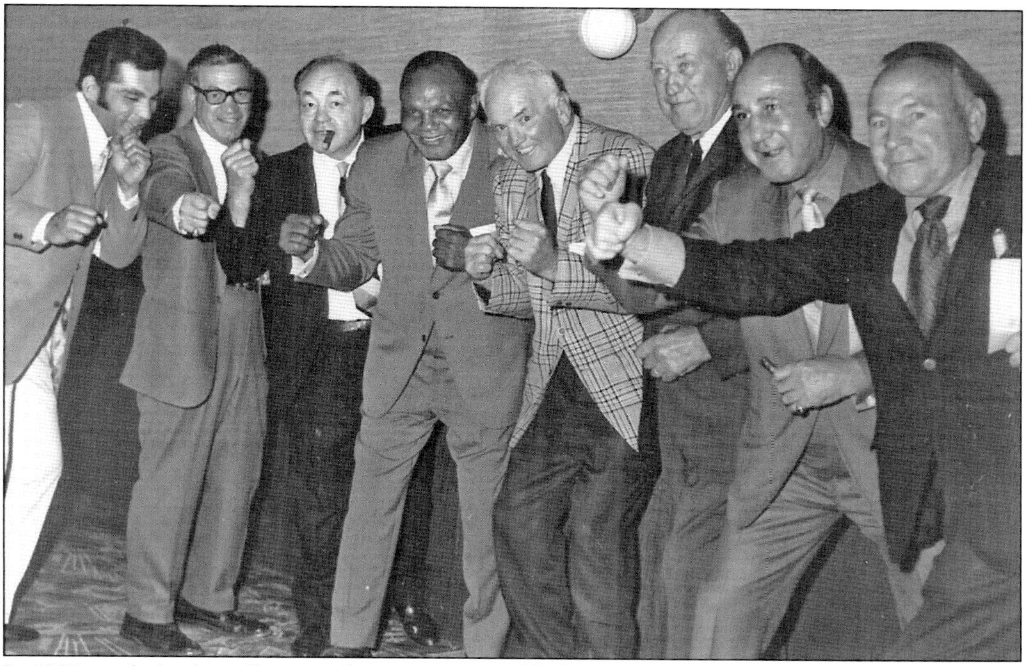

In 1970, a who's who of boxing champions assembled at the Mapes Hotel for the Golden Days of Boxing Banquet in honor of longtime boxing manager Ancil Hoffman. The champs included, from left to right, Willie Pastrano, Fred Aposteli, Tony Galento, Jersey Joe Walcott, James J. Braddock, Jack Sharkey, Jackie Fields, and Jimmy McLarnin. All except Galento were world champions. (Photograph courtesy of William Pettite.)

Heavyweight champion Jersey Joe Walcott (second from left) attended the Golden Days of Boxing Banquet at the Mapes Hotel in Reno. Judge William Pettite (far left) was the organizer of the event and the master of ceremonies at the banquet. Joe Conforte (second from right), owner of the Mustang Ranch brothel, was one of the event's sponsors. (Photograph courtesy of William Pettite.)

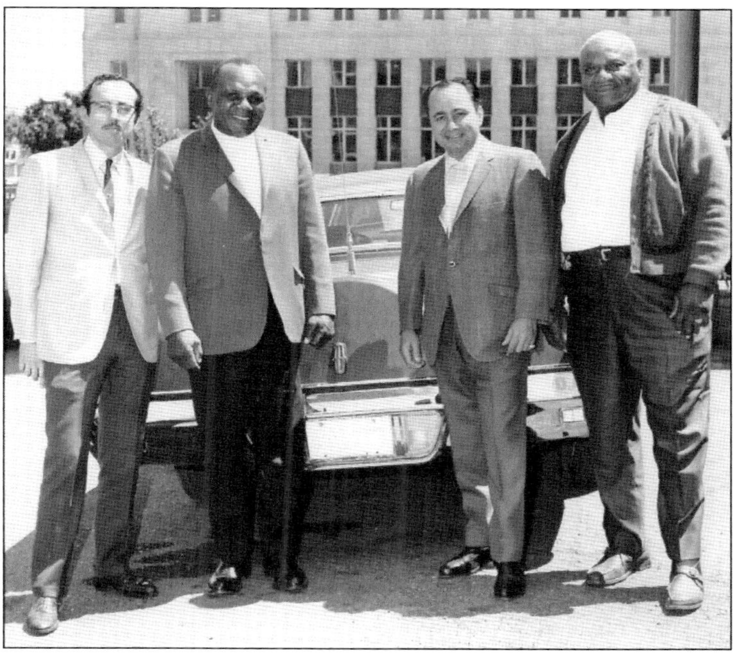

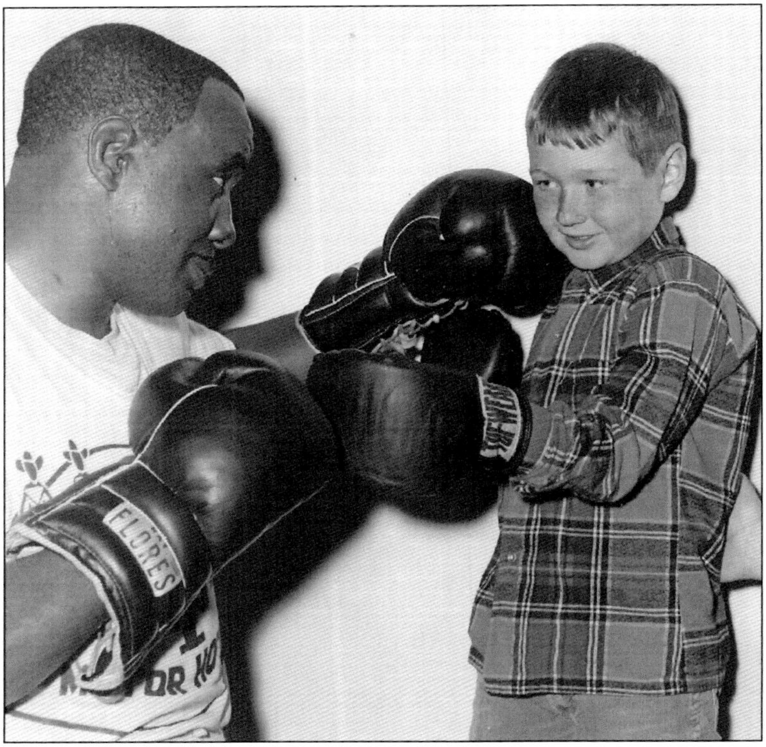

Known for his toughness, punching power, and menacing demeanor inside the ring, Sonny Liston, the heavyweight champion from 1962 to 1963, was all smiles outside the ring when he appeared in Reno in 1968 to take on Bill McMurray at the Centennial Coliseum. Liston trained daily at the Mapes Hotel in preparation for the fight and took some time to offer a few tips to Reno youngster Charles Kraemer. (Photograph courtesy of the *Reno Gazette-Journal*.)

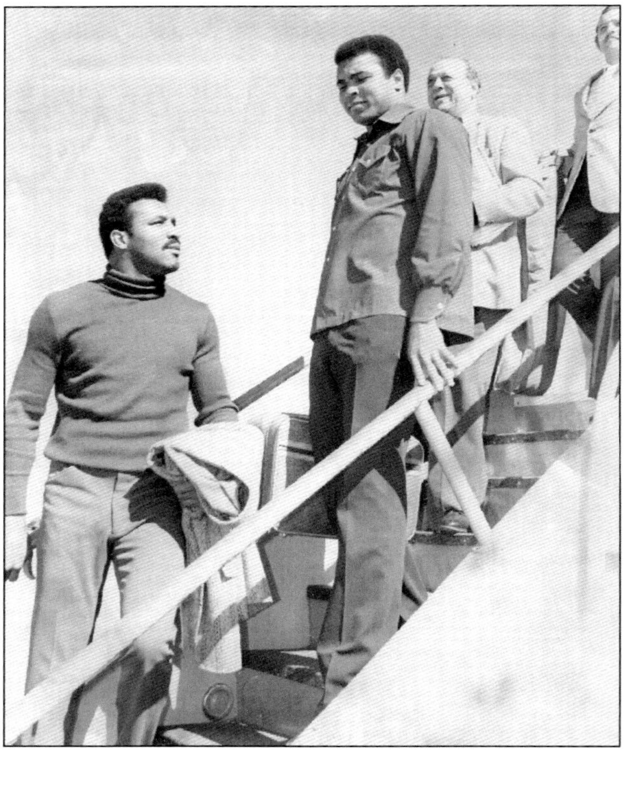

Muhammad Ali touched down at the Reno airport on November 14, 1972, in preparation for his bout against Bob Foster at Stateline a week later. Ali had lost the heavyweight championship to Joe Frazier a year earlier and was on the comeback trail. He had not lost his abilities to ridicule an opponent, however. At the Reno airport, Ali told reporters, "Bob Foster is too ugly to be the champ. He's not pretty." Ali won the fight with a seventh-round knockout. (Photograph courtesy of the *Reno Gazette-Journal*.)

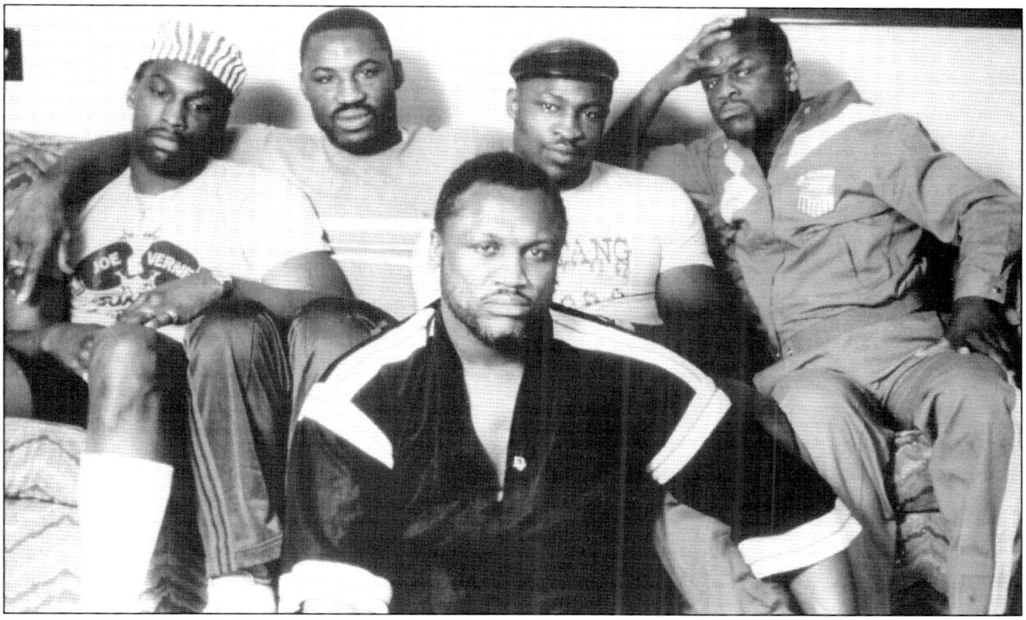

Joe Frazier, heavyweight champion from 1971 to 1973, had retired and become a trainer in 1985. His son, Marvis (second from left), became his protégé and took on fellow heavyweight James "Quick" Tillis on the undercard of the Larry Holmes–James "Bonecrusher" Smith fight at Lawlor Events Center. Marvis Frazier won a 10-round decision. (Photograph courtesy of the *Reno Gazette-Journal.*)

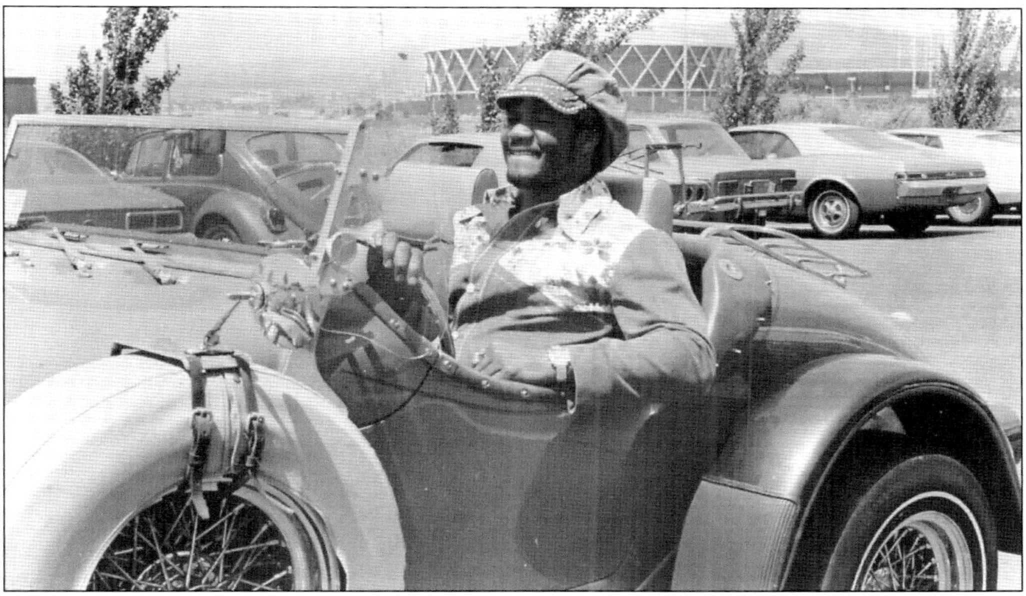

George Foreman traveled the country in his Rolls Royce after winning the heavyweight championship from Joe Frazier in January 1973 and pulled into Reno for an exhibition bout against three fighters at the Centennial Coliseum. The exhibition was a throwback to boxing champions of the 1920s and 1930s, who often fought exhibition bouts between their title tilts. (Photograph courtesy of the *Reno Gazette-Journal.*)

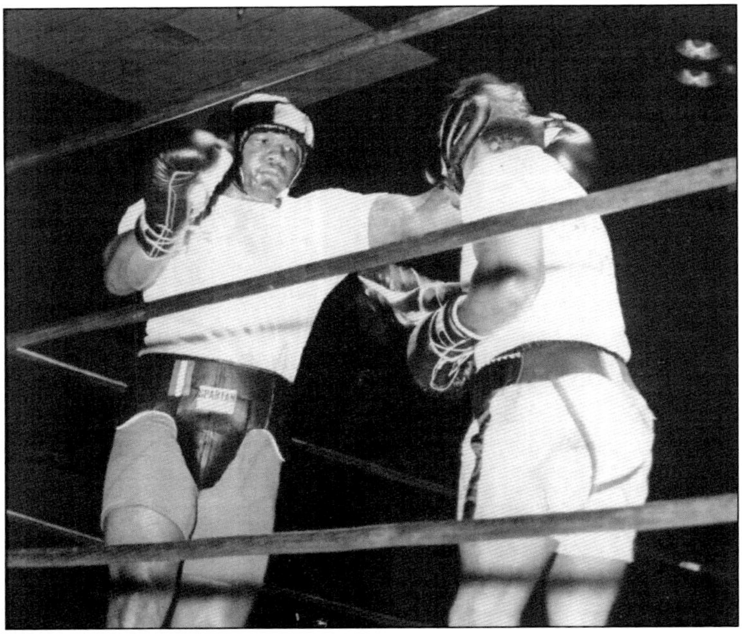

In 1973, George Foreman made his first in-ring appearance since winning the title in Reno. Foreman boxed two rounds each with Lonnie Bennett, Eddie "Bossman" Jones, and Terry Hinke at the Centennial Coliseum. He mostly clowned around throughout the exhibition and received a mixture of cheers and boos at the conclusion. (Photograph courtesy of the *Reno Gazette-Journal.*)

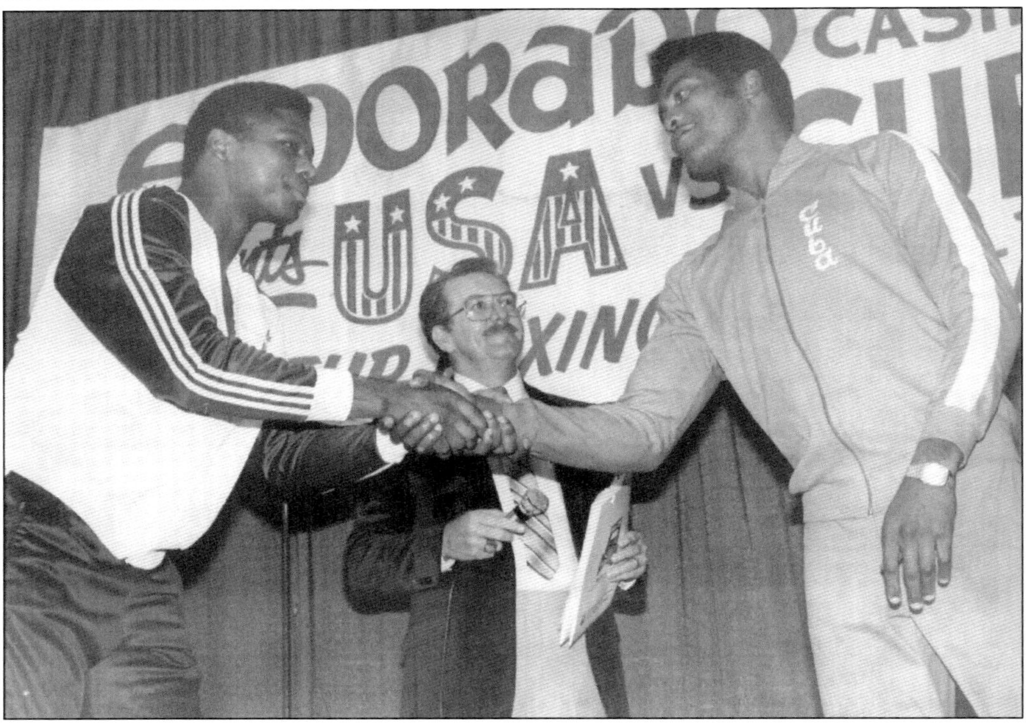

Reno was a destination venue not only for professional boxing but for the world's top amateurs as well. In 1984, a USA versus Cuba match pitted Olympic legend Teofilo Stevenson of Cuba against Olympic gold medalist Tyrel Biggs in the super heavyweight division. Stevenson, a three-time Olympic gold medalist, won a unanimous decision that was roundly booed by the Reno crowd. (Photograph courtesy of the *Reno Gazette-Journal.*)

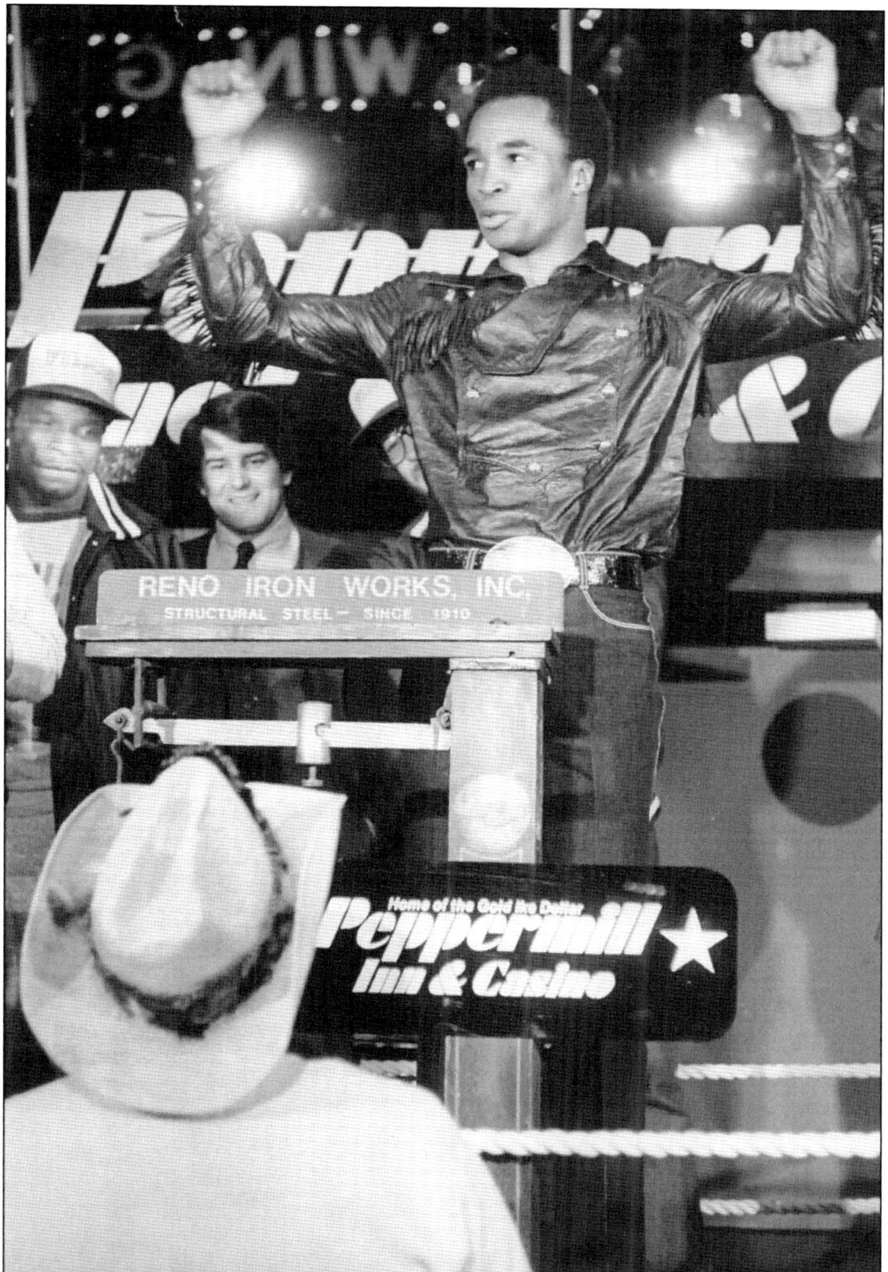

Sugar Ray Leonard was at the height of his popularity when he arrived in Reno for a February 15, 1982, world welterweight title fight against contender Bruce Finch at Reno's Centennial Coliseum. He weighed in for the bout on a Reno Iron Works scale at the Peppermill Hotel Casino. Leonard easily defeated Finch with a third-round knockout, but he also suffered a detached retina. He announced his retirement soon after, but like so many boxers before and after him, he came out of retirement and fought seven more times before retiring for good. (Photograph courtesy of the *Reno Gazette-Journal*.)

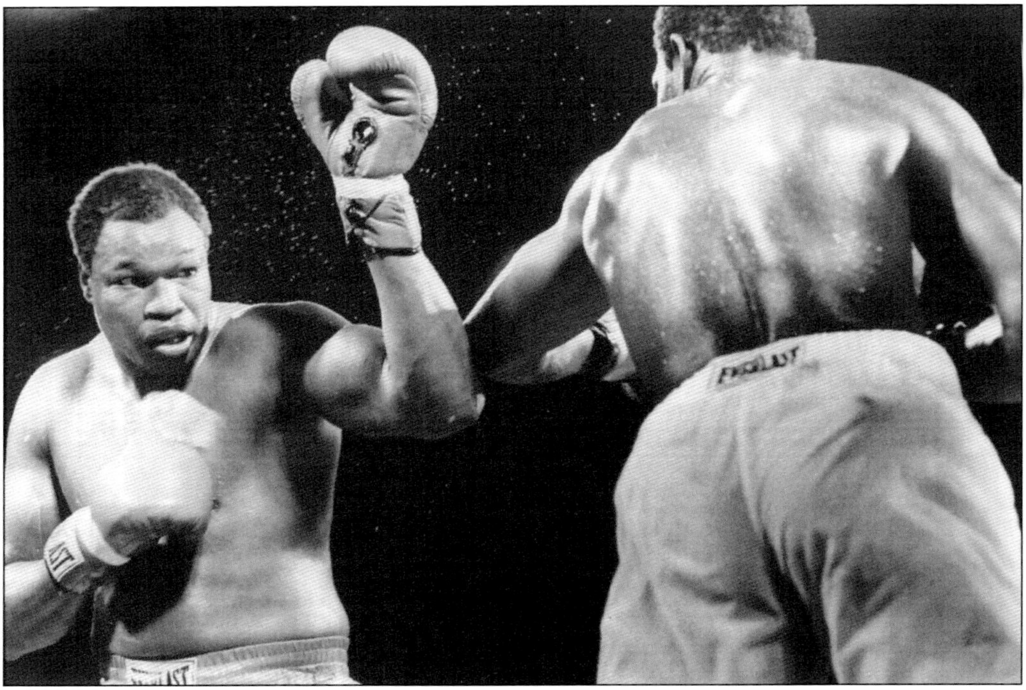

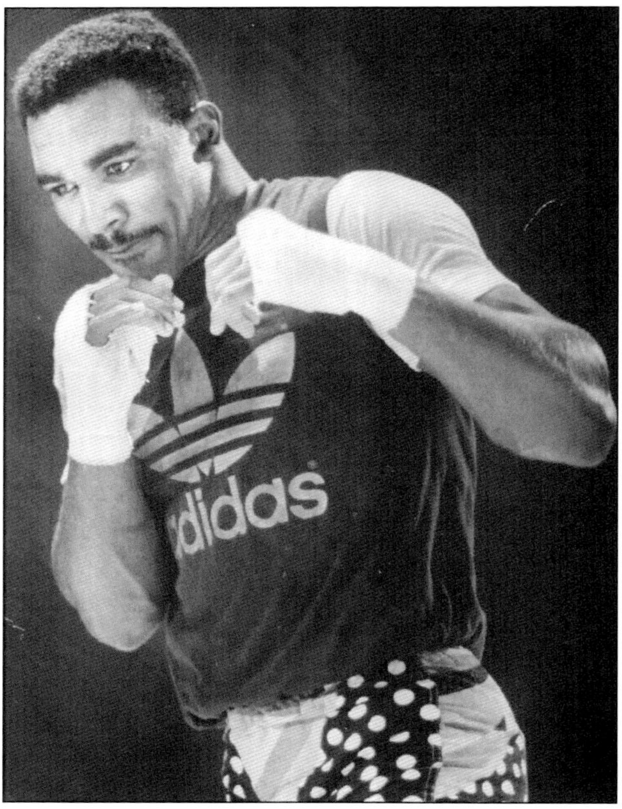

Larry Holmes, the heavyweight champion from 1978 to 1983, had history on the line when he faced Carl "The Truth" Williams at Reno's Lawlor Events Center on May 20, 1985. A lackluster Holmes won a controversial unanimous decision to improve his record to 48-0, one win short of Rocky Marciano's all-time record. Holmes would not tie the record, however, losing in his next bout to Michael Spinks. (Photograph courtesy of the *Reno Gazette-Journal*.)

Evander Holyfield, the only five-time world heavyweight champion, held the world cruiserweight title when he fought Henry Tillman at Bally's Hotel and Casino on February 14, 1987. Holyfield won by a technical knockout in the seventh round of the scheduled 15-round bout. Three years later, he became the undisputed heavyweight champion with a third-round knockout of Buster Douglas. (Photograph courtesy of the *Reno Gazette-Journal*.)

Nine

Disasters and Oddities

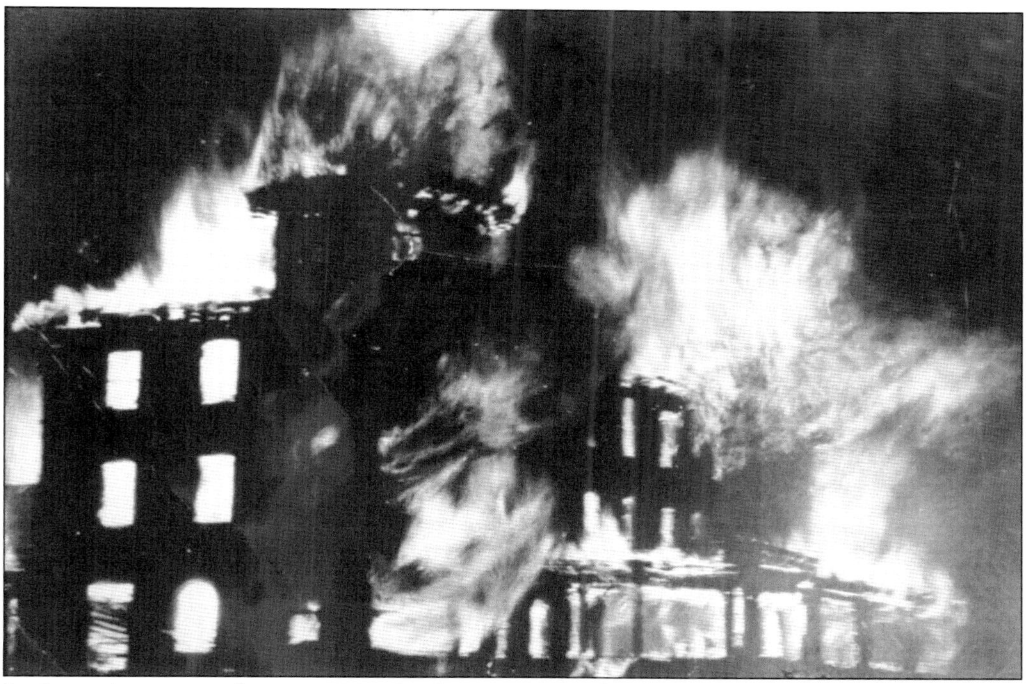

In the early morning hours on March 15, 1922, Reno's landmark Riverside Hotel went up in a raging inferno, destroying the three-story, 110-room hotel. Miraculously, Reno police chief John Kirkley reported the next day, all the hotel's guests and employees were able to escape the fire. The hotel's owner, Harry Gosse, estimated the loss at $250,000, only $100,000 of which was covered by insurance. The property stood vacant until 1926, when George Wingfield bought the property and built a new Riverside Hotel, which opened in 1927. (Photograph courtesy of the *Reno Gazette-Journal*.)

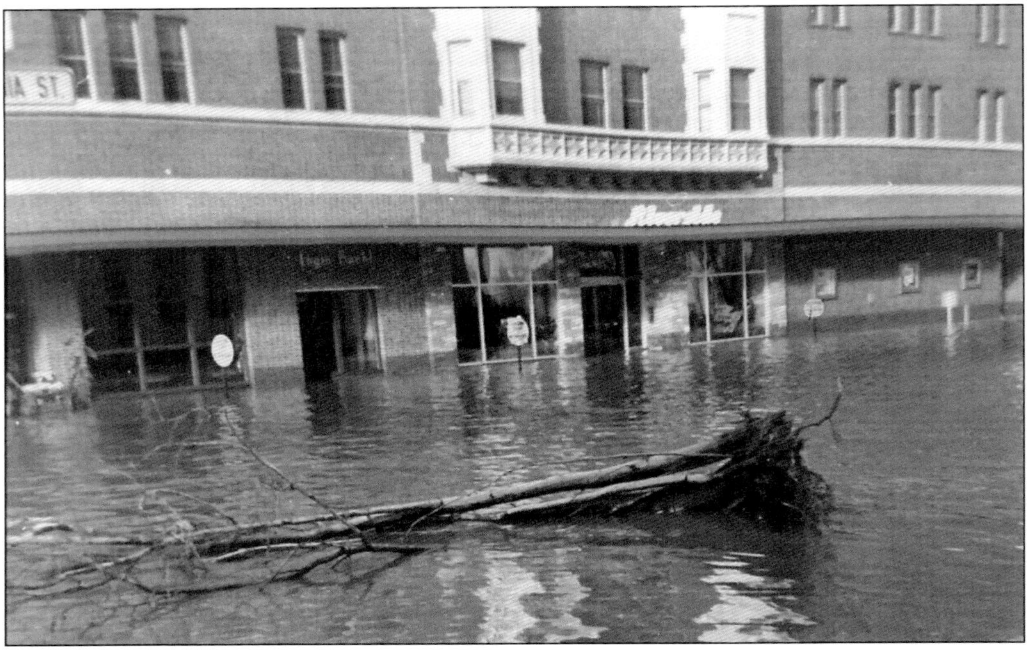

With the Truckee River running through the middle of town, Reno has always been susceptible to flooding. One of the worst came in 1950, when floodwaters jumped the banks of the river and encased downtown Reno. Above, floodwaters recede on the corner of Mill and Virginia Streets, but they are still halfway up the door frames of the Riverside Hotel. (Photograph courtesy of the *Reno Gazette-Journal.*)

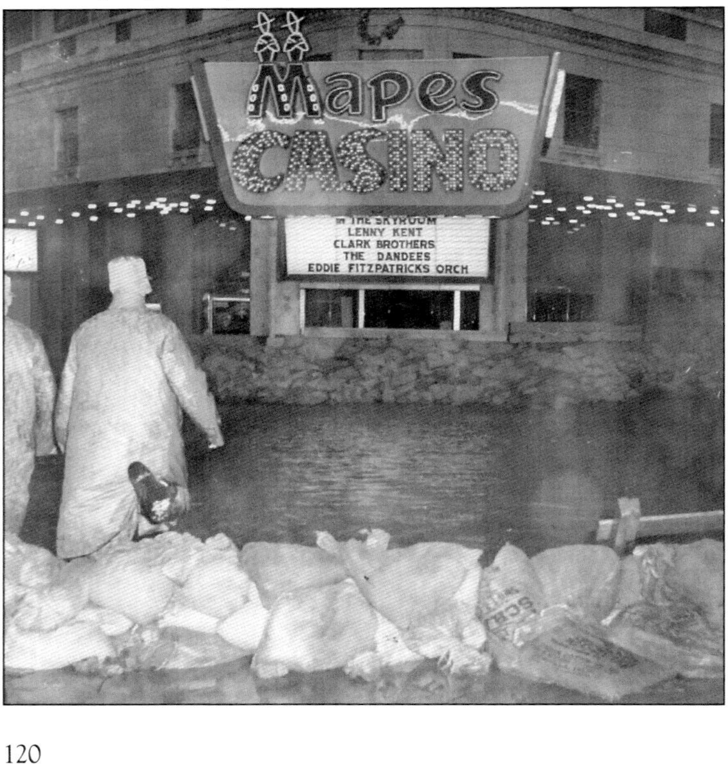

Frigid floodwaters ravaged downtown Reno two days before Christmas in 1955. A wall of sandbags protected the Mapes Hotel on the east side of Virginia Street. (Photograph courtesy of the *Reno Gazette-Journal.*)

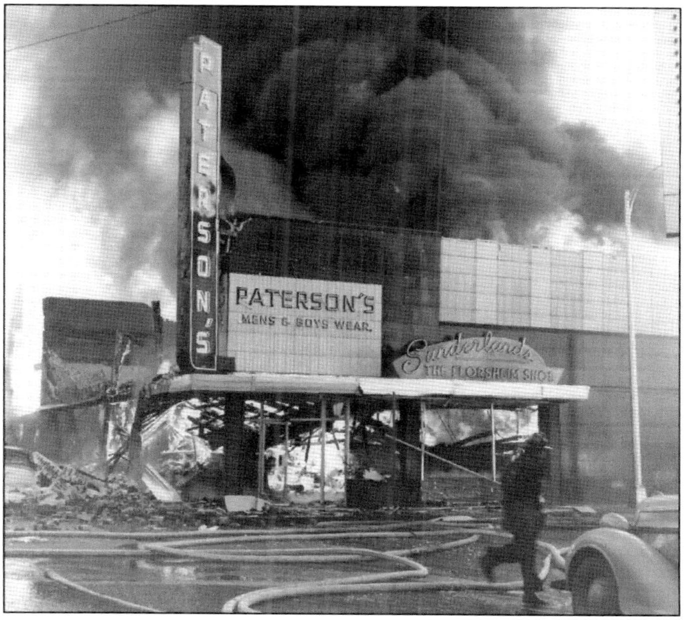

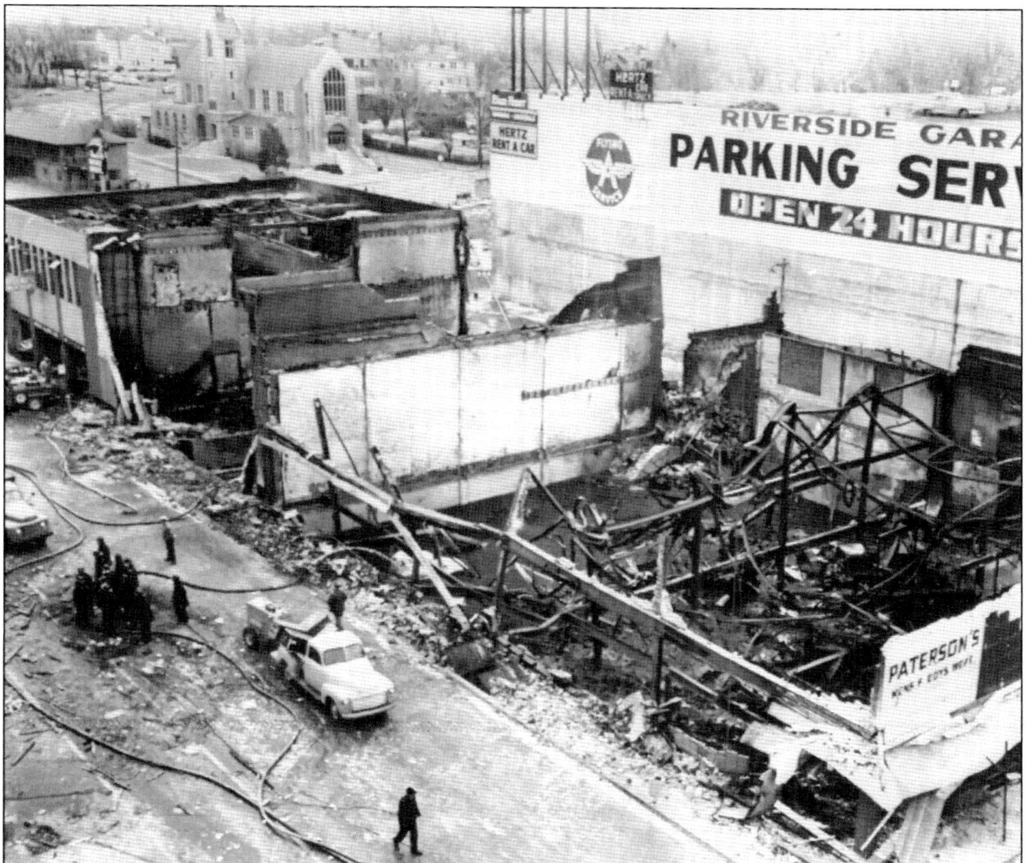

A trio of natural gas explosions rocked downtown Reno in the early afternoon on February 5, 1957, one of the worst disasters in the city's history. The blast, so powerful it registered on the seismograph at the University of Nevada, killed two people, injured 49, and destroyed much of a city block in the area of First and Sierra Streets. The blasts started massive fires, destroying a number of businesses, including Paterson's Men's and Boy's Clothing Store. (Photographs courtesy of the *Reno Gazette-Journal*.)

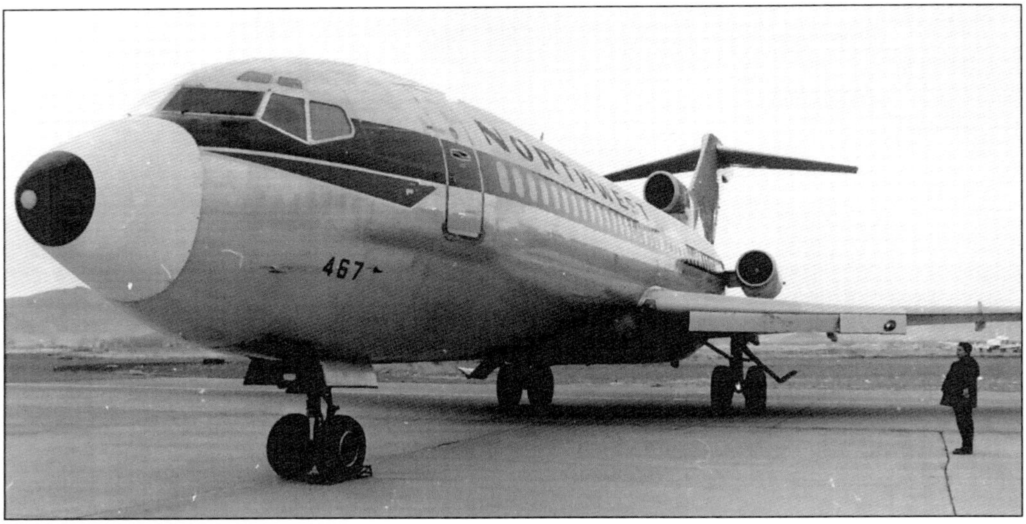

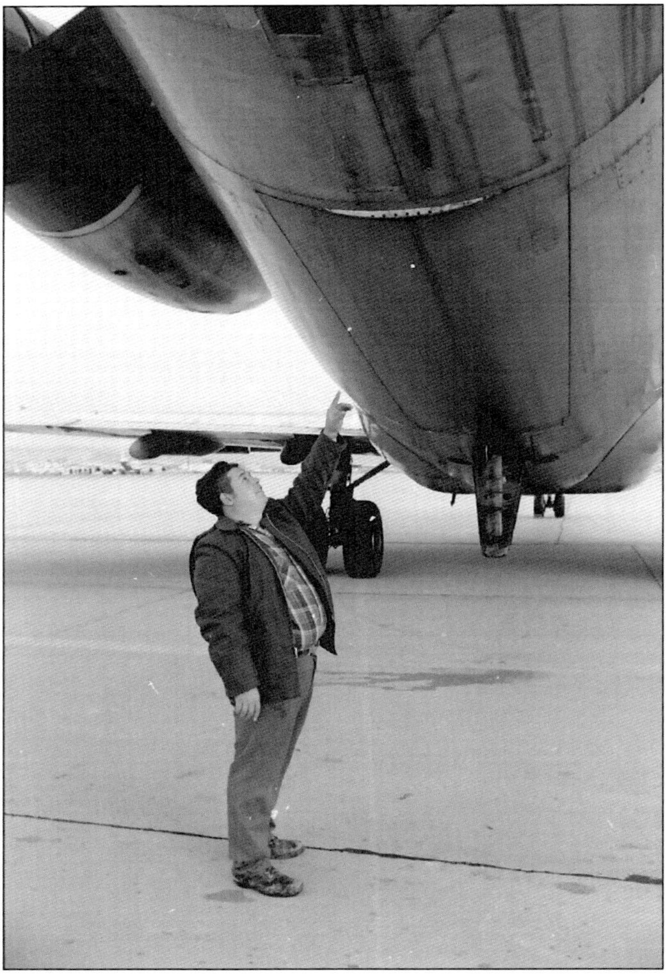

On November 24, 1971, Northwest Orient Airlines Flight 305 was scheduled for a 30-minute hop from Portland, Oregon, to Seattle, Washington, when a man dressed in a suit and carrying a briefcase bought a one-way ticket at the counter under the name Dan Cooper. He hijacked the plane during the flight, and after he received $200,000 in ransom money and four parachutes, the plane was sent to Reno. When the plane landed late that night, however, the FBI and local law enforcement swarmed the plane, only to discover the hijacker had jumped somewhere along the way, and the legend of D.B. Cooper was born. It remains the nation's only unsolved hijacking. (Photographs courtesy of the *Reno Gazette-Journal*.)

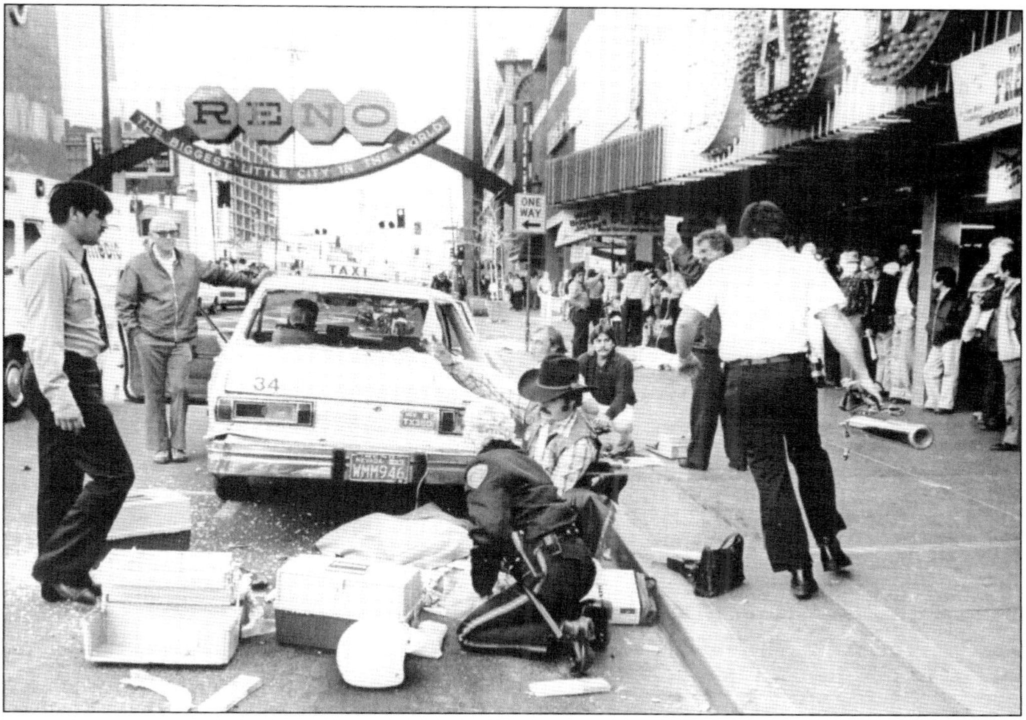

On Thanksgiving Day, 1980, Priscilla Ford drove her Lincoln Continental onto a busy sidewalk on Virginia Street in downtown Reno and accelerated. She killed five people instantly and injured 25, becoming one of Reno's most notorious murderers in the process. "It looked as though someone had gone through the streets with a lawnmower, mowing people down," a Canadian tourist told the *Reno Evening Gazette*. "It looked like a battlefield. There were bodies all over the place." Ford was convicted of murder and sentenced to death. She died on death row in Nevada State Prison. (Photographs by Marilyn Newton, courtesy of the *Reno Gazette-Journal*.)

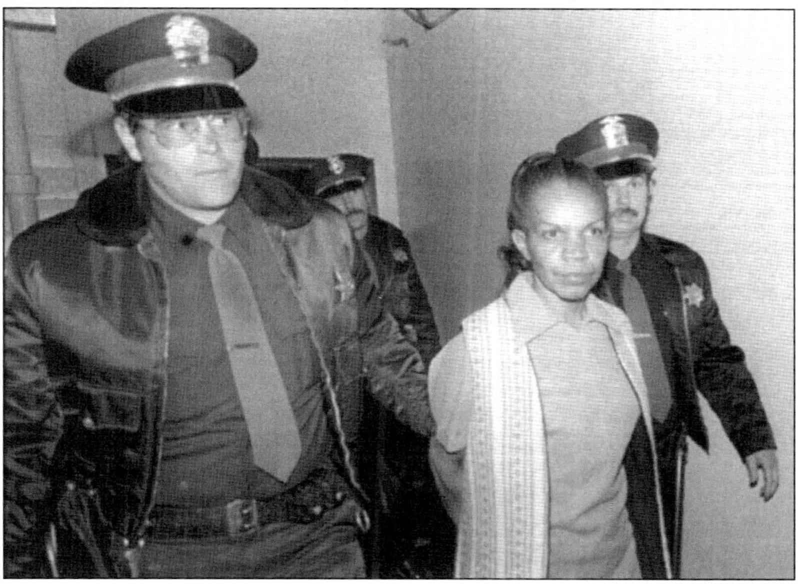

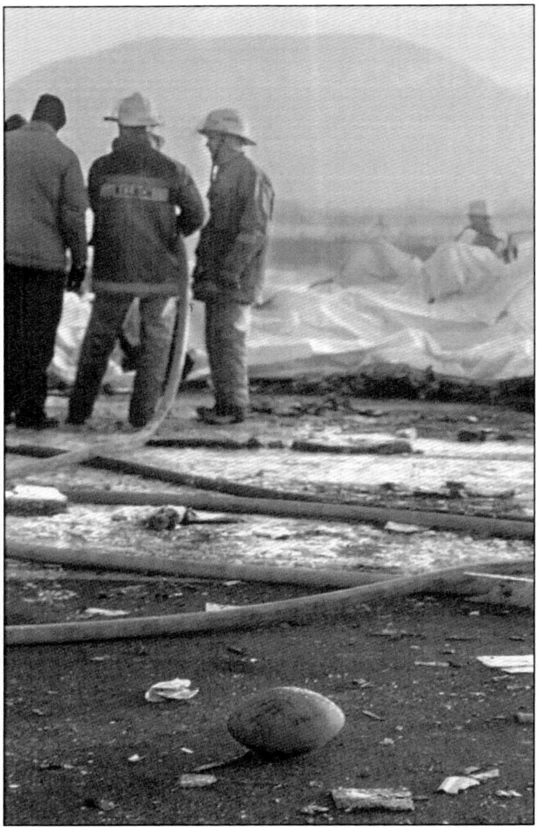

On January 21, 1985, Galaxy Airlines Flight 203 took off from Reno-Cannon International Airport at 1:03 a.m. and crashed into an RV dealership south of Reno moments later. The worst air crash in the city's history killed 70 people, most of them Minnesota residents who were in Reno for a Super Bowl celebration. The lone survivor of the crash was 17-year-old George Lamson Jr. (Photographs by Marilyn Newton, courtesy of the *Reno Gazette-Journal*.)

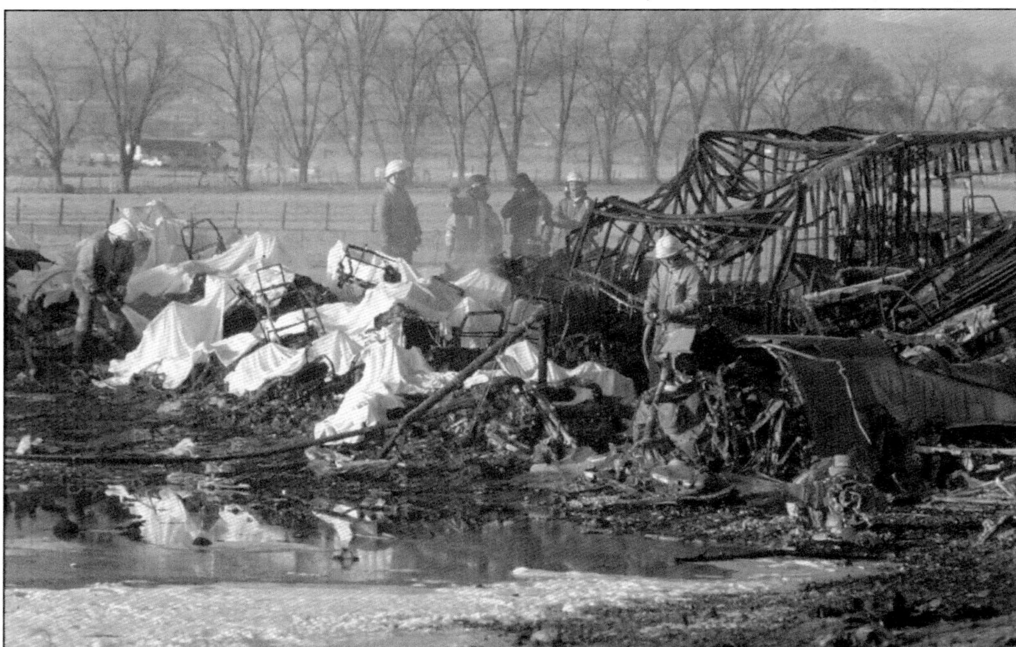

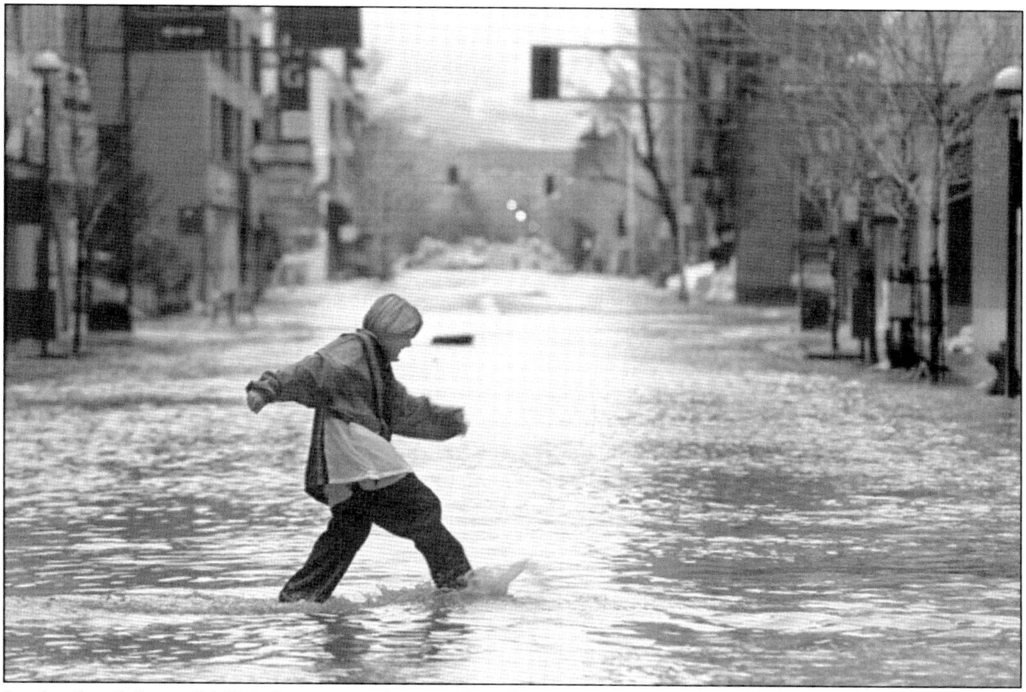

In the final days of 1996, Reno was slammed with a series of unseasonable subtropical rainstorms that melted layers of Sierra snowpack and set in motion the New Year's flood of 1997, one of the worst natural disasters in the city's history. All areas of the city were hard hit. Above, a youngster makes his way across First Street in downtown Reno. Below, a couple flees their flooded Hidden Valley home in a canoe. (Above, photograph by David B. Parker; below, photograph by Marilyn Newton, courtesy of the *Reno Gazette-Journal*.)

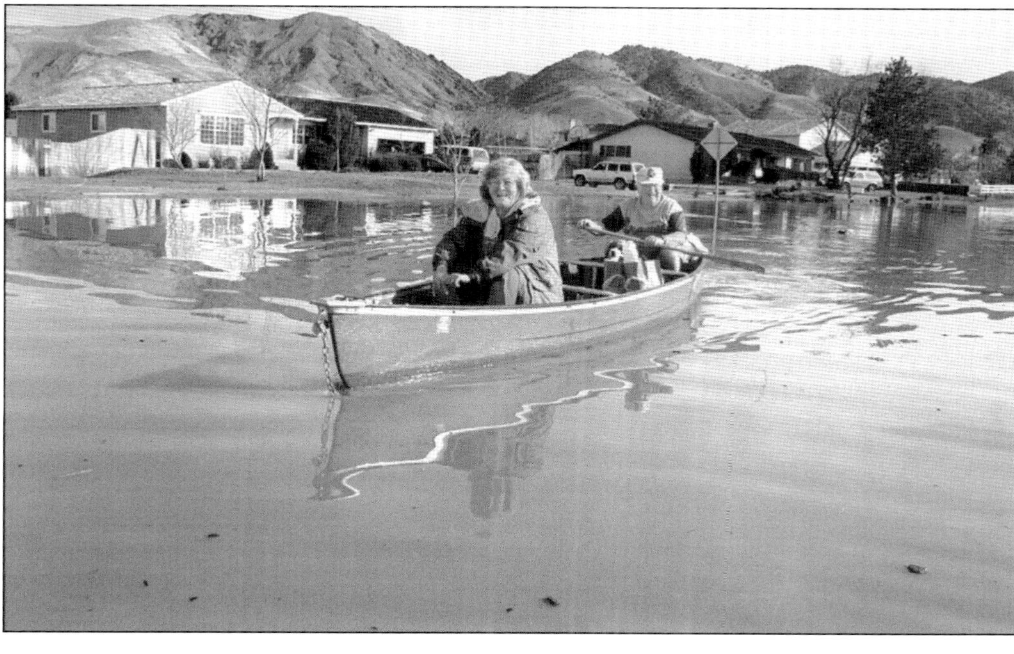

Bibliography

Clifton, Guy. *Dempsey in Nevada*. Reno: Jack Bacon & Co. and Baobab Press, 2007.

———. *Reno Rodeo: A History, The First 80 Years*. Reno: Reno Rodeo Foundation, 1999.

Cobb, Ty. *The Best of Cobbwebs*. Reno: The Black Rock Press, 1997.

Dondero, Don with Jean Stoess. *Dateline: Reno: Photography by D. Dondero*. Reno: self-published, 1991.

Hagar, Ray and Guy Clifton. *Johnson-Jeffries: Dateline Reno*. Battle Ground, WA: Pediment Publishing, 2010.

Kling, Dwayne. *The Rise of the Biggest Little City: An Encyclopedic History of Reno Gaming, 1931–1981*. Reno and Las Vegas: University of Nevada Press, 2000.

Land, Barbara and Myrick. *A Short History of Reno*. Reno and Las Vegas: University of Nevada Press, 1996.

Lear, Moya Olsen. *Bill and Moya Lear—An Unforgettable Flight*. Reno: Jack Bacon & Co., 1996.

Melton, Rollan. *Nevadans*. Reno and Las Vegas: University of Nevada Press, 1988.

Moe, Albert Woods. *Nevada's Golden Age of Gambling*. Seattle: Puget Sound Books, 2001.

Thomas, Henry W. *Walter Johnson: Baseball's Big Train*. Lincoln: University of Nebraska Press, 1995.

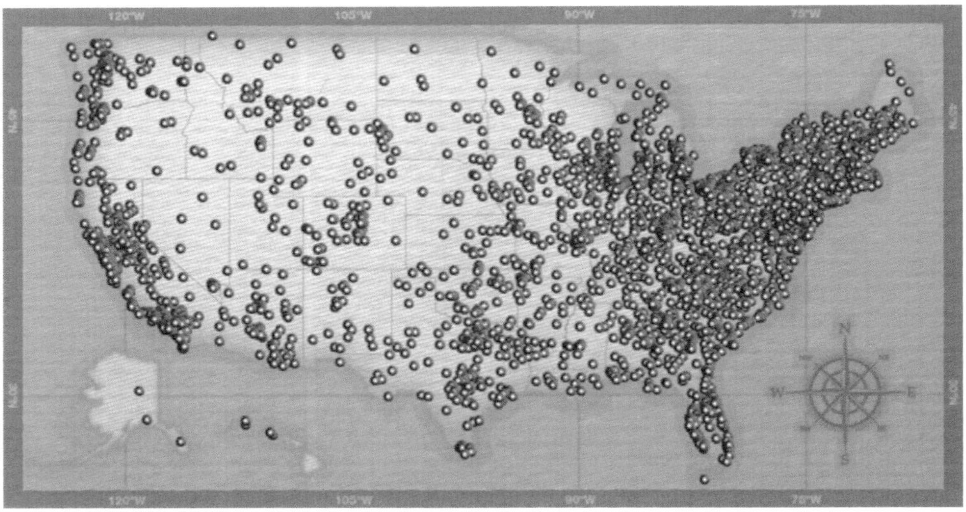